THE CHRISTIANS AS THE ROMANS SAW THEM

THE CHRISTIANS
AS THE ROMANS
SAW THEM

ROBERT L. WILKEN

YALE UNIVERSITY PRESS

NEW HAVEN AND LONDON

Designed by Sally Harris
and set in Galliard type.
Printed in the United States of America by
Edwards Brothers Inc., Ann Arbor, Michigan.

Library of Congress Cataloging in Publication Data

Wilken, Robert Louis, 1936–
   The Christians as the Romans saw them.

   Bibliography: p. 207.
   Includes index.
   1. Christianity—Controversial literature—History
and criticism. I. Title.
BL2756.W54 1984   270.1   83–12472
ISBN 0–300–03066–5
    0–300–03627–2 (pbk.)

22 21 20 19 18 17 16 15

To Don and Mary—
And to summers on Schoodic Lake

CONTENTS

ACKNOWLEDGMENTS

A number of friends and colleagues read all or part of the manuscript and provided helpful comments and criticisms. I wish in particular to thank Philip Devenish, Robert M. Grant, Dennis Groh, Stanley and Ann Hauerwas, Charles Kannengiesser, Richard J. Neuhaus, and Harold Remus.

I am also grateful to Charles Grench of Yale University Press for his interest in the book, to Barbara Folsom for her careful editing of the manuscript, and to David Hunter for preparing the index.

INTRODUCTION

How did Christianity appear to the men and women of the Roman Empire? How did it look to the outsider before it became the established religion of western Europe and Byzantium? The story of early Christian history has been told almost wholly on the basis of Christian sources. The Gospels of the New Testament, the letters of the apostle Paul, the writings of Ignatius of Antioch, Clement of Rome, Justin Martyr, Irenaeus, Tertullian, Origen—these and similar works, most of which have been studied for centuries, have provided us with our primary body of information about early Christianity. In recent years new documents such as the Gnostic manuscripts discovered at Nag Hammadi in Egypt have expanded the collection of sources. These works, written by Christians who were not part of the "mainstream," have given us new insight into the history and character of the early Christian movement. But even the Gnostic writings, though declared deviant and heretical by the leaders of what might be called the "great church," were still produced by Christians.

There is, however, another body of material that does not come from Christians. I am speaking of the observations of pagan observers of Christianity (Roman and Greek writers) which, either in offhand comments in works dealing with other topics, or in frontal attacks on Christianity, provide us with a unique perspective on the emerging church. Though most of this material is familiar to scholars and specialists in the field, it is seldom made available to the wider public, and even when it does find its way into books on the early Christian movement, it does not play a major role in shaping our view of Christianity.[1]

The observations of pagans are particularly valuable in the earliest period in Christian history because those who commented on the new movement had little prior knowledge on which to base their views. The first mention of the Christian movement by a Roman writer, Pliny, governor in the province of Bithynia (modern Turkey), was at the beginning of the second century. He called Christianity a "superstition." Later in the century Celsus, a Greek philosopher, wrote that Jesus was a magician and sorcerer. Do statements such as these reflect simple prejudice or slander, or do they tell us something about the kind of religion Christianity was during this period? What do comments of this sort mean in the world in which Christianity was first making its way?

Most of the comments of outsiders on Christianity have come down to us in fragmentary form. They appear either as casual and perfunctory observations in letters or essays or histories dealing with some other topic, or they derive from books attacking Christianity that were destroyed. When Christianity gained control of the Roman Empire it suppressed the writings of its critics and even cast them into flames. Yet the number of fragments that survive—ironically, in the works of Christians written to refute them—is considerable, and they offer a vivid and uncommon portrait of Christianity.

An early example is the book *True Doctrine*, written by Celsus against Christianity in approximately 180 C.E. Everything we know of Celsus's book comes from Origen, a Christian theologian and apologist from Alexandria. Origen wrote a massive defense of Christianity against Celsus (*Contra Celsum*) seventy years later. That the work still needed refutation seventy years after it was written is an indication of how seriously Christians took its arguments. In his book Origen cited Celsus at length and verbatim. If one analyzes these fragments of Celsus in Origen without the benefit of Origen's interpretation and

---

1. The standard work remains Pierre de Labriolle, *La Réaction païenne. Etude sur la polemique antichrétienne du Ier au VIe siècle,* 2d ed. (Paris, 1948). For recent surveys, see articles by Nestle, Benko, and Meredith in Suggestions for Further Reading.

rebuttal, and places Celsus's observations within the framework of the philosophical thinking of his time, it is possible, with some confidence, to reconstruct what he thought about Christianity, how it compared to other religious cults and the more traditional forms of religion, what Christians believed and how they lived, and why Christianity should be resisted.

Besides Celsus, two other major opponents of Christianity in the ancient world also write works devoted exclusively to Christianity. The first of these, Porphyry, a Neoplatonic philosopher, lived in the third century, and the other, Julian, a Roman emperor, reigned in the fourth century. These works, too, can be reconstructed through the books of Christian apologists who sought to refute their charges. Other than these writers, there are a number of authors from whom we have less information but who do help us to fill out the picture of the Christians as the Romans saw them. Among these are Pliny; Galen, the physician-philosopher who came to know Christians in Rome in the middle of the second century; and Lucian, the satirist who poked fun at the Christians, as he did at everything else in his world.

This book is a portrayal of pagan criticism of Christianity from its beginning in the early second century to the time of Julian in the late fourth century, a period of almost three hundred years. I base my discussion on what pagan observers themselves said and I seek to place their views within the context of their religious, intellectual, and social world. I have conscientiously refrained from viewing pagan observations in light of what Christians said or may have thought about them, or even in light of whether they are "true" or not—that is, whether they reflect what we think Christianity to have been or is. Much of what the pagan critics say is "true" but cannot be fitted into the Christian self-understanding. I am convinced that the perceptions of outsiders tell us something significant about the character of the Christian movement, and that without the views of those who made up the world in which Christianity grew to maturity, we will never understand what Christianity was or is. How something is perceived is an aspect of what it is. This is especially true in the social world, where the perception of others is an essential part of the reality people inhabit.

We have a distorted view of the history of early Christianity. The historian of the Roman Empire, who by training and perspective could view Christianity within the larger historical picture, has seldom bothered to look closely at the Christian sources. The student of Christianity, who does know the sources and the unique problems of early Christian history, is usually familiar with the pagan sources only at second hand and has inflated the Christian part of the canvas beyond all reasonable proportion. The historian of Christianity has given the impression that the rest of the canvas is simply background for the closeup—relegating the general history of the times to an introductory chapter of vague generalities.

In his recent book, *Paganism in the Roman Empire*, the historian Ramsay MacMullen makes an interesting observation concerning Adolf von Harnack's *The Mission and Expansion of Christianity in the First Three Centuries*, one of the classic studies of early Christianity published in this century. "Among its thousands of references to sources . . . I can find not one to a pagan source and hardly a line indicating the least attempt to find out what non-Christians thought and believed. Thus to ignore the prior views of converts or to depict the mission as operating on a clean slate is bound to strike an historian as very odd indeed."[2] Much has happened in the study of early Christianity since Harnack's day, and in the study of Roman history there has been a burgeoning interest in the religions of the Roman world, in Greco-Roman philosophy, and in the social world of the early Roman Empire. Yet little of this material actually makes its way into the general accounts of early Christianity.

This disjunction between Roman history and Christian history is also reflected in the ancient documents. For almost a century Christianity went unnoticed by most men and women in the Roman Empire. When the Christian movement first appeared, there was little common ground of understanding between Christians and non-Chris-

2. MacMullen, *Paganism in the Roman Empire* (New Haven, 1981), 206 n. 16.

tians. The earliest Christian writings, highly theological and directed primarily at Christian readers, present the life of Jesus and the beginning of the church as the turning point in history, whereas non-Christians see the Christian community as a tiny, peculiar, antisocial, irreligious sect, drawing its adherents from the lower strata of society. In the section on Palestine in his *Natural History*—a book written approximately a generation after the death of Jesus—the elder Pliny does not even mention Jesus or the beginnings of Christianity. By that time many of the books of the New Testament had already been written. The first mention of the Christian movement in a Roman writer does not occur until eighty years after the beginning of Christianity.

One of my purposes in writing this book is to bring the world of ancient Rome into closer conjunction with that of early Christianity. By focusing on the comments of Roman and Greek writers on Christianity, I show how pagans thought about religion and philosophy and the society in which they lived, while at the same time shedding light on early Christianity. The specificity of pagan observations on Christianity allows a unique perspective unavailable in other writings from the period. I hope to provide the student of Christianity with an unusual vantage point from which to view early Christianity and to locate the Christian movement within the world in which it arose.

The book also has a theological purpose. I originally began to study pagan criticism of Christianity because I was interested in the early Christian apologists, those Christian thinkers who sought to present an intelligible and reasonable case for Christian claims within the language and the ways of thinking of the Greco-Roman world. The more I read the apologists, however, the more I realized that they could not be understood without first studying the attitudes of outsiders to Christianity, the ideas the apologists were trying to combat as well as the beliefs they thought compatible with Christianity and in whose framework they presented the Christian message. Most of the early apologists were brought up as pagans and only converted to Christianity later in life. The spiritual and intellectual world in which they were nurtured remained a part of their thinking after they became Christians.

I intended to return to the apologists after I had completed the study of the pagan authors, but I found the pagan material so interesting that this book is concerned only with it. Yet what the pagan critics say about Christianity is not insignificant for Christian theology. Many of the themes which have played a role in the history of Christian thought and are still debated today were first adumbrated in the dialogue between Christianity and the classical intellectual tradition. Some of these are: faith and reason, the relation of God to the world, *creatio ex nihilo* (creation out of nothing), the relation of Christianity to Judaism, the status of· Jesus and his relation to God, the historical reliability of the Scriptures, Christianity and civil religion, and revelation of God in history.

In some cases—for example, the doctrine of creation out of nothing—it was a pagan critic who first grasped that Christian statements about God required a new view of the process of creation. Several decades before Christian thinkers had given attention to the problem, Galen pointed out the philosophical difficulties of the biblical presentation of creation. Christian thinkers were forced to think through their views with greater care. Not long after pagans had raised the issue in debates with Christians, Christian theologians began to assert, for the first time in the history of Christian thought, that creation out of nothing is a fundamental doctrine. In this case, as well as in others, the commentaries of pagans are necessary to understanding how and why Christian doctrines came to take the form they did.

I have written this book with the general reader in mind and with an eye to students of Christian history and theology. It is based on my own reading of the ancient sources, but it is not intended as a scholarly monograph and much of what I say will be familiar to scholars in the field. My procedure has been the following. I have selected five major figures, three from the second century—Pliny the Younger, Galen, Celsus—one from the third century—Porphyry—and one from the fourth century—Julian—and I have centered my discussion on their views, using the comments of others to fill out the picture. I have not tried to cover everything but to present the attitudes of Romans to Christianity through the eyes of these key figures. The sources themselves are intrinsically interesting, but by focusing on individual persons about whom we have fairly extensive information I have sought to give concreteness and life to the narrative. In chapters 2 and 3 I depart from this scheme somewhat to develop two important aspects of the story: the role of religious associations in the Roman world and the attitude toward superstition, the earliest characterization of the Christian movement. These topics are suggested by the observations of Pliny discussed in chapter 1. The term *Romans* in the title refers to the Roman Empire and its inhabitants. Many of the authors discussed in the book wrote in Greek.

ABBREVIATIONS

References to ancient sources are given in the body of the text. For the major figures discussed in the book—for example, Pliny or Celsus—information concerning texts and translations is given in the appropriate chapter. Many of the other Greek and Roman authors are available in the bilingual editions of the *Loeb Classical Library* (Cambridge: Harvard University Press). In the case of lesser-known authors, I have given the name of the editor.

Christian writings are cited either in the *Patrologia Graeca (PG)* and *Patrologia Latina (PL)* of J. G. Migne, *Patrologiae cursus completus* (Paris, 1844 ff.), or in modern critical editions such as *Sources chrétiennes* (Paris, 1941 ff.) and *Corpus Christianorum* (Turnhout and Paris, 1953 ff.).

Abbreviations of ancient works are taken from the standard lexica: *A Greek English Lexicon*, comp. Henry George Liddell and Robert Scott, rev. Henry Stuart Jones with the assistance of Roderick McKenzie (Oxford, 1968); *Oxford Latin Dictionary*, ed. P. G. W. Glare (Oxford, 1982); *A Patristic Greek Lexicon*, ed. G. W. H. Lampe (Oxford, 1961); and *Dictionnaire Latin-Français des Auteurs Chrétiens*, ed. Albert Blaise and Henri Chirat (Turnhout, Belgium, 1954).

I PLINY: A ROMAN GENTLEMAN

R OUNDING CAPE MALEA, THE SOUTHERNMOST TIP OF the Greek Peloponnese, in mid-August 111 C.E., Pliny's ship sailed into the dark waters of the Aegean Sea. A few days later the party from Rome put in at Ephesus, a Greek city on the western coast of Asia Minor where the traveler could pick up one of two roads leading to the East. When Pliny departed from Rome several weeks earlier, he had planned to disembark at Ephesus and proceed by carriage to his destination in Bithynia, a Roman province some two hundred miles to the northeast on the shores of the Black Sea; but the weather was sweltering and shortly after his party had begun the overland trip he came down with a fever. An aristocratic Roman gentleman who seldom traveled at all, Pliny was accustomed to spending the summer in the comfort of one of his country villas. Overcome by heat and fever, he changed plans, hired a small boat, and made the remainder of the trip by coaster.

On September 17 he arrived in Bithynia to assume his post as governor of the province and representative of the emperor M. Ulpius Trajan. In the first of some sixty letters he was to write Trajan during the next year and a half, he reported that he had already set about one of his chief assignments, the examination of the financial affairs of the cities in Bithynia. "I had hoped to arrive earlier, but I cannot complain of the delay as I was in time to celebrate your birthday in my province, and this should be a good omen. I am now examining the finances of the town of Prusa, expenditures, revenues, and sums owing, and finding the inspection increasingly necessary the more I look into their accounts" (*Ep.* 10.17).

I

THE MAKING OF A ROMAN OFFICIAL

When Pliny left that summer for Asia Minor, he looked back with satisfaction on a notable career in public life. Appointment as the emperor's legate was only the most recent and, Pliny thought, long deserved honor he had received in the thirty years since he first held public office. He had been born fifty years earlier in 62 C.E. in Comum, a town at the foot of the Alps not too far from present-day Milan, and he first entered public life in 79–80. Little is known of Pliny's father, but his mother's family belonged to the landed municipal gentry of northern Italy. Her brother, G. Plinius Secundus (the Elder), adopted Pliny (the Younger) as a youth, providing him with the family pedigree necessary for advancement in public life.

Pliny's uncle, the author of a monumental encyclopedia in thirty-seven books, the *Natural History*, was a distinguished Roman citizen of the senatorial class. On good terms with several emperors, he was said to have had the custom of visiting the emperor Vespasian before daybreak (the Romans rose early) to discuss matters of state; he dedicated his *Natural History* to another emperor, Titus. The elder Pliny died in 79 C.E. in the lava and flames spewing from the eruption of Mount Vesuvius. His scientific curiosity had led him too close to the object of his study. From him Pliny inherited the family's Tuscan estate, worth 400,000 sesterces a year. Thus, through his mother's family Pliny acquired the requisites for a successful career: good family and wealth.

As was the custom among aristocratic Romans, Pliny received his early education at home from private tutors. Even when their children were infants, wealthy Romans were careful to see that they were assigned nurses who spoke correctly. From the very beginning it was thought important that a child become accustomed to a style of speech that would not have to be unlearned at some later date. In Pliny's day Roman education consisted chiefly of the study of rhetoric, the skill an enterprising young man would need most for a life in the law courts or a position in the civil bureaucracy. Grammar, recitation, analysis of classical literary texts, imitation of the great stylists—these comprised the chief part of Pliny's education. At the age of fourteen he was sent to Rome for advanced study in rhetoric under Quintilian, the greatest rhetorician in Roman history, a man who held a chair endowed by the emperor and from whom Pliny acquired a love of language and literature. By his own admission his greatest pleasure came from discussing the literary qualities of speeches delivered by himself or his friends before the senate, reading poetry to his wife in the evening, or spending long afternoons walking about the gardens of his villa listening to Greek or Latin verse or prose.

Although Pliny harbored literary ambitions, after little success at writing verse, he contented himself with the writing of letters. These letters, comprising nine books of twenty to thirty letters each from various periods in his life, and a tenth book of sixty letters written to Trajan while Pliny was governor in Bithynia-Pontus, are the chief source for Pliny's life and our surest guide to the man, the world he inhabited, and the scope of his interests.[1] Commenting on these letters, Ronald Syme, the biographer of Tacitus, a contemporary and close friend of Pliny's, wrote:

> [Pliny] displays people in their daily pursuits or confronting the important events of upper and middle class life in a stable society characterized by ease and refinement. Betrothal and matrimony, wills and bequest, the illness of a friend or bereavement in a family, the first flowering of poetical or oratorical genius, the early stages of youthful ambition in the career of honors, the multifarious occupations enjoined by metropolitan life, the ceremonial obsequies of illustrious men—such are among the subjects of Pliny's epistolary essays.[2]

When his education was completed, Pliny's career began on a conventional note. He became an advocate before the centumviral court, a lower tribunal hearing cases of property and inheritance. He stayed

---

1. Text of Pliny's letters, R. A. B. Mynors, ed., *Epistularum libri decem* (Oxford, 1963). Citations are from the English translation by Betty Radice, *The Letters of the Younger Pliny* (New York: Penguin Books, 1963).
2. Ronald Syme, *Tacitus* (Oxford, 1958), 1: 97; on Pliny's life, see pp. 75–85. Also M. Shuster, in Pauly-Wissowa, *Realencyclopädie der classischen Altertums-Wissenschaft* (Stuttgart, 1951), 21.1: 439 ff. Several inscriptions on Pliny are conveniently translated in Radice, 303–04.

there only a short time, for he had not yet served in the army. As military experience was a prerequisite for a successful political career, Pliny went to Syria to serve as tribune in a unit stationed there. But military service held little interest for him. Lacking any desire to command legions or to become a military hero, he discovered that he could put his administrative and financial skills to work even while in the army. He arranged an assignment away from the troops auditing the accounts of auxiliary legions.

Pliny's brief tour of duty in Syria was the only time in his life he lived outside of Italy until his appointment as governor in Asia Minor in 111 C.E. He shuttled back and forth between Rome and his several country residences, and on occasion he traveled to his hometown of Comum in northern Italy; but until he was almost fifty, except for this brief stint in the army, he never resided anywhere except Rome. His geographical home was also his spiritual home. Pliny made no grand tour of the Mediterranean for pleasure or for adventure; he did not make the trek to Athens, as had some Romans, to study philosophy, nor to Egypt to seek the wisdom of the Orient. His world was that of the privileged upper class of Rome, his values those of the political and moral traditions of his ancestors, and his intellectual horizon that of Latin rhetorical education. At one time in his life he seems to have been on friendly terms with a group of philosophers, but the chief business of Pliny and his friends was politics and the administration of the civil and financial affairs of Rome. A conservative by education and by temperament, Pliny was secure in the world he inherited from his family, his fellow aristocrats, and his countrymen. "Pliny moves among active professional men who take their responsibilities seriously; many of them owe their position in the Senate to the Emperor's recognition of their merit, and none can afford to squander his capital or neglect his obligations."[3]

How long Pliny stayed in Syria we do not know. He seems to have become bored rather quickly with life in a military garrison and grew eager to return home to begin his political career in government. On

3. Radice, 26.

return to Rome, he was appointed to the quaestorship, the first office in the course of honors and the traditional door through which men made their way to the senate. Pliny was in his mid-twenties. The quaestor was a low-level magistry in the civil service, though Pliny's appointment was singular in that he was designated *quaestor augusti* (quaestor of the emperor), an honor reserved for men of birth. At the time Pliny assumed this position the truculent and ruthless Domitian was ruling. As quaestor of the emperor, Pliny had the delicate task of conveying Domitian's messages to the senate, where many of his opponents could be found. But Pliny survived under Domitian, no doubt partly because of his youth but also because he had already learned the political arts of compromise and flattery.

Moving quickly up the political ladder, Pliny became tribune of the people, an office more important in name than in influence. But it too was a stepping stone to a more prestigious appointment. Always earnest, Pliny took his position seriously and later claimed, somewhat dreamily, that as tribune he had given up all his private court work to serve the people as a whole "rather than give my professional service to a few."

After his term as tribune Pliny became praetor, the highest honorary office in Rome next to the consulship. He then accepted a number of administrative posts in the government—first as prefect for military finances and later as prefect of the state treasury. In the first position he managed a pension fund for disabled soldiers, a place he held until 96 C.E., the year Domitian was assassinated. Though Pliny had prospered under Domitian, like most well-placed Romans he was relieved at the emperor's death. Domitian had not only banished some rhetoricians and philosophers from Rome, he had also arbitrarily and indiscriminately exiled distinguished citizens, accused some of his own provincial governors of conspiracy, and driven from public life good and able men. "He robbed Rome of her best and noblest sons, unopposed. No hand was raised to avenge them," wrote the poet Juvenal. In this atmosphere of fear and suspicion good men were unwilling to speak their minds to friends lest they be implicated as traitors and summarily whisked off to exile or death.

In 100 C.E. Pliny became consul with his long-time friend Cornutus Tertullus. Largely ceremonial, the office of consul had little to do with the actual governing of the empire. Its tenure lasted two months and its duties included presiding over the senate, conducting trials, and arranging for games and festivals in honor of the emperor. But, like a number of the other offices held by Pliny, it opened the way to further advancement. After his consulship, the last office in the *cursus honorum*, Pliny was still a young man—not yet forty. He returned to private legal practice to await a new appointment from the emperor. Since the accession of Trajan to the imperial throne in 98 C.E., Pliny had been waiting to receive appointment to one of the official state priesthoods, a customary and coveted honor.

The priesthoods, divided into four chief colleges, were public offices held by persons of high birth who had rendered distinguished service to the city. That there were only sixty offices for two to four hundred eligible men made the honor particularly desirable. Often one had to wait years before a position became vacant. Because the Romans thought that the official cults were an integral part of the public life of the city, they took it for granted that the priesthoods should be offered to the most prominent social and political figures. The practice had been defended by Cicero, who said that the "most distinguished citizens safeguard religion by the good administration of the state and safeguard the wise conduct of religion" (*Dom.* 1). In Rome the practice of religion was a public matter.

Pliny's appointment dragged on for several years, but when it was offered it was more than he had hoped for. In 103 he was nominated to fill the vacant position of Julius Frontinus, an eminent and distinguished citizen, who had held the augurate, the same priesthood held by Cicero, the great Roman statesman and orator, a hundred and fifty years earlier. And to his great delight Pliny was appointed at an earlier age. The comparison did not escape him. To a friend he wrote: "Thank you for your very proper congratulations on my appointment to the office of augur. . . . As I have reached the same priesthood and consulship at a much earlier age than [Cicero] did, I hope I may attain to something of his genius at least in later life" (*Ep.* 4.8). His comment sounds vain and self-serving, but the sensibilities of the Romans were different from ours. They openly praised their own accomplishments and were not embarrassed to seek glory. To another friend, Tacitus the historian, Pliny once wrote, "I believe that your histories will be immortal; a prophecy which will surely prove correct. That is why (I frankly admit) I am anxious to appear in them" (*Ep.* 7.33).

Shortly after his appointment as augur, Pliny was elected president of the curators of the Tiber, the board responsible for keeping the riverbanks in repair and maintaining Rome's sewer system. In a modern city he would have been head of the sanitation department or the environmental protection administration. Pliny's skills lay in finances, management, and law, and these could be adapted to fit various administrative jobs. Practical and businesslike, he was thoroughly suited to the position and he enjoyed its challenge.

But eventually he grew restless, not so much with the job as because of his own ambitions. He realized that he was approaching that time in life when a major political and administrative appointment should be forthcoming. For a man in his position, the most predictable next step would be a position as governor in one of the provinces. In anticipation of such an appointment, his letters reflect a growing interest in provincial matters and an increasing preoccupation with the qualities necessary for holding the office. Pliny was not disappointed. In 109 (or 110), he was appointed as the emperor's personal legate in the Asian province of Bithynia-Pontus. He joined an exclusive club of several dozen men who held Rome's power in distant lands and who were symbols of authority as well·as judges and arbiters in legal matters in the provinces. Assuming that this would be his last official position before retirement, Pliny was determined that his career culminate in a distinguished tenure of office. He would be no "ugly Roman." His rule would be wise, just, understanding, respectful of local traditions, honest. In a letter to a friend who governed Achaea in Greece, Pliny enunciated the principles he thought should guide the office. He urged Maximus to have regard for the local gods, to honor the legends of the people's past, not to detract from their dignity or pride, not to be domineering.

No one who bears the insignia of supreme authority is despised
unless his own meanness and ignobility show that he must be the
first to despise himself. It is a poor thing if authority can only test
its powers by insults to others, and if homage is to be won by ter-
ror; affection is far more effective than fear in gaining you your
ends. Fear disappears at your departure, affection remains, and
whereas fear engenders hatred, affection develops into genuine
regard. Never, never forget (I must repeat this) the official title
you bear, and keep clearly in mind what it means and how much
it means to establish order in the constitution of free cities, for
nothing can serve a city like ordered rule and nothing is so precious as freedom. [*Ep.* 8.24]

With these thoughts revolving in his mind, Pliny began to make plans
for his trip to Asia Minor.

TRAVELS OF A PROVINCIAL GOVERNOR

Bithynia-Pontus lay on the northern coast of Asia Minor. Two provinces, each with its own history prior to annexation to the Roman
Empire but now linked together in one administrative unit, comprised
a narrow strip of land some fifty to seventy miles wide along the
southern shore of the Black Sea. Bithynia in the west was more popu-
lous and Hellenized, while Pontus had only a few major cities and still
bore traces of the native culture. The land was mountainous but broken up with valleys and plains suitable for farming and ample pastures
for grazing. Wool from the sheep was widely sought, especially in the
neighboring provinces, where it was quite scarce. Rich forests on the
mountains provided good timber for shipbuilding as well as for furni-
ture, the maple and mountain nut trees being especially suitable for
the building of tables, according to the geographer Strabo (*Geography*
12.3.2). The abundance of the land, combined with good fishing off
the coast, made Bithynia-Pontus commercially important for the Roman world.

Nicomedes IV, king of Bithynia, had bequeathed the area to Rome in 75 B.C.E. when Rome was extending her empire into the eastern Mediterranean. A few years later, in 64 B.C.E., Rome annexed Pontus. During the reorganization of the empire under Augustus in 27 B.C.E. the area had become a senatorial province, which meant its governor was appointed by and responsible to the senate rather than to the emperor. Trajan's decision to send Pliny as his own personal representative in the early second century C.E. indicated that he thought the province needed much closer supervision than it had received to date.

Pliny arrived in Bithynia at a time Edward Gibbon called the happiest in mankind's history. "In the second century of the Christian Era," he writes,

> the empire of Rome comprehended the fairest part of the earth, and the most civilized portion of mankind. The frontiers of that extensive monarchy were guarded by ancient renown and disciplined valor. The gentle but powerful influence of laws and manners had gradually cemented the union of the provinces. Their peaceful inhabitants enjoyed and abused the advantage of wealth and luxury. The image of a free constitution was preserved with decent reverence; the Roman senate appeared to possess the sovereign authority, and devolved on the emperors all the executive powers of government. During a happy period of more than fourscore years, the public was conducted by the virtue and abilities of Nerva, Trajan, Hadrian, and the two Antonines.[4]

Gibbon's glowing description of the second century is exaggerated, but from Pliny's perspective the account of life at that time would not be far from the truth. The turbulence of the last fifty years—conflict and dissent at home, troubles on the frontiers, civil war, and especially the bitterness and resentment over the arbitrary and capricious rule of Domitian—had given way to a time of peace, prosperity, and stability. The emperor Trajan, though a soldier from Spain, was remembered by later generations as a symbol of kindliness. Crabby old Juvenal the satirist might have thought the world was badly out of joint—

---

4. Edward Gibbon, *The History of the Decline and Fall of the Roman Empire*, 6 vols. (London [1910], 1978), vol. 1, chap. 1, "Introduction."

all those Greeks and Syrians filling up Rome with their strange and arcane practices—but Pliny supported and encouraged the new generation and did not think that the men of the past were superior to those of the present. He looked out on a world where things were better than they had been for generations.

The cities in the area to which Pliny was sent were prospering, but some had misused their resources. Overly enthusiastic about outdoing their neighbors with a new amphitheatre or a more spacious gymnasium, some cities simply lacked the funds to carry out their construction projects. Building permits were required to prohibit construction when "it is a matter of rivalry with another city." Ordinary building remained unregulated, but competitive building was curtailed. "Those poor Greeks all love a gymnasium," said the emperor Trajan. The rivalry of these ancient cities is reminiscent of large corporations exhibiting their corporate egos in shimmering glass towers surrounded by pink terrazzos, marble fountains, and bronze sculptures.

A primary reason for sending Pliny to Bithynia-Pontus was to inspect the cities and help them deal with their financial woes. But there were other problems. The emperor had heard reports of political unrest and factionalism. A contemporary of Pliny, Dio Chrysostom, was troubled by the growing number of political factions vying with each other and causing unnecessary divisions within the cities. Sedition is perhaps too strong a word, but Dio was concerned enough to make a number of public speeches in which he warned against conducting the affairs of the city "by means of political clubs" (*Or.* 45.8). How much better, he said, would it be if citizens lived together in harmony rather than abusing each other. There were also signs of social unrest. After a hike in prices in Nicomedia, one of the chief cities of Bithynia, the council had difficulty controlling the populace and had to appeal to the Roman proconsul to restore authority. It may be that one of Pliny's directives from Trajan was to dissolve all "associations" or "clubs," whether political or not, in the hope of keeping order in the province.

As governor, Pliny's assignments were the following: (1) to look into the irregularities in the handling of funds (some cities were on the verge of bankruptcy); (2) to examine the municipal administration of the cities; (3) to put down any political or potentially political disorders; (4) to deal with whatever criminal cases were pending; (5) to investigate the military situation in the provinces.

Pliny began his tour of the province in Prusa, a city in the western sector of Bithynia. His activities there are illustrative of the problems he faced as governor and his style of administration. After examining the finances of Prusa, he discovered that private individuals had been embezzling public funds designated for building purposes. He wrote to Trajan, who advised him to put the financial affairs of the city in order. Then he learned that there was a problem with wardens at the local jail and wrote Trajan for a directive. A prefect from the coast called on Pliny and requested that more soldiers be assigned to him. Trajan replied that he also heard from the prefect and told Pliny to decide whether the prefect really needed more soldiers or whether he simply wanted to extend his authority. "The public interest must be our sole concern," wrote Trajan, "and as far as possible we should keep to the rule that soldiers must not be withdrawn from active service." Finally Pliny inspected the public bath and forwarded to Rome the request of the city to build a new one. Trajan replied that the city could build the bath as long as it did not strain the city's finances (*Ep.* 10.17–24). With matters such as these occupying his time and energy, Pliny moved on to the next city on his itinerary, Nicomedia.

Nicomedia, the capital city of the province of Bithynia, had long been one of the favorite cities of the Roman emperors. Already at the time of Augustus its citizens had erected a temple to Rome and another to Augustus, and over the years Nicomedia overshadowed its neighboring cities in the scale and extent of its public buildings. Nevertheless, its finances had not been well managed and there were social problems, such as a near riot over food, mentioned earlier. When Pliny first arrived there he dealt with a number of perfunctory matters, but during a brief trip to Claudiopolis, a nearby city, a more serious problem arose. A large fire had ravaged the central city, destroying a number of private houses, a clubhouse for elder citizens, and a large temple of Isis. After investigating the aftermath of the fire, Pliny concluded that it would not have caused such extensive damage had the people been better organized to deal with fires. There was no public firefighting organization, and since no one was responsible, nothing was done. "It is generally agreed that people stood watching the disaster without bestirring themselves to do anything to stop it. Apart from this, there is not a single fire engine anywhere in the town, not a bucket nor any apparatus for fighting a fire. These will now be provided on my instructions" (*Ep.* 10.33).

Should there not be some public organization for fighting fires? Pliny thought that the most reasonable solution was to organize an "association of workers to fight fires (*collegium fabrorum*) to avoid any future calamities." In the western provinces and in Rome organizations of firemen were common. In his letter to Trajan he makes such a request. "Will you consider whether you think a company of firemen might be formed, limited to 150 members? I will see that no one shall be admitted who is not genuinely a fire-fighter (*faber*), and that the privileges granted shall not be abused; it will not be difficult to keep such small numbers under observation" (*Ep.* 10.33).

The request sounds innocent enough, but Pliny's cautious phrasing of his letter indicates that he knew Trajan might object to the formation of any association, no matter how harmless it appeared. It was precisely associations such as these, originally organized for nonpolitical purposes, that had led to trouble in the province. Furthermore, since the days of the late republic, the activities of clubs and associations had been restricted. All were subject to a system of licensing to prevent clubs from becoming a political nuisance, but Trajan thought that greater restrictions were necessary.

I have received your suggestion that it should be possible to form a company of firemen at Nicomedia on the model of those existing elsewhere, but we must remember that it is societies like these which have been responsible for political disturbances in your province, particularly in its cities. If people assemble for a common purpose, whatever name we give them and for whatever reason, they soon turn into a political club (*hetaeria*). It is a better policy then to provide the equipment necessary for dealing with fires, and to instruct property owners to make use of it, calling on the help of the crowds which collect if they find it necessary. [*Ep.* 10.34]

The term used in this letter for "club," *hetaeria*, is the same word Pliny was to use later when he wrote to Trajan about the Christians. It may seem surprising that the same term used to describe a firemen's association would also be used to describe a group of Christians, but in the circumstances, and from Pliny's perspective, the designation was appropriate, as we shall see when we discuss this aspect of his letter in the next chapter. Trajan had good reasons for prohibiting the organization of a firemen's association. Associations of this sort organized by members of the same trade or occupation did not restrict their activities to matters of "professional" interest. The clubs were also social organizations, and the members met together regularly for food and drink, fun and relaxation, and support in times of trouble. As a consequence, they were a natural breeding ground for grumbling about the conduct of civic affairs and they often became involved in politics. Clubs would support candidates for local office, sponsor campaigns, and post campaign slogans on the walls of local buildings. Ancient placards attest to the political activity of such associations: "The fruit dealers unanimously urge the election of Marcus Holconius Priscus as duovir with judicial power." "The goldsmiths unanimously urge the election of Gaius Cuspius Pansa as aedile." "The worshippers of Isis unanimously urge the election of Gnaeus Helvius Sabinus as aedile."[5] Trajan thought the clubs had gotten out of hand in Bithynia and he wished to halt their growth.

After spending more than a year in the western half of the two provinces, Pliny gradually made his way to the distant cities in Pontus in the east. Here he found problems not unlike those in Bithynia. In Sinope, a beautiful city on a peninsula in the Black Sea and one of the chief trading centers of the area—it was also the home of Marcion, an early Christian heretic—Pliny was presented with a problem in the

5. H. Dessau, *Inscriptiones latinae selectae* (Berlin, 1906), nos. 6411a, 6419e, 6420b.

water supply for the city. He immediately proceeded to examine the terrain around Sinope and then proposed that a survey be taken to discover whether the land, which happened to be quite marshy, could support the weight of an aqueduct to bring fresh water into the city (*Ep.* 10.90–91). Clearly Trajan had sent the right man to Bithynia, for it was just such problems as these that Pliny was well equipped to handle.

Traveling even farther eastward along the coast, Pliny came to Amisus, an old Greek city that had fallen under Roman domination in the first century B.C.E. There he had to deal with a situation somewhat similar to that in Nicomedia. The local citizens had made a request that "benefit societies" be permitted in the city. Even though Trajan had made quite clear in his earlier rescript that new associations would not be permitted, Pliny nevertheless passed on the request to Trajan because of the unique status of the city. Amisus was a "free and confederate city," which meant that it had special privileges—notably freedom from the intervention of the provincial governor in internal affairs. It was allowed to follow its own laws as it had before the coming of the Romans; only its foreign policy was subject to Roman domination. For this reason Pliny realized that any attempt to enforce the imperial rescript on associations was a touchy matter with the citizens. Another factor influencing Pliny's handling of the matter was that the societies about which the citizens made the request were "benefit societies." The term he uses is *eranus,* a different word from the somewhat more political term *hetaeria.* Benefit societies were a distinct class of societies, usually made up largely of poor people who banded together to help one another, especially in meeting funeral expenses and caring for each other in times of need. They also met together, however, for communal dining and recreation. Potentially they were as disruptive as the group in Nicomedia.

Following his normal procedure, Pliny wrote Trajan to transmit the request of the citizens. Trajan replied: "If the citizens of Amisus, whose petition you send with your letter, are allowed by their own laws, granted them by formal treaty to form a benefit society, there is no reason why we should interfere; especially if the contributions are not used for riotous and unlawful assemblies, but to relieve cases of hardship amongst the poor. In all other cities which are subject to our own law these institutions must be forbidden." Though Trajan would clearly have preferred to restrict the activities of private associations in all cities, he did not proscribe the group in Amisus. He acknowledged that clubs could become troublesome, but he respected the unique status of Amisus (*Ep.* 10.92–93).

A CHRISTIAN ASSOCIATION

After Amisus, Pliny's itinerary is uncertain. The next geographical reference in his letters is to Amastris (*Ep.* 10.98), a city almost a hundred miles west of Amisus on the road back to Bithynia. Between the letter written at Amisus and the letter from Amastris, Pliny wrote his famous letter (*Ep.* 10.96) about the Christians. Because he does not mention the city from which it was written, assuming no doubt that Trajan would know where he was, we cannot say whether Pliny's dealings with the Christians took place in Amisus, Amastris, or some other town between the two. We can only say that the letter was written from one of the coastal cities of northern Pontus in the fall of A.D. 112.[6]

Shortly after Pliny's arrival in the city, a group of local citizens approached him to complain about Christians living in the vicinity. What precisely the complaint was we do not know, but from several hints in the letter it is possible to infer that the charge was brought by local merchants, perhaps butchers and others engaged in the slaughter and sale of sacrificial meat. Business was poor because people were not making sacrifices. Toward the end of the letter, written after Pliny had dealt with the problem, he observed that the "flesh of sacrificial victims is on sale everywhere, though up till recently scarcely anyone could be found to buy it." No doubt some trouble had arisen between

6. Discussion of Pliny's letter and Trajan's reply is extensive. See especially A. N. Sherwin-White, *The Letters of Pliny: A Historical and Social Commentary* (Oxford, 1966); Rudolf Freudenberger, *Das Verhalten der römischen Behörden gegen die Christen im 2. Jahrhundert* (Munich, 1967). Among the older works E. G. Hardy, *Christianity and the Roman Government* (London, [1894] 1934), is particularly valuable.

Christians and others in the city. This was unusual. In most areas of
the Roman Empire Christians lived quietly and peacably among their
neighbors, conducting their affairs without disturbance. The letter of
1 Peter, however, written late in the first century to Christians living
in Pontus and Bithynia (as well as other places in Asia Minor), does
mention that people "speak against [Christians] as wrongdoers" (1 Peter 2:12).[7] Only in those places where friction existed were local magistrates inclined to bring charges against Christians or to initiate legal
action. What specifically caused the hostility in Pontus, however, Pliny
does not say.

Pliny was not unfamiliar with Christianity, but there is no mention
of Christians in any of his other letters, and his knowledge of the new
movement must have been slight and largely second-hand.

I have never been present at an examination of Christians. Consequently, I do not know the nature or the extent of the punish-
ments usually meted out to them, nor the grounds for starting an
investigation and how far it should be pressed. Nor am I at all
sure whether any distinction should be made between them on
the grounds of age, or if young people and adults should be
treated alike; whether a pardon ought to be granted to anyone re-
tracting his beliefs, or if he has once professed Christianity, he
shall gain nothing by renouncing it; and whether it is the mere
name of Christian which is punishable, even if innocent of crime,
or rather the crimes (*flagitia*) associated with the name. [*Ep.* 96]

Pliny knew that on previous occasions Roman officials had had to
deal with troublesome foreign religious groups—for example, the
Druids, the Bacchae, the Jews. Livy, the Roman historian, whose
writings Pliny knew, recounts a particularly well-known case early in
the second century B.C.E., when the Roman senate suppressed the
spread of Bacchic rituals in Italy. The cult's nocturnal rites, which had
been transplanted from Greece to Etruria in Italy, shocked sober Ro-

---

7. See the interesting social analysis of 1 Peter in John H. Elliott, *A Home for the
Homeless: A Sociological Exegesis of 1 Peter, Its Situation and Strategy* (Philadelphia, 1981).

man sensibilities. According to Livy, the secret ritual included the "pleasure of wine and feasts" and ecstatic dancing in the forest outside the city. The description of the Bacchic orgies in Livy's history, written during the reign of Augustus (27 B.C.E.–14 C.E.), influenced later Roman attitudes toward foreign religious groups. Some of the things reported by Livy—for instance, the mingling of males with females, the abandonment of modesty, the indiscriminate defilement of women–appear in reports about the Christians. In the case of the Bacchae, Roman officials took a firm line, banning the Bacchanalia from Rome and Italy. The only concession was that if the rite had been practiced for a long time, and therefore had become traditional, it would be permitted so long as participants registered before the praetor of the city, who would in turn report to the senate. The number of participants was to be strictly limited and the group was not allowed to have a "common purse or a master of sacrifices or a priest" (Livy 39.18).

When Pliny was informed of the presence of the Christian group in Bithynia, it is possible that he saw similarities between the Christians and the Bacchae. He knew that Christians met together for a secret ritual and he must have wondered what went on in those gatherings. He may also have heard other rumors about the new religion. He indicated that he expected to find evidence that Christians were guilty of "crimes." He did not, however, specify what these crimes were. They could have been ordinary offenses such as robbery, theft, adultery, and fraud, but he could also have heard tales about debauchery and infanticide in connection with Christian rites.

Not so long after Pliny, Christians were accused of clandestine rites involving promiscuous intercourse and ritual meals in which human flesh was eaten, the so-called Thystean banquets (Thystes, who seduced his brother's wife, was invited to a banquet in which his sons were served up to him) and Oedipean unions (Athenagoras, *Legatio* 3.1; 31–32). By the late second century such charges had become widespread. There is no way of knowing whether stories of this sort were already circulating in Pliny's time, but in his letter to Trajan a statement that Christians only "took food of an ordinary, harmless kind" suggests that he may have heard rumors of sinister activities in the Christian gatherings. Charges of immorality and licentiousness were often brought against deviant individuals or groups. The later accounts of Christian wantonness are often quite specific and the accusations often follow a common pattern. For example, a Greek romance written by a certain Lollianus, recently discovered on a second-century papyrus from Cologne, may shed some light on the background of accusations that Christians engaged in promiscuous intercourse or ritual murder. The papyrus describes an elaborate rite of initiation which included the ritual murder of a young boy, the removal of the victim's heart, an oath, eating of the heart and drinking of the blood, and sexual intercourse. The sacrificial murder is described as follows.

At this moment another naked man arrived with a purple belt around his loins. He threw the boy's body on its back, struck it, opened it, removed the heart and placed it over the fire. Then he took the roasted heart off the fire and cut it into halves. He sprinkled it with barley and drenched it with oil. When it was sufficiently prepared, he distributed portions of it to the initiates, and when they were holding them (in their hands), he made them swear an oath by the blood of the heart, not to leave in the lurch nor to betray . . . , even if they would be arrested or if they would be tortured or if their eyes would be dug out.[8]

Of course we cannot say that Pliny had so monstrous a ritual in mind. If so, it would explain why he acted so precipitously. But it seems unlikely. We do know that such accusations were made later. Minucius Felix, a third-century Latin apologist, gave a lurid account of Christian debauchery which he claims to have derived from Marcus Cornelius Fronto (100–166 C.E.), a Latin rhetor and tutor of Marcus Aurelius.

8. Text, translation, and discussion of the Cologne papyrus in Albert Henrichs, "Pagan Ritual and the Alleged Crime of the Early Christians: A Reconsideration." In *Kyriakon. Festschrift Johannes Quasten* (Münster, 1970), 18–35 (citation on p. 30).

A young baby is covered over with flour, the object being to deceive the unwary. It is then served before the person to be admitted into the rites. The recruit is urged to inflict blows onto it—they appear to be harmless because of the covering of flour. Thus the baby is killed with wounds that remain unseen and concealed. It is the blood of this infant—I shudder to mention it—it is this blood that they lick with thirsty lips; these are the limbs they distribute eagerly; this is the victim by which they seal their covenant. . . .

On a special day they gather in a feast with all their children, sisters, mothers—all sexes and all ages. There, flushed with the banquet after such feasting and drinking, they begin to burn with incestuous passions. They provoke a dog tied to the lampstand to leap and bound towards a scrap of food which they have tossed outside the reach of his chain. By this means the light is overturned and extinguished, and with it common knowledge of their actions; in the shameless dark with unspeakable lust they copulate in random unions, all equally being guilty of incest, some by deed, but everyone by complicity. . . . [*Octavius* 9.5–6][9]

Once the suspicion had been aroused that Christians engaged in clandestine rites, tales of this sort could spread. The possibility, however, must not be ruled out that there was some basis for such accusations. A number of Christian writers mention bizarre rites practiced by certain libertine groups, for example, the Gnostic sect known as the Carpocratians. Clement of Alexandria, writing in the early third century, says that the Carpocratians celebrated a "love-feast" in which the participants had intercourse "whenever they will and with whom they will" (*Strom.* 3.2.10). Justin Martyr, writing in the middle of the second century, had heard stories about Christian groups who "upset the lamp" to engage in intercourse and partake of human flesh (1 *Apol.* 26.7). He was concerned that people not think this behavior charac-

9. Translation of Minucius by G. W. Clarke, *The Octavius of Marcus Minucius Felix,* Ancient Christian Writers, no. 39 (New York, 1974). Discussion of the passage cited on pp. 221 ff.

teristic of all Christians. But the most dramatic account comes from a later Christian author, Epiphanius of Cyprus, who claimed to have knowledge of a Christian group called the Phibionites which practiced ritual intercourse and the eating of an unborn child.

When they thus ate together and so to speak filled up their veins from the surplus of their strength they turn to excitements. The man leaving his wife says to his own wife: "Stand up and perform the agape with the brother." Then the unfortunates unite with each other, and as I am truly ashamed to say the shameful things that are being done by them, because according to the holy apostle the things that are happening by them are shameful even to mention, nevertheless I will not be ashamed to say those things which they are not ashamed to do, in order that I may cause in every way a horror in those who hear about their shameful practices. After they have had intercourse in the passion of fornication they raise their own blasphemy to heaven. The woman and the man take the fluid of the emission of the man into their hands, they stand, turn toward heaven, their hands besmeared with the uncleanness, and pray as people called *stratiotikoi* and *gnostikoi,* bringing to the father the nature of all that which they have on their hands, and they say: "We offer to thee this gift, the body of Christ." And then they eat it, their own ugliness, and say: "This is the body of Christ and this is the Passover for the sake of which our bodies suffer and are forced to confess the suffering of Christ." Similarly also with the woman when she happens to be in the flowing of the blood they gather the blood of menstruation of her uncleanness and eat it together and say: "This is the blood of Christ." [*Panarion* 26.4–5]

How much should be made out of reports of this sort is a matter of debate. Epiphanius claims to have reliable information, but he lived in the fourth century. He is a distant witness to the situation in Pliny's time. The pagan critic Celsus, writing in the late second century, hints that certain Gnostic groups, among which he includes the Carpocratians, engaged in immoral and iniquitous practices, but his comments are vague (*c. Cels* 5.62–63). Further, the reports in Christian writers about deviant Christian groups (Justin Martyr, Clement of Alexandria) are sharply polemical and follow the same stylized pattern as the accusations of pagans against the Christians. Nevertheless, though we are dealing with stereotyped criticism, I do not think we should dismiss such reports out of hand. If certain libertine Christian groups did practice ritual intercourse, as such practices came to be known they contributed to rumors that all Christians were guilty of crimes. The rumors may have been fueled by the practices of these extremist and fringe groups.[10] If a Christian sect in one city celebrated the Eucharist without clothes, or participated in a ritual in which human semen was offered to God and consumed, it is not difficult to imagine how stories would spread that Christians in general were depraved and guilty of unspecified "crimes." Outsiders could hardly be expected to distinguish one Christian group from another.

The background sketched above cannot be simply read back into Pliny's response to the Christians in Pontus at the beginning of the second century. As we have seen, most of the information on Christian "crimes" comes from later sources. But that Pliny makes a point of explaining to Trajan that the Christian "food" was harmless intimates that rumors were already circulating. It would not be long before rumors were rife, and, whatever their origin or truth, they played a part in shaping the milieu in which the Christian movement made its way. If such rumors had not been circulating it is doubtful that Christian apologists would have repeated the accusations. On the other hand, it must be noted—indeed emphasized—that the accusations of promiscuity and ritual murder appear *only* in Christian authors. They are *not* present in the writings of pagan critics of Christianity.[11]

10. For a discussion of libertine Christian groups as well as a translation of key texts, see Stephen Benko, "Pagan Criticism of Christianity during the First Two Centuries A.D." *Aufstieg und Niedergang der römischen Welt*, ed. H. Temporini and W. Haase (Berlin, 1980), 23.2: 1081–89. Also Benko's article, "The Libertine Gnostic Sect of the Phibionites according to Epiphanius." *Vigiliae Christianae* 21 (1967): 103–19.

11. In Celsus's book against the Christians there is no mention of Christians engaging in promiscuous rites. In his response to Celsus, Origen mentions the "rumor" that Christians "turn out the light and each man has sexual intercourse with the first woman he meets," but he does not attribute it to Celsus (*c. Cels.* 6.27). It may be that the omission is insignificant and due to the fragmentary transmission of the writings of pagan

To return to Pliny. Although he expected to find evidence of Christian crimes, he found none. He discovered instead that the rites were innocuous.

They declared that the sum total of their guilt or error amounted to no more than this; they had met regularly before dawn on a fixed day to chant verses alternately among themselves in honor of Christ as if to a god, and also to bind themselves by oath, not for any criminal purpose, but to abstain from theft, robbery, and adultery, to commit no breach of trust and not to deny a deposit when called upon to restore it. After this ceremony it had been their custom to disperse and reassemble later to take food of an ordinary harmless kind.

All Pliny found was a *superstition*, a foreign cult.

As a result Pliny was unsure how to deal with the problem. He referred the matter to Trajan, but, and this is curious, he did not wait for a reply before acting. Even before he dispatched his letter he had decided on a preliminary course of action, and only after he had carried it out did he seek advice and direction. His behavior appears impulsive and out of character with his customary deliberateness, but it may suggest that he had received intense pressure from local magistrates and that the situation required immediate action. Or it may be that Pliny knew more about former trials of Christians than he let on and that he was confident of the legal grounds for his action.[12]

His first step, after hearing the charges, was to summon the Christians. The group included old and young alike, that is, families, persons who were openly associated with the Christian movement, people who had once been Christians but were so no longer, and people from different social classes. There is no hint that the Christians had

---

critics, but it may also be that serious critics had more important things to say against Christianity.

12. On the legal basis for persecution of Christians, see Timothy Barnes, "Legislation against the Christians," *Journal of Roman Studies* 58 (1968): 32–50; also P. Keresztes, "The Imperial Roman Government and the Christian Church. I. From Nero to the Severi. II. From Gallienus to the Great Persecution," *Aufstieg und Niedergang der römischen Welt* (Berlin, 1980), 23.2: 247–315; 375–86.

anything to do with Jews or that they came from Jewish background. It is likely that some were converted Jews, but Pliny treated the Christians as an independent sect. The majority of the group came no doubt from humble backgrounds, freedmen and slaves, working people engaged in menial tasks, artisans. In any case, this frightened and somewhat confused band of uneducated provincials straggled into the chamber where the mighty governor from Rome presided.

The Romans sometimes followed a trial procedure known as *cognitio extra ordinem*. This procedure, simpler and more efficient than ordinary trials, did not require the several judges and lawyers or a jury. The *cognitio extra ordinem* simply required that the party or parties appear before the governor and that he hear the evidence and adjudicate the matter on his own authority. Pliny first asked each person if he were a Christian while at the same time warning him that if he answered yes he would be executed. After asking him the first time he put the same question a second time, and then a third time.

When he had received a definite yes from some members of the group, Pliny sent them off to be executed. In his letter to Trajan, he had requested whether the "mere name of Christians . . . is punishable, even if innocent of crime, or rather the crimes (*flagitia*) associated with the name" is cause for punishment. But he proceeded on the assumption that Christians were culpable for the sake of the name alone. No doubt Pliny had a precedent in mind (his action is confirmed by Trajan), and on this basis he acted. He did, however, express some uncertainty. "Whatever the nature of their admission, I am convinced that their stubbornness and unshakeable obstinacy ought not to go unpunished." Contempt and defiance of a magistrate was sufficient grounds for punishment. A similar charge occurred in several acts of the martyrs. "Since they remained unbending, obstinate, I have condemned them," said another Roman magistrate. A proconsul in Sardinia accused several communities of *contumacia* (obstinacy) because they refused to observe a regulation concerning civic boundaries. On occasion, magicians were charged with the same offense.

Among those brought before Pliny some held Roman citizenship. His *imperium* as provincial governor did not allow him to convict Roman citizens and summarily send them away to be executed. Accordingly, he put these few people in prison, added their names to a list of other citizens already in jail, and prepared to have them sent to Rome for trial. What happened to them we do not know.

At this point Pliny apparently turned to other affairs in the city, as he had done in other places on his trip eastward. But soon afterward the matter of the Christians came up again. Now their status became much more of a public matter because other citizens began to bring further charges. Pliny was not surprised. "Now that I have begun to deal with this problem, as so often happens, the charges are becoming more widespread and increasing in variety." Though he does not say so explicitly, Pliny's comments imply that the Christians in the city were unpopular with the local citizenry. We can guess some of the reasons: the Christians kept to themselves; they were scornful of the traditional worship and gods; they made converts chiefly among the lower classes, rejecting efforts to discuss their religion with educated people; they asked others "only [to] believe, do not ask questions"; and they were suspected of committing unspecified "crimes." Yet, in spite of such attitudes there is little evidence of persecution of Christians, and the instances we do know of are sporadic and confined to particular locales. Apparently the Christians in Pontus had irritated the local citizenry to such a degree that they immediately took the opportunity offered by Pliny's presence to rid themselves of the sect.

The new charges took the form of an anonymous pamphlet containing the names of a number of supposed Christians. This group differed from the first in several respects. The list included the names of some people who denied that they were Christians. Others at first admitted that they were Christians and later denied it, claiming that they had once belonged to the sect but had left it two or more years before. Some said they had been Christians many years ago but had given it up over twenty years before. No doubt Christians would have called these people "apostates" because they had rejected their earlier faith. But viewed historically and sociologically rather than ecclesiastically or theologically, another explanation may be more to the point. Even in this early period of Christian history, not everyone who became a

Christian remained a Christian for the rest of his or her life. Some people initially joined the Christian sect because they found the figure of Jesus attractive, others because they were persuaded of the superiority of the Christian way of life by the behavior of a friend, others because they had married Christians. But in an age when religious distinctions were often blurred, people changed allegiances often and sometimes belonged to more than one religious group in the course of a lifetime. Consequently, there was much movement in and out of religious associations and across organizational lines. When Christianity did not meet some people's expectations, they lost interest.

OFFERINGS OF WINE AND INCENSE

This fuzziness on the edges of the Christian sect presented Pliny with a new problem. How was he to know when people were telling the truth? What would happen if, after leaving the city, those who claimed they were not Christians took up Christianity again and reorganized a Christian group? What was to stop people from saying they were not Christians to save their lives but later promoting the beliefs they denied? He solved his dilemma by a "test" designed to determine who was and was not a Christian. He had statues of the emperor Trajan and of the Capitoline gods—Jupiter, Juno, and Minerva—brought into the room. Those who had already admitted that they were Christians he sent off to be executed, as he had done with the first group. Those who denied the charge he asked to repeat after him a "formula of invocation to the gods" and "to make an offering of wine and incense" to Trajan's statue. He also ordered them to "revile the name of Christ."

Pliny's use of this test is puzzling. Christian tradition has romanticized the martyrs who refused to throw a pinch of incense on the flames of Roman altars, but most of these accounts come from a later period, not from Pliny's time. The idealized portrait of the martyr has created the impression that the use of such "tests" was common and widespread practice in the Roman Empire. Yet the procedure followed by Pliny has few, if any, real precedents in Roman history. It is in part due to Pliny's actions in Pontus and in part to the publication of his correspondence that this practice gained such attention. Nevertheless, how the "test" came to be used in the first place requires some sort of explanation.

The phrase used by Pliny, "make offerings of wine and incense," has a long history in Roman religion. Centuries earlier, on the occasion of national catastrophes such as natural disasters or defeat in war, or at times of public jubilation, as victory in war, the people of Rome flocked to the temples to beseech the gods for aid or to celebrate their good fortune. On these occasions the supplicants used the common form of unbloody offerings of wine and incense, as they were accustomed to do in their homes when worshipping the family Lares. What originally occurred only on exceptional occasions gradually became regularized as a common form of worship. Supplications (the technical term) became a standard type of religious act to commemorate memorable events such as the birth or accession of an emperor, the anniversary of a battle, and similar occasions. Because an offering that consisted of pouring wine over an altar and dropping grain was much less expensive than the slaughter and roasting of a pig or a bull, it gained in popularity as a simple form of devotion to the gods. It could, for example, accompany other public and ritual occasions. In the time of Emperor Augustus, the historian Suetonius reports that Augustus provided that "before taking his seat each member [of the senate] should offer incense and wine at the altar of the god in whose temple the meeting was held" (Suet. *Aug.* 35.3). Augustus's successor, Tiberius, himself followed this practice on accession to the throne. "On the first day that he entered the senate after the death of Augustus, to satisfy at once the demands of piety and religion, he offered sacrifice . . . with incense and wine."

As the ritual became more popular, Roman authorities initiated the practice of setting aside days on which the populace could make such offerings. After the victory of Gnaeus Pompeius in the Mithraditic war (63 B.C.E.) ten days were set aside for *supplicationes*. As the practice of offering supplications was used more frequently on occasions such as this, the distinction between supplications offered to the gods and those offered to outstanding men became blurred. Cicero, for example, proudly notes that the senate ordered supplications after he exposed the Catiline conspiracy. Following these precedents, supplications began to occur on inscriptions honoring the exploits of emperors. In the famous inscription found at Ankara (ancient Ancyra) in Turkey, in which Augustus recounts his own accomplishments, he says: "For successes achieved on land and on sea by me or through my legates under my auspices the senate decreed fifty-five times that supplication be offered to the immortal gods. Moreover, the number of days on which, by decree of the senate, such supplication was offered was 890."[13] At another point in the same inscription he mentions that citizens, individually and as members of municipalities, prayed for his health at temples and shrines. Events in the life of the emperor— his birth, military victories, the anniversary of his accession—become occasions for supplications. Pliny regularly notes such occasions in his letters.

Practices of the sort mentioned above, when joined to the popular perception that one should not shun the civic cult, may lie behind Pliny's use of a test involving the offering of bread and wine. What seems new in Pliny's action was the use of a ritual act of offering incense and wine as a test of religious allegiance. He may have gotten the idea from what he had heard about trials of Christians under the emperor Domitian several decades earlier. Flavia Domitilla and her husband Flavius Clemens were condemned on a charge involving "atheism," and this probably involved some association with Judaism, a superstition in the eyes of the Romans (Suet. *Dom.* 15; Dio Cassius 67.14.2). Speaking of this affair, Sherwin-White, the historian of Roman law and commentator on Pliny's letters, said that Pliny "could hardly have been absent."[14] It is also possible that the Book of Revelation refers to such a practice when the author writes that some had been executed "for the sake of God's word and their testimony to Jesus, those who had not worshipped the beast and its image or received

13. Text in V. Ehrenburg and A. H. M. Jones, *Documents Illustrating the Reigns of Augustus and Tiberius* (Oxford, 1949), 4.
14. Sherwin-White, 695.

its mark on forehead or hand" (Rev. 20:4). Whatever the precedent, Pliny had discovered a simple but effective test to determine who was a Christian, though the practice did not become as widespread or as significant as generally thought.[15] This information could assist a magistrate in bringing judicial action against the Christians.

As was Trajan's custom, he replied to Pliny's letter, and his letter is included in the collection of Pliny's correspondence.

> You have followed the right course of procedure, my dear Pliny, in your examination of the cases of persons charged with being Christians, for it is impossible to lay down a general rule to a fixed formula. These people must not be hunted out; if they are brought before you and the charge against them is proved, they must be punished, but in the case of anyone who denies that he is a Christian, and makes it clear that he is not by offering prayers to our gods, he is to be pardoned as a result of his repentance however suspect his past conduct may be. But the pamphlets circulated anonymously must play no part in any accusation. They create the worst sort of precedent and are quite out of keeping with the spirit of our age. [*Ep.* 10.97]

So Trajan supported Pliny's actions, while insisting, as Pliny had, that the Christians be treated fairly and not made to suffer from calumny or slander.

Once Pliny had resolved the matter to his satisfaction, he went about his business as before, without making any mention of Christianity again. He continued his tour of the cities, and the remaining letters in the collection deal with the same kinds of problems that had required his attention earlier. One city needed help in securing funds to cover a stream which had become a filthy sewer; in another he was asked to forward a request to grant Roman citizenship to three provincials; in Amisus the public prosecutor brought a claim to Pliny about a large sum of money owed to the city for twenty years; and in

---

15. Robert M. Grant, "Sacrifices and Oaths as Required of Early Christians," in *Kyriakon. Festschrift Johannes Quasten* (Münster, 1970), 12–17.

another he wrote Trajan for his advice on whether someone elected to the local council should have to pay an entrance fee.

The letter about the Christians comes close to the end of Pliny's correspondence with Trajan and his stay in Bithynia-Pontus. Sometime during the next year he died without having the chance to return to Rome. We are fairly certain of the date of his death, 113 c.e., as several of his last letters mention the anniversary of Trajan's accession to the purple (January 28) and the annual "vows" (prayers) for the well-being of the state (January 3). "We have prayed the gods to preserve you," he writes Trajan, "and the state in prosperity and safety, and to show you the favor you deserve for your many great virtues, and above all for your sanctity, reverence, and piety" (*Ep.* 100; 102). Since Pliny's letters stop before Trajan's birthday in September 113, it is presumed that he died sometime between January and September of that year.

Pliny's work remained unfinished. He was succeeded as governor of Bithynia-Pontus by Cornutus Tertullus, a friend who had held the consulship with him some years earlier but was twenty years his senior. Pliny's honors had come to him early. Few held the consulship at the age of thirty-nine, and few held two treasury posts in succession, as he did. Measured against his contemporaries, Pliny was a most successful public servant and career diplomat, but he also led an exemplary life, embodying the highest ideals of ancient Rome. Hardly an arresting figure, he is nevertheless a splendid representative of his age; and more than anyone in his day he reflects those traits which made Rome great: he was honest and just, generous, loyal, free from corruption, devoted to the public good, respectful of inherited ways, and pious toward the gods. And, as the following inscription testifies, he was well remembered by his fellow citizens:

> Gaius Plinius Caecilius Secundus, son of Lucius of the tribe Oufentina, consul; augur; praetorian commissioner with full consular power for the province of Pontus and Bithynia, sent to that province in accordance with the Senate's decree by the Emperor Nerva Trajan Augustus, victor over Germany and Dacia, the Fa-

ther of his Country; curator of the bed and banks of the Tiber and sewers of Rome; official of the Treasury of Saturn; official of the military Treasury; praetor; tribune of the people; quaestor of the Emperor; commissioner for the Roman knights; military tribune of the Third Gallic legion; magistrate on board of Ten; left by will public baths at a cost of . . . and an additional 300,000 sesterces for furnishing them, with interest on 200,000 for their upkeep . . . and also to his city capital of 1,866,666 ⅔ sesterces to support a hundred of his freedmen, and subsequently to provide an annual dinner for the people of the city. . . . Likewise in his lifetime he gave 500,000 sesterces for the maintenance of boys and girls of the city, and also 100,000 for the upkeep of the library. . . .[16]

16. *Corpus inscriptionum latinarum* 5.2 (Berlin, 1877), no. 5262; trans. Radice, 303.

II CHRISTIANITY AS A BURIAL SOCIETY

B
Y THE EARLY PART OF THE SECOND CENTURY, WHEN
Pliny was living in Asia Minor, Christian groups could be
found in perhaps forty or fifty cities within the Roman
Empire. Most of these groups were quite small, some
numbering several dozen people, others as many as several hundred.
The total number of Christians within the empire was probably less
than fifty thousand, an infinitesimal number in a society comprising
sixty million. The Jews, by contrast, were a significant minority numbering four to five million. Most inhabitants of the Roman Empire
had never heard of Christianity, and very few had had any firsthand
contact with Christians. Even among educated people little was
known about the Christian movement.

Early in the second century, however, Greek and Roman authors
began to take notice of the new movement. What we have from these
observers are little more than casual comments made in passing in
writings that are concerned with other matters. It is not until later in
the century that a pagan observer (Celsus) made a serious effort to
study the new movement and to acquaint himself at first hand with its
practices and beliefs. Nevertheless, these first comments, though perfunctory and indifferent, and often based on hearsay, are significant,
for they give us clues as to how Christianity was perceived at the time
it was first coming into public view. Viewed from the Christian perspective, some of the observations of outsiders seem misinformed and
distorted, especially when measured against other knowledge about
the Christian movement; but from the perspective of the society in

which Christians lived, they reflect conventional attitudes and are neither inaccurate nor unfair.

Appearances, it is sometimes said, are deceiving. Knowledge based
on what one sees and hears is thought to be superficial, for what one
sees and hears is never the sum of things. Yet is it not equally true that
how something appears, how it is perceived by others, is an aspect of
what it is? This is especially true in the social world, where the attitudes of others, and the roles assigned by society to individuals or
groups, define and shape identity. How much more is this the case
when one is speaking of a tiny minority that is unable to shape the attitudes of the larger society toward itself. The perceptions of others,
mistaken or not, create the world that men and women inhabit, and it
is ill-advised to think that the self-understanding of the early Christian
movement was formed independently of the attitudes and perceptions
of outsiders.

In his letter to the emperor Trajan, Pliny used two terms to characterize the Christians, "superstition" (*superstitio*) and "political club"
(*hetaeria*). The first, *superstitio*, appears in two other contemporary
writers, Tacitus and Suetonius, referring to Christianity, and syn-
onyms of the second occur in other writers from the period, which
means that Pliny's observations not only furnish us with a clue to
how he perceived the Christians, but also give us some inkling of how
the society at large viewed them. An examination of the social and religious background of these terms will provide us with a starting point
for how the Greeks and Romans saw Christianity in the early second
century, when the Christian movement was first beginning to emerge
into public view. "Political club" will occupy us in this chapter and
"superstition" in chapter 3.

CHURCH OR POLITICAL CLUB?

By the time Pliny had come into contact with Christianity, most
Christians had adopted the term *ecclesia*, the word translated as
"church," to refer to themselves. Whether Christians were speaking of
the local gathering in a particular city or town or to the network of

Christians scattered throughout the Mediterranean world, they used this term to describe their conventicles. A Christian bishop in Rome, for example, began his letter to Corinth as follows. "The church (*ecclesia*) of God which sojourns in Rome to the church of God which sojourns in Corinth" (1 *Clem.* 1.1). The book of Acts, written about the same time, i.e., at the end of the first century, speaks of "the church throughout Judaea, Galilee, and Samaria" (Acts 9 : 31).

The Romans did *not* use the term *ecclesia* to refer to the new movement. They simply called it "Christian." Indeed, this term, *Christianus*, which would become the characteristic name for the followers of Jesus, was first used by outsiders (Acts 11 : 26). Pliny, too, calls them *Christiani*, identifying them by reference to their founder, just as the followers of Pythagoras were called Pythagoreans, the followers of Epicurus, Epicureans, the worshipers of Dionysus, Dionysiacs. Had Pliny heard the term *ecclesia*, he would have been puzzled, for in common usage in Greek and Latin *ecclesia* referred to the political assembly of the people of a city, as contrasted with the smaller group of elected officials who comprised the council (*boule*). In a letter to Trajan written a few weeks after the affair with the Christians, Pliny refers to the vote of the "local *boule* and *ecclesia*" (*Ep.* 10.11). A passage such as the following, taken from the book of Colossians, would have been inexplicable to him: "Now I rejoice in my sufferings for your sake, and in my flesh I complete what is lacking in Christ's affliction for the sake of his body, that is the church (*ecclesia*)" (Col. 1 : 24).

Besides the specific name *Christiani*, Pliny also used the general term *hetaeria* to identify the Christian group.

They [the Christians] also declared that the sum total of their guilt or error amounted to no more than this; they had met regularly before dawn on a fixed day to chant verses alternately among themselves in honor of Christ as if to a god, and also to bind themselves by oath. . . . After this ceremony it has been their custom to disperse and reassemble later to take food of an ordinary, harmless kind; but they had in fact given up this practice since my edict, issued on your instructions, which banned all *hetaerias*.

The term *hetaeria*, a transliteration into Latin of a Greek word, is usually rendered as "political club" or "association." As we have seen in the previous chapter, it is the same word used by Pliny in another letter to Trajan to refer to a firemen's association in Nicomedia. *Hetaeriae* had the potential of becoming political and thereby of disturbing the life of a city. Because such groups promoted factionalism in the cities and sometimes bred social or political unrest, Roman officials discouraged their formation.

Although the term *hetaeria* highlights the political aspects of these associations, most clubs were not political, as Trajan recognized. Associations had existed in the Roman world since the third century B.C.E. According to tradition, some of them were supposed to have been founded at the time of the establishment of the city of Rome. The legendary king Numa was said to have divided the citizens into *collegia* (associations) according to their crafts: flute-players, goldsmiths, carpenters, dyers, leather-workers, coppersmiths, potters. Each group was supposed to have been assigned its appropriate function and its distinctive god or goddess and religious rites. It is, however, more likely that the associations did not emerge until a much later time, when Rome had grown much larger and people were seeking opportunities for recreation and fellowship among those with whom they worked and with whom they shared certain interests. Associations often assumed the responsibility of providing a decent burial for their members. Customarily, an association would adopt a particular god or goddess as patron, and when the members gathered for a communal meal they celebrated religious rites in honor of the patron deity. Though the associations were frequently composed of men from the same trade, they were not guilds or embryonic trade unions. Their purpose was social, recreational, and religious.

Similarly, in the Greek world, especially from the third century on, as the city (*polis*) lost its importance as the primary focus of identity for citizens, clubs and associations began to spread. The Greek clubs were more varied than the Roman—some organized around trades and occupations, some explicitly religious, for instance, the *Dionysiastai, Herakleistai* (worshipers of Dionysus or Heracles), some named after their founders, and others simply groups of people who came together for fun and fellowship. There were associations of wool-workers, weavers, bankers of Delos, bakers, fishermen, beekeepers, greengrocers, *Aigyptioi* (Egyptians), *Salaminioi*, and many others. All combined religious worship and social intercourse, and they sometimes offered commercial advantages and education. Almost all of these societies were local and drawn from people living in a specific city. They were not "international," that is, a group of associations bound together in an organization extending across the Mediterranean world. At most they included people from within a specific island or province. They were generally small, with an average membership under fifty; a few had memberships of several hundred. In the life of these associations religion played an important role. Even more than in the Roman *collegia*, religion stood in the foreground of the Greek associations, writes Poland, a historian of the associations: "Indeed in the case of many associations these religious relations are the only thing about which we have any information."[1]

A SENSE OF BELONGING

In the first centuries of the Common Era associations became a familiar feature in the cities of the Roman Empire. The bulk of their members were drawn not from the upper classes, which had other outlets for socializing and amusement, but from the craftsmen and artisans, merchants and shopkeepers, some of whom were freedmen or slaves, or who because of their birth and education did not have the means to enter the world of the upper classes. This class of people, uneducated or only partly educated, was cut off from the cultural and social life enjoyed by men such as Pliny. The wealthy purchased the skills of craftsmen to decorate their houses, and they profited from the marketing and sale of fine cloth, oils, perfumes, and precious stones bought and sold by enterprising businessmen and merchants, but they scorned the people themselves. Buying and selling was not the business of a

---

1. Franz Poland, *Geschichte des griechischen Vereinswesens* (Leipzig, 1909), 173.

man of Pliny's background; the only occupations worthy of a person of high birth were politics, agriculture, and soldiering. Cicero not only scorned the occupations of custom collecting and usury, he also considered manual labor and the business of merchants vulgar. Even less respectable than these were fishmongers, butchers, cooks, poulterers.

From people such as these the associations drew their members. They knew they did not have the respect of the wealthy and powerful; but they could get together with friends and neighbors on a regular basis to share a meal, spend an evening in each other's company, or comfort a grieving friend when his wife died. The associations gave men and women a sense of belonging. "Individually weak and despised, they were finding the means of developing an organization, which at once cultivated social feeling, heightened their self-respect, and guarded their collective interest."[2]

The associations can be divided into three main types: (1) professional corporations, as for example, a guild of shipowners, fruit merchants, wool-workers, or plasterers; (2) funerary societies whose chief purpose was to provide burial expenses for deceased members and to insure that each member received a decent burial; (3) religious societies composed of the worshipers of a particular deity, such as the devotees of Bacchus or Isis. Seldom, however, were the activities of an association limited to one of these functions. Most combined several, if not all, of them. All types included some form of religious worship. Jupiter Optimus Maximus was the favorite of ironworkers, butchers, perfumers; Minerva, of fullers and hemp makers; Hercules, of carpenters, clothiers, and bakers. An association of fullers might, for example, serve as a burial society for its members and be dedicated to Minerva.

An interesting and quite complete inscription from Lanuvium, a town in Italy southeast of Rome, dated 136 c.e., provides us with a good example of how an association was organized and what some of its activities were.[3] This particular society was dedicated to the god-

---

2. Samuel Dill, *Roman Society from Nero to Marcus Aurelius* (London, 1911), 256.
3. Text of inscription in H. Dessau, *Inscriptiones latinae selectae* (Berlin, 1906), no. 7212. Translation in Napthali Lewis and Meyer Reinhold, *Roman Civilization* (New York, 1955), 2:272–75.

dess Diana and was "licensed" by the Roman senate. The decree of the senate read: "These are permitted to assemble, convene, and maintain a society; those who desire to make monthly contributions for funerals may assemble in such a society, but they may not assemble in the name of such society except once a month for the sake of making contributions to provide burial for the dead." The inscription includes the bylaws of the society, which begin with the following statement:

> May this be propitious, happy and salutary to the Emperor Caesar Trajanus Hadrian Augustus and to the entire imperial house, to us, to ours, and to our society, and may we have made proper and careful arrangements for providing decent obsequies at the departure of the dead. Therefore we must all agree to contribute faithfully, so that our society may be able to continue in existence a long time. You, who desire to enter this society as a new member, first read the by-laws carefully before entering, so as not to find cause for complaint later or bequeath a lawsuit to your heir.

The bylaws themselves read in part:

> It was voted unanimously that whoever desires to enter this society shall pay an initiation fee of 100 sesterces and an amphora of good wine, and shall pay monthly dues of 5 copper coins. It was voted further that if anyone has not paid his dues for six consecutive months and the common lot of mankind befalls him, his claim to burial shall not be considered, even if he has provided for it in his will. It was voted further that upon the decease of a paid-up member of our body there will be due him from the treasury 300 sesterces, from which sum will be deducted a funeral fee of 50 sesterces to be distributed at the pyre [among those attending]; the obsequies, furthermore, will be performed on foot.
> It was voted further that if a member dies farther than twenty miles from town and the society is notified, three men chosen from our body will be required to go there to arrange for his funeral; they will be required to render an accounting in good faith to the membership, and if they are found guilty of any fraud they shall pay a quadruple fine; they will be given money for the fu-

neral expenses, and in addition a round-trip travel allowance of 20 sesterces each. But if a member dies farther than twenty miles from town and notification is impossible, then his funeral expenses, less emoluments and funeral fee, may be claimed from this society, in accordance with the by-laws of the society, by the man who buries him, if he so attests by an affidavit signed with the seals of seven Roman citizens, and the matter is approved, and he gives security against anyone's claiming any further sum.

It was voted further that if a slave member of this society dies, and his master or mistress unreasonably refuses to relinquish his body for burial, and he has not left written instructions, a token funeral ceremony will be held.

It was voted further that if any member takes his own life for any reason whatever, his claim to burial [by the society] shall not be considered.

It was voted further that if any slave member of this society becomes free, he is required to donate an amphora of good wine.

It was voted further that if any master, in the year when it is his turn in the membership list to provide dinner, fails to comply and provide a dinner, he shall pay 30 sesterces into the treasury; the man following him on the list shall be required to give the dinner, and he [the delinquent] shall be required to reciprocate when it is the latter's turn.

Calendar of dinners: March 8, birthday of Caesennia . . . his father; November 27, birth of Antinous; August 13, birthday of Diana and of the society; August 20, birthday of Caesennius Silvanus, his brother; . . . birthday of Cornelia Procula, his mother; December 14, birthday of Caesennius Rufus, patron of the municipality.

Masters of the dinners in the order of the membership list, appointed four at a time in turn, shall be required to provide an amphora of good wine each, and for as many members as the society has a bread costing 2 copper coins, sardines to the number of four, a setting, and warm water with service.

It was voted further that any member who becomes *quinquen-*

nalis in this society shall be exempt from such obligations for the term when he is *quinquennalis,* and that he shall receive a double share in all distributions.

It was voted further that if any member desires to make any complaint or bring up any business, he is to bring it up at a business meeting, so that we may banquet in peace and good cheer on festive days.

It was voted further that any member who moves from one place to another so as to cause a disturbance shall be fined 4 sesterces. Any member, moreover, who speaks abusively of another or causes an uproar shall be fined 12 sesterces. Any member who uses any abusive or insolent language to a *quinquennalis* at a banquet shall be fined 20 sesterces.

It was voted further that on the festive days of his term of office each *quinquennalis* is to conduct worship with incense and wine and is to perform his other functions clothed in white, and that on the birthdays of Diana and Antinous he is to provide oil for the society in the public bath before they banquet.

As can be seen from this inscription, the burial society at Lanuvium provided far more than insurance against burial expenses. The regular meetings were occasions for eating and drinking, conversation, recreation. These meetings not only provided relief from the daily round of work; they also provided friends and associates for mutual support, an opportunity for recognition and honor, a vehicle by which ordinary men could feel a sense of worth. The society also gave people an opportunity for religious worship in a setting that was supportive, personal, and familiar. "When the brotherhood, many of them of servile grade, met in full conclave in the temple of their patron deity, to pass a formal decree of thanks to a benefactor, and regale themselves with a modest repast, or when they passed through the street and the forum with banners flying, and all the emblems of their guild, the meanest member felt himself lifted for the moment above the dim, hopeless obscurity of plebian life."[4]

4. Dill, 256.

The associations enriched the lives of men and women by providing a social unit more inclusive than the family yet smaller than the city. Like the many voluntary organizations that exist today, from the VFW to bowling clubs, they offered a sense of belonging, relief from the routine and responsibilities of family life, and the company of friends. The associations were larger than the narrow confines of the family yet intimate enough for one to feel at home in them. Here one could mark life's occasions—birthdays and anniversaries—and at the same time celebrate the particular festivals associated with one's society—the birthday of Diana, the emperor, or distinguished citizens. The societies met regularly; they had rules and regulations governing their activities; they conducted business affairs in orderly fashion; on special days the members feasted and drank good wine; there were offices to be held, honors to be received; and one could be confident that, at the time of death, one's fellows would see to it that one received a decent burial. The society to which one belonged was a cohesive group that became the focal point for many of the ordinary as well as extraordinary events of life. In it the craftsman, the merchant, the worker became "somebody." Men from this class, writes Jean Waltzing, a historian of the Roman associations,

> were placed always at the bottom of the political and social ladder; they saw in the association the only means to escape their isolation and weakness, to acquire some little consideration and even a little influence, finally to create for themselves in the society, in the city, an honorable place. . . . Religion, taking care of funerals, the desire to be stronger, to defend their interest, to elevate themselves above the common herd, the desire to fraternize and to make their difficult existence more pleasant—such were the diverse sources of that powerful need of association which worked in the popular class.[5]

5. J. P. Waltzing, *Etude historique sur les corporations professionelles chez les romains* (Brussels, 1895–96), 1:332.

A BACCHIC SOCIETY

The society at Lanuvium was organized primarily to provide a decent burial for its members, but as we have seen, the regular meetings of the society included religious worship. There were other associations whose primary purpose was religious. It is among these associations that we find the closest parallel with the Christians. One of the most interesting of which we have firsthand information is the society of Bacchi (*Iobacchi*)—that is, a cult to Dionysus. This society had existed in Athens for many years, and on the occasion of the resignation of its president and the appointment of a new one, the society decided to inscribe its status on a stone. Fortunately, it also included a brief extract of the minutes from the meeting at which the new president was appointed, which took place sometime in the latter part of the second century, shortly before 178 C.E.[6]

To good luck. In the archonship of Arrius Epaphroditus, on the eighth day of the month Elaphebolion, a meeting was convened for the first time by the priest who had been nominated by Aurelius Nicomachus, who had served as vice-priest for seventeen years and as priest for twenty-three years and had in his lifetime resigned his position, for the honor and glory of the Bacchic Society, in favour of the most excellent Caludius Herodes.

As the new president, Herodes, nominated the outgoing president for vice-president, he read the statutes and the group shouted its approval. "These are what we always observe." "Hurrah for the priest! Revive the statutes; you ought to. Long life to the Bacchic Society, and good order. Engrave the statutes. Put the question." Then followed a resolution: "Whoever wishes the statutes which have been read to be ratified and engraved on a column will raise his hand. All hands were raised." Then some shouted, "Long life to the most excel-

6. Text in *Inscriptiones graecae* II–III², 1, 2 (Berlin, 1916), no. 1368; translation and discussion in M. N. Tod, *Sidelights on Greek History* (Oxford, 1932), 71 ff. For another interesting inscription of a religious organization from this period, see S. C. Barton and G. H. R. Horsley, "A Hellenistic Cult Group and the New Testament Churches," *Jahrbuch für Antike und Christentum* 24 (1981): 7–41.

lent priest Herodes! Now you are in fortune; now we are the first of all Bacchic Societies. Hurrah for the vice-priest! Let the column be made." Having decided to engrave the statutes, the vice-priest ordered that the mandate be carried out: "The column shall rest upon the pillar, and the statutes shall be engraved; the officers will take care to prevent any infringement of them."

Next come the statutes themselves, which give us a clear picture of the workings of the society, how one became a member, what went on in meetings, how disputes were settled, and so on. The statutes begin with the rules for admission: "No one may be an Iobacchus unless he first lodge with the priest the usual notice of candidature and be approved by a vote of the Iobacchi as being clearly a worthy and suitable member of the Bacchic Society. The entrance fee shall be fifty denarii and a libation for one who is not the son of a member, while the sons of members shall lodge a similar notice and pay, in addition to twenty-five denarii, half the usual subscription until the attainment of puberty."

Then followed the regulations for meetings: "The Iobacchi shall meet on the ninth of each month and on the anniversary of its foundation and on the festivals of Bacchus and on any extraordinary feast of the god, and each member shall take part in word or act or honorable deed, paying the fixed monthly contribution for the wine." The statutes went on to set down regulations for those who failed to pay the dues and those who had: "When anyone has lodged his application and has been approved by vote, the priest shall hand him a letter stating that he is an Iobacchus, but not until he has first paid to the priest his entrance fee, and in the letter the priest shall cause to be entered the sums paid under one head or another."

From time to time there was strife in the meetings, somewhat on the order of those Paul described in his letter of admonition to the Christians at Corinth. "When you assemble as a church I hear there are divisions among you. . . . When you meet together it is not the Lord's supper that you eat. For in eating, each one goes ahead with his own meal, and one is hungry and another is drunk" (1 Cor. 11 : 18–21). The Iobacchi statutes read: "No one may either sing or create a disturbance or applaud at the gathering, but each shall say and act his allotted part with all good order and quietness under the direction of the priest or the arch-bacchus. . . . If anyone start a fight or be found acting disorderly or occupying the seat of any other member or using insulting or abusive language to anyone, the person so abused or insulted shall produce two of the Iobacchi to state upon oath that they heard him insulted." Penalties follow. A few lines later the statutes also list penalties for those who bring disputes to the public courts instead of settling them within the society, a problem also faced by Christian groups (1 Cor. 6).

As to the activities at the meetings, the statutes assert:

And no one shall deliver a speech without the leave of the priest or of the vice-priest on pain of being liable to a fine of thirty light [small] drachmas to the Society. The priest shall perform the customary services at the meeting and the anniversary in proper style, and shall set before the meeting the drink-offering for the return of Bacchus and pronounce the sermon, which Nicomachus the ex-priest inaugurated as an act of public spirit. And the arch-bacchus shall offer the sacrifice to the god and shall set forth the drink-offering on each tenth day of the month Elaphebolion. And when the portions are distributed, let them be taken by the priest, vice-priest, arch-bacchus, treasurer, bucolicus, Dionysus, Core, Palaemon, Aphrodite and Proteurynthmus. . . .

The society not only celebrated Bacchic festivals and anniversaries, but also events in the lives of its members.

And if any of the Iobacchi receives any legacy or honor or appointment, he shall set before the Iobacchi a drink-offering corresponding to the appointment—marriage, birth, Choes, coming of age, citizen-status, the office of wand-bearer, councillor, president of the games, Panhellen, elder, *thesmothetes,* or any magistracy whatsoever, the appointment as *sunthytēs* or as justice of the peace, the title of *ieroneikēs,* or any other promotion attained by any Iobacchus.

There was one person in the society especially designated to keep order in meetings. He was assisted by two "bouncers," called "horses," whose job was to throw out troublemakers. The society also included a treasurer, whose responsibility was to purchase oil, out of his own pocket, for the lights on regular meeting days and on special days when honors or appointments were celebrated. Finally, the statutes made provisions for the death of members. "And if any Iobacchus die, a wreath shall be provided in his honor not exceeding five denarii in value, and a single jar of wine shall be set before those who have attended the funeral; but anyone who has not attended may not partake of the wine."

To the casual observer, the Christian communities in the cities of the Roman Empire appeared remarkably similar to religious associations such as the one described above or to a burial society such as the one at Lanuvium. Like these other associations, the Christian society met regularly for a common meal; it had its own ritual of initiation, rules, and standards for members; when the group came together, the members heard speeches and celebrated a religious rite involving offerings of wine, prayers, and hymns; and certain members of the group were elected to serve as officers and administrators of the association's affairs. It also had a common chest drawn from the contributions of members, looked out for the needs of its members, provided for a decent burial, and in some cities had its own burial grounds. Like the followers of Heracles who were called Heraclists, the devotees of Asclepius called Asclepiasts, or the followers of Isis called Isiacs, the Christians were called *Christiani*. The Christian communities, writes the Roman social historian Jean Gagé, "offered at first glance an astonishing resemblance to a type of fraternal association, namely the funerary or burial society."[7]

AN OBSCURE AND SECRET ASSOCIATION

Besides Pliny, other pagan observers in the second century used the language of associations to identify Christianity. Lucian, a satirist who

7. Jean Gagé, *Les Classes sociales dans l'empire romain* (Paris, 1964), 308.

wrote humorous essays and dialogues about life in the Roman world in the second century, pokes fun at the gullibility of the Christians. In referring to their leaders, he uses the term *thiasarchēs* to describe the head of the association of Christians who worship "the man who was crucified in Palestine" (*Peregrinus* 11). Later in the century Celsus, whose work I shall discuss extensively in a later chapter, also used the language of associations to describe Christianity. In a passage arguing that the Christian claim that Jesus rose from the dead can hardly be taken seriously as Jesus appeared only to his followers, he writes, "At the time when he was disbelieved while in the body, he preached without restraint to all; but when he would establish a strong faith after rising from the dead, he appeared secretly to just one woman and to those of his own association." One of the chief points of Celsus's book against Christianity is that Christians formed "associations contrary to the laws" (*c. Cels.* 1.1). Instead of joining in with the public religious rites of the cities, like other associations, they refused to have anything to do with others and carried on their affairs in the fashion of an "obscure and secret association" (*c. Cels.* 8.17).

That Christianity appeared to outside observers as an association devoted to the worship of Christ or as a burial society did not imply that such associations were illegal. Though Celsus attempted to present the Christian society as illegal and disruptive of the well-being of the city, in Pliny's letter the legality of Christianity as an unlicensed association is not the issue. Celsus is making a debater's point. To call Christianity a burial association was not a negative judgment. Indeed, such a characterization helped people to place the Christian groups within a familiar frame of reference and gave outsiders a sense of what went on in its meetings and what one could expect if one were to join.

That such was the case can be seen in a Christian writer, Tertullian, who self-consciously presented Christianity as a *collegium* (association) in his *Apologeticum* (Apology), a work designed to defend and explain Christianity to outsiders and win converts to the new movement. His point is that Christianity is not an illegal association, and he seems to be responding to the charge that it, like other associations, was politically divisive. But in answering these charges he uses the language of the association as a vehicle to present a portrait of the Christian move-

ment to outsiders. Christianity, he argues, is an association devoted
not to political maneuvering or clandestine activities but to inculcating
moral principles in its members and training people to live virtuously.
Let me, says Tertullian, describe to you the "business of the Christian club (*factio*)."

> We are an association (*corpus*) bound together by our religious
> profession, by the unity of our way of life and the bond of our
> common hope. . . . We meet together as an assembly and as a so-
> ciety. . . . We pray for the emperors. . . . We gather together to
> read our sacred writing. . . . With the holy words we nourish our
> faith. . . . After the gathering is over the Christians go out as
> though they had come from a "school of virtue."

No one suffers harm from these assemblies, he concludes, for when
the virtuous gather together it "should not be called a political club
but a council" (*Apol.* 39).

This chapter in Tertullian's *Apology* is filled with a host of technical
terms used in connection with associations. The Christian community
is called *factio Christiana* (Christian party), *corpus* (association), *secta
Dei* (sect or school of God), *coitio Christianorum* (meeting of Christians), *curia* (council or senate). Tertullian also used familiar terms to
refer to the offerings of Christians: *arca* (chest), *honoraria* (gifts), *stips*
(contribution). He shuns familiar Christian words for the church—
for example, *ecclesia*—or images from the Bible in favor of terms such
as *corpus*—association, club, or school. His language would be quite
intelligible to anyone in the Greco-Roman world whether one was acquainted with Christianity or not. Like other associations, he argues
that the Christian community had a common chest, regular meetings
for worship and festive meals, official leaders, and—perhaps, though
Tertullian does not mention it—a common place of burial.

In comparison to the rich imagery for the church in the New Testament and in other early Christian writers, including Tertullian in other
treatises, his description of the church in this chapter is social and
nontheological. In effect, he commends Christianity to others because
it is a good association that can help people achieve a devout and

moral life. Like other men and women, he says, we have our religious allegiance; we follow a certain way of life defined by our tradition; we, too, seek to live a life of piety toward the gods and philanthropy toward others; in our gatherings we exhort one another to live according to these ideals; we have our own scriptures and leaders who preside over our assemblies. We are not a fly-by-night sect, a newcomer which sprang up only a few years ago: "We date the origin of our teaching . . . from the reign of Tiberius" (*Apol.* 7.3), who lived two centuries earlier.

Tertullian, an apologist writing a tract in defense of Christianity, singles out a common social designation of the sect in the Roman world to present his faith to outsiders. In doing so, he provides additional evidence that when the Christian movement began to appear to public view in the second century it was perceived by outsiders as a religious association or burial society, whose founder was Jesus and which resembled other societies that could be found in the cities of the Roman world. Of course, Tertullian was not content to let Christianity be seen simply as one association among others. Later in his apology he argues for the superiority of the Christian association.

My purpose here, however, is not to analyze the response of Christians to the attitudes and observations of outsiders. I wish only to note how one apologist took the social descriptions of outsiders as a starting point for his apologetic efforts. If Tertullian was to make a credible case for the truth of Christianity, he had first to show its similarity to other accepted religious and social groups within the empire. What others thought about Christianity was a factor in shaping how Christians would think about themselves and how they would present themselves to the larger world. A similar process can be seen in the characterization of Christianity as a superstition.

III THE PIETY OF
THE PERSECUTORS

FTER PLINY HAD PASSED JUDGMENT ON THE SECOND group of Christians brought before him, he decided to interrogate two Christian slavewomen. He had heard rumors about Christian rites and wished to inquire further into what the Christians actually did when they gathered together. The women told him that when Christians assembled they shared a common meal, sang hymns, prayed, and exhorted one another to live God-pleasing lives. After the interview Pliny wrote Trajan to report that he had not turned up any new information. All he found, wrote Pliny, was a "depraved superstition carried to extravagant lengths." What did it mean, in the second century of the Roman Empire, to call Christianity a superstition?

The use of the term "superstition" (*superstitio*) would be less significant were it not that two other Roman writers living at the same time also employed it to refer to the Christians. In his *Annales,* a history of the Roman Empire in the first century C.E., Tacitus, a close friend and colleague of Pliny, mentioned the Christians in his account of the burning of Rome under Nero. Tacitus, born five years before Pliny, had grown up in the same world, received a similar education, and pursued a similar career. At approximately the same age he too had become a provincial governor. By temperament he was more skeptical than Pliny, and his intellect more inquisitive, but he was shaped by the same moral and intellectual values.

In his *Annales* Tacitus intended to document the transformation of Roman life as a result of the establishment of the rule of one man, the emperor. He looked back wistfully on the days of the Republic before the accession of Augustus, and he wanted to show that the moral sensibilities of the leaders of the state had been dulled by the new form of government. Christianity is not part of Tacitus's history. Except for the one reference in the *Annales,* he shows no interest in the new movement. When he adverts to Christians in the book it is not because he is interested in Christianity as such or aimed to inform his readers about the new religion, as, for example, he did in a lengthy discussion of the Jews in another work, the *Histories* (5.1–13), but because he wished to make a point about the extent of Nero's vanity and the magnitude of his vices, and to display the crimes he committed against the Roman people. On the basis of Tacitus's account of the burning of Christians, later Christian tradition created a fantastic picture of persecution after the burning of Rome; but his account was written sixty years later, and the sparsity of detail in the text should caution one from making too much of the event. Tacitus's account tells us more about Roman attitudes in his own time, the early second century, than it does about the misfortunes of Christians during Nero's reign. It is clear that the incident is extrinsic to Tacitus's chief interest.

Yet, precisely because Tacitus is disinterested his testimony is more interesting, for it reflects how another person living at the same time as Pliny viewed the Christian movement.[1] The *Annales* was written within five, at most ten, years of Pliny's encounter with the Christians in Bithynia. "Their originator, Christ," writes Tacitus, "had been executed in Tiberius's reign by the governor of Judaea, Pontius Pilatus. But in spite of this temporary setback the deadly superstition [*superstitio*] had broken out afresh, not only in Judaea (where the mischief had started) but even in Rome. All degraded and shameful practices collect and flourish in the capital." Tacitus describes the execution of the Christians, but he makes it clear that it is not for their "incendiarism" that they are being killed, but because of their "antisocial tendencies" (literally, "hatred of mankind") and the savagery of

---

1. Tacitus knew the letters of Pliny and may have read the letter on the Christians before writing his *Annales*. See H. Fuchs, "Tacitus über die Christen," *Vigiliae Christianae* 4 (1950): 72.

Nero. "It was felt that they were being sacrificed to one man's brutality rather than to the public interest" (*Annales* 15.44).

Another Roman historian, friend and correspondent of Pliny and fifteen years his junior, Suetonius, also mentioned the Christians in passing in his book on the lives of the Roman emperors. Though Suetonius's *Lives of the Caesars* is not always a trustworthy source of information, it reflects, like the writings of Pliny and Tacitus, the outlook of the same generation of Romans. In a passage referring to the execution of Christians under Nero, Suetonius wrote, "Punishment was inflicted on the Christians, a class of men given to a new and mischievous *superstition*" (*Nero* 16).[2] Thus the three Roman writers who mention Christianity at the beginning of the second century agree in calling the new movement a *superstitio*.

ROMAN RELIGION AND CHRISTIAN PREJUDICE

In its most common and familiar sense, the term *superstition* referred to beliefs and practices that were foreign and strange to the Romans. What was foreign and strange, of course, was defined by whoever was making the judgment, but to a Roman senator, or to members of the ruling classes of Rome, *superstition* designated the kinds of practices and beliefs associated with the cults that had penetrated the Roman world from surrounding lands. The religion of the Celts in the British Isles, the practices of Germanic tribes in northern Europe, the customs of the Egyptians—all seemed superstitious to the Romans. According to Tacitus, one of the reasons why Egypt needed the firm rule of the

2. Besides this passage from *Nero*, Suetonius (*Claud.* 25) mentions a certain Chrestus. "Since the Jews constantly made disturbances at the instigation of Chrestus (*impulsore Chresto*), he [Claudius] expelled them from Rome." From the context it is clear that Claudius is speaking of Jews, and it may be that Chrestus, a not uncommon name, was simply a Jewish troublemaker about whom we have no further information. On the other hand, this may be a misspelling, based on a mispronunciation, of "Christus," and Suetonius might have been speaking of Christians in Rome who were followers of Christ but were not distinguished from Jews. In confirmation of the latter view, Tertullian says that the term *Christianus* was sometimes mispronounced as *Chrestianus* (*Apol.* 3). On the use of the term *Chrestianus*, see Fuchs, 69–74. On the Suetonius passage, see H. Janne, "Impulsore Chresto," *Mélanges Bidez* (Annuaire de l'Institut de philologie et d'histoire orientales 2, Brussels, 1934): 531–53.

Romans was that "superstitious and irresponsible excesses" divided and unsettled the region. Sarapis, an Egyptian god, he called "the favorite God of a nation addicted to superstitions." Jews were placed in the same class, religiously speaking, as the Egyptians. In 19 C.E. the Roman senate ordered four thousand ex-slaves "tainted with the superstition of the Egyptians and Jews" to be transported to Sardinia to quell the brigandage and thievery rampant on the island. The assumption that the Jews were superstitious was not an abstract judgment based on hearsay or rumor. Jews could be found in most of the larger cities of the empire and a large Jewish community dwelt in the city of Rome itself. Over the course of generations Romans had occasion to observe Jewish practices at first hand, for example, the refusal to eat pork, circumcision, the keeping of the Sabbath, the celebration of holidays and festivals. "Some, whose lot it was to have Sabbath-fearing fathers," wrote Juvenal,

> worship nothing but clouds and the numen of the heavens, and think it as great a crime to eat pork, from which their parents abstained, as human flesh. They get themselves circumcised, and look down on Roman law, preferring instead to learn and honor and fear the Jewish commandments, whatever was handed down by Moses in that arcane tone of his—never to show the way to any but fellow believers (if they ask where to get some water, find out if they're foreskinless). But their fathers were the culprits; they made every seventh day taboo for all life's business, dedicated to idleness." [*Satire* 14]

Plutarch, a Greek writer living at the beginning of the second century, also ridiculed the fanaticism of Jews who refused to fight because an attack took place on the Sabbath (*De superst.* 169c).

Tacitus's *Histories,* his account of the years from the Roman civil war in 69 C.E. to the reign of Domitian at the end of the century, includes a fuller, though not less judgmental, account of the Jews. "Among the Jews all things are profane that we hold sacred; on the other hand, they regard as permissible what seems to us immoral." He finds Jewish practices offensive, in part because he can see no genuine religious grounds for their customs, and in part because he believed that they had introduced their idiosyncratic customs to wall themselves off from others. Nevertheless, Tacitus realized that the religion of the Jews could not easily be compared to that of other peoples. "The Egyptians worship a variety of animals and half-human, half-bestial forms, whereas the Jewish religion is a purely spiritual monotheism. They hold it to be impious to make idols of perishable materials in the likeness of man; for them, the Most High and Eternal cannot be portrayed by human hands and will never pass away. For this reason they erect no images in their cities, still less in their temples." In spite of this insight into the nature of Jewish worship, Tacitus had no words of praise for the religion of the Jews, even though many intellectuals in his time were beginning to be attracted to the philosophical concept of one supreme spiritual deity. For Tacitus, however, the Jewish cult was "perverse and degraded" (*Hist.* 5.5) and Jews were thought to be a "people prone to superstition and the enemy of true religion" (*Hist.* 5.13).

Jewish religion was foreign and non-Roman. It was "novel" (*Hist.* 5.4) and contrary to the customs of other peoples. If one reads the passage from the *Histories* closely, it is clear that Tacitus's criticism of Judaism is not simply cultural or social. It is true that Jewish religion was "other" and that it deviated from the norms familiar to people in the Roman world. The Jews did not fit into Greco-Roman society, they lived as a people apart, and their religious practices had vulgar origins. But Tacitus also seems to be making a religious judgment about Judaism, or, to put the matter more correctly, his social and religious judgments are intimately related to one another. I do not want to make Tacitus more of a theologian than he was, but if we are to understand what the Romans meant by superstition, we will have to say something about the positive side of Roman religion and how it differed from our conceptions.

Much as Roman civilization is celebrated and admired in the West, in the learned as well as in the popular culture, little is said about Roman religion, and what is said is seldom complimentary. The Romans were thought to excel in law, in political sagacity, in their skill and foresight in constructing roads, in their administrative accomplishments and tolerant rule over many disparate peoples. But Roman religion is thought to have been cold and lifeless, lacking in emotive appeal, ritualistic. R. M. Ogilvie wrote:

> Latin poetry is studded with the names of gods and Roman works of art, in particular the great public monuments, like the Altar of Peace with its magnificent sculptures . . . regularly depict religious scenes. But it is difficult for us to feel that this world of gods and goddesses is more than decoration. The influence of Christian education and tradition is so strong that we cannot imagine that the pagan gods ever had any real meaning or that people could actually believe in their existence or their power.

Nevertheless, the Romans "were able to feel emotionally excited about the traditional stories of the gods, even when, with the rational side of their minds, they would dismiss them as fictions. So if we are to understand the history of the first century B.C. and of the first century A.D., we must try to get under the skin of the Romans, see how their religion worked and appreciate how they thought about it."[3]

The task of understanding and appreciating Roman religion is not made easy by the Christian apologetic tradition, especially the early writers who wrote books and essays criticizing it and defending the new Christian movement. Among these apologists the man with the greatest influence has been Augustine who, in his *City of God*—the full title of which is *City of God against the Pagans*—discussed Roman religion in detail and at length. Augustine ridiculed the Roman gods and tried to show that educated Romans did not actually "believe" in their power and influence in human affairs; rather, they thought that "belief" in the gods was "useful" or advantageous to the life of society and to the state. Traditional Roman religion had emphasized the *utilitas* (usefulness) of religious belief for the well-being of the Roman commonwealth, and one of the outstanding theoreticians of Roman religion, Terentius Varro (116–27 B.C.E.) had developed a theology of Roman religion based on this conception.

This idea of the "usefulness" of religious belief rested on an under-

3. R. M. Ogilvie, *The Romans and Their Gods* (New York, 1969), 1.

standing of the intimate relation between religion and the social order, but it was presented by Augustine as a cynical and manipulative exploitation of religion for political ends. According to Augustine, Varro "almost admits the falsity" of the tales of the gods. His work shows that "ostensibly religious rites may have been invented in cases where lies about the gods were thought to bring advantage to the citizens" (*De civ. D.* 3.4). Considering this point of view, it is hardly surprising that Augustine, and the intellectual tradition that followed him, had difficulty in taking Roman religion seriously. Even many modern scholars see Roman religion as chiefly political, a "religion of loyalty" to the state and its institutions that involved few authentic religious impulses and feelings. Yet, unless we dismiss what the Romans themselves say, we must look a bit more closely and probe more deeply. Roman religion preserved a genuine religious sensibility.[4]

THE PRACTICE OF RELIGION

The term used most frequently to designate the religious attitudes of men such as Pliny and Tacitus was *piety* (*pietas* in Latin, *eusebeia* in Greek). An illustration of Roman "piety" can be found in Tacitus's account in his *Histories* of the rebuilding of the Capitol, the temple to Jupiter Optimus Maximus, Juno, and Minerva, which stood on one of the hills of Rome. The temple had been destroyed in the civil wars of 68–69 C.E., Tacitus describes the ritual of rededicating the ground on which the temple was to be reconstructed as follows:

> Responsibility for the reconstruction of the Capitol was conferred on Lucius Vestinus, a man of the equestrian order. He summoned the diviners who advised that the remains of the earlier shrine should be dumped in the marshes and the temple rebuilt on the same foundations so far as these remained; it was the will of the gods that the ancient plan should be preserved unaltered.

4. Joseph Vogt, *Zur Religiosität der Christenverfolger im römischen Reich,* Sitzungsberichte d. Heidelberger Akademie der Wissenschaft, phil.-hist. Klasse (Heidelberg, 1962), p. 28. See also L. F. Janssen, "Superstitio and the Persecution of the Christians," *Vigiliae Christianae* 33 (1979): 131–59.

The whole area which was to be dedicated as the site of the temple was marked off by a continuous line of fillets and garlands, and on 21 June, under a cloudless sky, soldiers, who bore auspicious names, entered the precincts bearing boughs of olive and laurel and followed by the Vestal Virgins with boy and girl attendants who had both parents alive. All these carefully sprinkled the site with water drawn from springs and rivers. Then the praetor Helvidius Priscus, guided in the ritual by the pontifex Plautius Aelianus, purified the area by the sacrifice of pig, sheep and ox, and offered up the entrails upon a turf altar, praying to Jupiter, Juno and Minerva, as the deities that ruled the empire, that they would vouchsafe to prosper the labors now begun, and forasmuch as the building of their holy house had been undertaken by the piety (*pietas*) of men, to exalt the same by their divine assistance. Then the praetor laid his hand upon the fillets around the foundation stone, to which ropes were secured. In the same instant, the other officials, the priests, senate, knights and a large proportion of the populace eagerly and gladly took the strain and hauled the enormous block of stone into place. Everywhere they cast into the foundations offerings of gold and silver—nuggets of unrefined metal in the natural state. The diviners' instructions were that the building should not be desecrated by the use of stone or gold intended for any other purpose. Some addition was made to its height. This, it was felt, was the only change that religious feeling (*religio*) permitted, and the only respect in which the earlier temple had been wanting in splendor. [*Hist.* 4.53]

In this account the rebuilding of the Capitol is at once a religious and a civic occasion. It is religious in that the rebuilding of the temple was an act of piety toward the gods, but it is civic in that it was a public occasion involving the *populace as a whole* and was presided over by the representative of the people and the political head of the empire, the emperor. Priests, senators, equestrians, soldiers, and large numbers of the people took part in the event, and a praetor, an honorary position held only by distinguished Roman civil servants, offered sacrifices of a pig, a sheep, and an ox, and prayers were offered to the three Capitoline gods, Jupiter, Juno, and Minerva, beseeching their aid and protection for Rome. Tacitus described a religious ceremony that embraced all the citizens, not simply the members of a particular religious community or association.

Originally the word *piety* was used to designate the honor and respect one showed to members of one's family, children to parents, children and parents to grandparents, and everyone to one's ancestors. But the term came to be used in a wider sense, designating loyalty and obedience to the customs and traditions of Rome, to inherited laws, to those who lived in previous generations—in short to the "fatherland." As time went on, the term acquired a more specifically religious sense, meaning reverence and devotion to the gods and to the ritual or cultic acts by which the gods were honored, as for example the offering of sacrifices. But the older sense of the word was never lost. *Piety* embraced both the sense of reverence for the traditions of the family and city and the more specifically cultic sense. "Separation of the concept of piety into a familial and a cultic half is clearly a product of modern sensibilities; in antiquity piety formed a unity."[5]

Many coins from the first three centuries of the Roman Empire bear the word *pietas* or some combination of words with *pietas*, for example, *pietas augusta*. On some coins with these legends the bust of an emperor appears on one side, and on the obverse are stamped pictures of liturgical instruments used for offerings and sacrifices. Others depict the emperor standing beside an altar or making an offering; some feature animals being readied for sacrifice. Other coins bear the imprint of a female figure whose hands are uplifted in a gesture of prayer. With the female figure, legends such as *vota publica* (public prayer), *pietas*, *pietas augusta* are to be found. *Vota publica* were offered on official holidays and anniversaries. For example, a Roman military calendar discovered at an army station at Dura Europos on the eastern border of the empire in Mesopotamia designates 3 January as a holiday for "vows fulfilled and offered for the preservation of our

5. C. Koch, "Pietas," in Pauly-Wissowa, *Realencyclopädie der classischen Altertums-Wissenschaft* (Stuttgart, 1951), 22: 1230.

Lord Marcus Aurelius Severus Alexander Augustus and for the eternity of the Empire of the Roman people." Sacrifices accompanied the prayers: "To Jupiter, best and greatest, an ox; to Juno, a cow; to Minerva, a cow."[6] For soldiers garrisoned far from home, these holidays and the sacrifices accompanying them were occasions not only for an expression of public piety but also for good eating and hearty drinking.

Roman religion was not, however, confined to the public realm. It also played a part in the life of the family, in associations and clubs, as we saw in the previous chapter, and in the personal lives of individuals. Epitaphs on tombs in antiquity, as well as today, reflect the personal religious beliefs and values by which people sought to live their lives. "Here lies Anymore, wife of Marcus, most good and beautiful, wool spinner, pious (*pia*), modest, careful, chaste, stay-at-home."[7] But it was in its public function that Roman religion had its most characteristic *Sitz im Leben,* in beliefs about the empire and the divine providence that insured the peace and prosperity of an emperor's rule, in education and military training, on coins, in the public monuments and statues which lined the streets and adorned the marketplaces and public buildings. The hallowing of the ground for the Capitol was, as we have seen, a religious event, but it was also one of high political significance. Tacitus called its destruction "the most lamentable and appalling disaster in the whole history of the Roman commonwealth" (*Hist.* 3.72).

Not only *were* the Romans religious, they also *considered* themselves religious. They thought that religious devotion set them apart from other peoples. "If we care to compare our national characteristics with those of foreign peoples," writes Cicero, "we shall find that, while in all other respects we are only the equals or even the inferiors of others, yet in the sense of religion, that is in worship for the gods, we are far superior" (*Nat. D.* 2.8). According to an ancient legend, when King Numa founded the city of Rome he established "fear of the gods

6. A. D. Nock, "The Roman Army and the Religious Year," *Harvard Theological Review* 45 (1952): 187–252.
7. H. Dessau, *Inscriptiones latinae selectae* (Berlin, 1906), no. 8402.

(*metus deorum*)" as one of the principles that should govern its life
(Livy 1.19). Dionysus of Halicarnassus, a Greek rhetorician who lived
in Rome for many years and was an enthusiast for things Roman,
wrote:

> Among the Romans there are no processions performed in
> mourning habits with expressions of sorrow and attended by the
> plaints and lamentation of women bewailing the disappearance of
> deities, such as the Greeks carry out in commemorating the rape
> of Proserpina and the adventures of Bacchus and many other
> things of the same nature. Nothing is to be seen among them
> (though their manners are now corrupted) of enthusiastic trans-
> ports of corybantic mysteries, no promiscuous vigils of men and
> women in the temples, nor any extravagances of this kind. But all
> reverence is shown to the gods, both in words and actions, be-
> yond what is practiced among either Greeks or Barbarians." [*Ant.*
> *Rom.* 2.19.2–3]

Cicero says that by establishing the Roman religion, Numa laid the
foundation for the city of Rome (*Nat. D.* 3.5).

In the cities of the ancient world, religion was inextricably inter-
twined with social and political life. One did not speak of "believing in
the gods" but of "having gods," just as a city might "have laws or customs." Piety toward the gods was thought to insure the well-being of
the city, to promote a spirit of kinship and mutual responsibility, indeed, to bind together the citizenry. "In all probability," wrote Cicero,
"disappearance of piety towards the gods will entail the disappearance
of loyalty and social union among men as well, and of justice itself, the
queen of all the virtues" (*Nat. D.* 1.4). If one were to single out one
idea that captured the religious sense of the Romans it would be divine providence, the notion that the gods exercised influence over the
affairs of men and the events of history. For this reason the gods were
worthy of worship and devotion. Thus Cicero wrote:

> There are and have been philosophers who hold that the gods ex-
> ercise no control over human affairs whatever. But if their opin-

ion is the true one, how can piety, reverence or religion exist? For all these are tributes which it is our duty to render in purity and holiness to the divine powers solely on the assumption that they take notice of them, and that some service has been rendered by the gods to the race of men. But if on the contrary the gods have neither the power nor the will to aid us, if they pay no heed to us at all and take no notice of our actions, if they can exert no possible influence upon the life of men, what ground have we for rendering any sort of worship, honor or prayer to the immortal gods? Piety, however, like the rest of the virtues, cannot exist in mere outward show and pretence; and with piety, reverence and religion must likewise disappear. And when these are gone, life soon becomes a welter of disorder and confusion." [*Nat. D.* 1.3–4]

Like *pietas, providentia* also appeared on Roman coins from the period. The gods were thought to preserve the city of Rome and to insure the orderly transition from one emperor to another. Through the providence of the gods the earth came to life each spring, the wheat bloomed, the trees bore fruit, and the heavens opened to provide rain. On some coins an eagle was shown flying down to the emperor with the scepter of Rome in his beak, symbolizing the peaceful transition of power through the *providentia* of the gods. On others, the emperor was presented as the restorer of the whole world (*restitutor orbis terrarum*) because of the *providentia deorum.*[8] Even attention to the smallest details, the minutiae of religious ceremonies (for example, the feeding of chickens or heeding the cry of a bird), was a mark of piety that contributed to the well-being and success of the Roman Republic (Livy 6.41.8).[9] Within this framework of "belief" it was possible to distinguish true from false practices, religion which fostered traditional beliefs and that which undermined the wisdom of the past.

8. M. P. Charlesworth, "Providentia and Aeternitas," *Harvard Theological Review* 29 (1936): 187–252.

9. Karl Koch, *Religion. Studien zur Kult und Glauben der Römer* (Nürnberg, 1960), 178–79.

Hence it was not inappropriate to contrast genuine religion and superstition. "Religion has been distinguished from superstition not
only by philosophers but by our ancestors," says Cicero. For *superstition* implied "groundless fear of the gods" whereas religion consisted
in "pious worship of the gods" (*Nat. D.* 1.117; 2.72). The superstitious person engaged in religious practices that neither honored the
gods nor benefited men and women.

Because the discussion of piety began with Pliny, a Roman who
wrote in Latin, I have concentrated on the attitude toward it reflected
in Latin sources. But in the world in which Christianity arose similar
attitudes and ideas could be found in other parts of the Roman world.
In the Greek cities of the eastern Mediterranean, for example, the term
"piety" (*eusebeia*) bore many of the same overtones. It was used in a
public sense to characterize the attitude of the *ephebes* (teenage boys)
on the completion of their athletic and military training. An inscription from Athens in the first century B.C.E. describes the elaborate ceremonies that took place on the day the young men were presented to
the city. There were a parade with full military dress, the bearing of
torches, races and other athletic contests, public sacrifices of bulls and
calves, the offering of libations. On being presented to the council and
the people, the ephebes were crowned with golden crowns and honored "on account of their piety (*eusebeia*) towards the gods and respect
(*philotimia*) for the council and people."[10]

Toward the end of the first century of the Common Era a Greek
philosopher, a contemporary of Pliny and Tacitus, wrote a little treatise on superstition (*deisidaimonia*). The work is usually attributed to
Plutarch (50–120 C.E.), a native of Greece.[11] Plutarch had traveled
widely in Egypt and Italy, and he wrote widely on moral and religious

10. *Inscriptiones graecae* (Berlin, 1916), II-III², 1, 2, no. 1029. Cf. also nos. 1009,
1036.
11. Text of *On Superstition* and translation can be found in Frank Cole Babbit, ed.,
Plutarch's Moralia (Cambridge: Loeb Classical Library, 1962), 2: 454–95. For a discussion of the work and of the question of authenticity, see Morton Smith, "De Super-
stitione (*Moralia* 164E–171F)," in Hans Dieter Betz, *Plutarch's Theological Writings
and Early Christian Literature,* Studia ad Corpus Hellenisticum Novi Testamenti (Leiden, 1975), 1–35.

topics. A pious and devout adherent of the ancient religion of Greece, he served as priest at Delphi, the great religious shrine in central Greece. He wrote books on the Egyptian religion of Isis and Osiris and on religious oracles, as well as on other topics. The treatise *On Superstition,* whether by Plutarch or not, is interesting as a reflection of a spiritually sensitive Greek thinker on superstition and piety. He does not, however, mention Christianity.

According to Plutarch, superstition sets people off from the rest of society because the superstitious person does not use his intelligence in thinking about the gods. Instead he creates fearful images and horrible apparitions that lead to bizarre and extreme behavior. The superstitious man is also fanatical. His feelings toward the gods are exaggerated; he worships them with excessive awe; and he believes that one's lot in life is dependent not on what one does—namely, on human responsibility—but on the decrees of fate and fortune over which one has no control. The superstitious man "enjoys no world in common with the rest of mankind" (166c). To him the gods are "rash, faithless, fickle, vengeful, cruel and easily offended," for they deal capriciously and arbitrarily with men and women (170e).

Because superstition leads to irrational ideas about the gods, the inevitable consequence is atheism. "Atheists do not see the gods at all," but the superstitious man "thinks they exist" and conjures up false ideas about them. He imagines fickle and willful gods who deal with men as playthings and shuns the ideas of philosophers and statesmen who try to show that "the majesty of God is associated with goodness, magnanimity, kindliness and solicitude." For this reason, says Plutarch, "it occurs to me to wonder at those who say that atheism is impiety and do not say the same of superstition." The atheist "thinks there are no gods" but the superstitious person "believes in them against his will, for he is afraid not to believe." Hence superstition must be driven out, for it is the "seed from which atheism springs" (167 d-e). There is "no infirmity comprehending such a multitude of errors and emotions, and involving opinions so contradictory, or rather antagonistic, as that of superstition." It is a worse evil than atheism, because instead of producing genuine religion it eventually leads men and women to have doubts about the very existence of the gods. For in trying to "escape superstition," people "rush into a rough and hardened atheism, thus overlapping piety (*eusebeia*) which lies between them (171f)."

"WE TOO ARE A RELIGIOUS PEOPLE"

It is unlikely that Pliny or Tacitus had read Plutarch's essay on superstition. Yet this work reflects a common fund of attitudes and ideas shared by educated men and women. In matters of religion the Romans were very conservative, suspicious of innovations and mistrustful of new religious ideas and practices. One should not, wrote Plutarch, "distort and sully one's own tongue with strange names and barbarous phrases, to disgrace and transgress the god-given ancestral dignity of our religion (*eusebeia*)" (166b). The primary test of truth in religious matters was custom and tradition, the practices of the ancients. "There was very little doubt in people's minds that the religious practices of one generation should be cherished without change by the next. . . . To be pious in any sense, to be respectable and decent, required the perpetuation of cult," writes Ramsay MacMullen.[12] In philosophical matters one might turn to intellectuals and philosophers, but in religious questions one looked to the past, to the accepted practices handed down by tradition, and to the guarantors of this tradition, the priests. Just as in public life the Romans were wary of the *novus homo*, the new man who had only achieved wealth and position, so in religion conservatism ran even deeper.

Compare, for example, the presumed speech of Maecenas to the emperor Augustus as recorded by the historian Dio Cassius. Both Maecenas and Agrippa had appeared before Augustus, one arguing the merits of monarchical rule, the other of democratic rule. In his speech Maecenas advises Augustus how to achieve immortality as the emperor of Rome. Do not, he says, allow honors to be conferred on you, for nothing can be greater than that which you already possess. Do not allow gold or silver images to be made or temples built.

---

12. Ramsay MacMullen, *Paganism in the Roman Empire* (New Haven, 1981), 2.

If you wish to become immortal pursue a life of virtue and worship the divine according to the tradition of your fathers. . . .
Those who attempt to distort our religion with strange rites you
should abhor and punish, not merely for the sake of the gods, but
such men by bringing in new divinities in place of the old, persuade many to adopt foreign pactices, from which spring up con-
spiracies, factions and political clubs which are far from profitable
to a monarchy. Do not therefore permit anyone to be an atheist
or a sorcerer." [Dio Cassius 52.36.2]

This text from Dio, who was a native of Bithynia, the province in
which Pliny served as governor, was written in the early third century,
but it could almost be taken as a commentary on the response of Pliny
to the Christian groups there.

Given this attitude that religion is a patrimony from the past which
sustains the life of the state, it was inevitable that the piety of the persecutors would conflict with the new movement that had begun in
Palestine. The Christians were seen as religious fanatics, self-righteous
outsiders, arrogant innovators, who thought that only their beliefs
were true. However, the Roman belief in divine providence, in the necessity of religious observance for the well-being of society, and in the
efficacy of traditional rites and practices, was no less sincere than the
beliefs of the Christians. As a Roman proconsul put it at the trial of a
Christian in North Africa, "If you make fun of things we hold sacred I
will not allow you to speak." How presumptuous, thought the Romans, that the Christians considered themselves alone religious. As a
Roman official aptly remarked at the trial of the Scillitan martyrs, "We
too are a religious people."

We must take these claims seriously. As tempting as it may be to
those who have been nurtured on the personal religion of our culture,
Roman religion cannot be reduced, as Augustine attempted, to politics or statecraft. The religion of the Romans was, to be sure, inextricably bound up with the life of the state, with the idea of Rome and
the fortunes of the empire, but such was the case with most religions
in the ancient world. In his now-classical study, *Conversion*, A. D.
Nock, historian of Roman religion, showed that in ancient times reli-

gion and society were always thought to complement each other. When a person moved from one city to another, he or she adopted the gods of the new city. The idea of "conversion"—that is, a conscious and individual decision to embrace a certain creed or way of life—was wholly foreign to the ancients. Hence we find there neither the intense personal experience nor the metaphysical or theological speculation that is taken for granted in Christianity. The classical scholar, Agnes Kirsopp Michels, says: "Of course if one studies Roman religion looking for original metaphysical concepts or an interest in the transcendental one will be disappointed, as one would be in looking for these things anywhere else in Roman culture. . . . That does not mean that it was lifeless or unsatisfying to the Romans themselves, but that one has been asking the wrong questions, and therefore failing to discover what its positive values were to those who created it."[13]

By the standards of religion familiar to most Westerners, and because of our propensity to view religion as a private and individual experience, the religious attitudes of the Romans seem superficial and emotionally unsatisfying. If, however, one views them as a form of public piety, ancient Roman religion is quite intelligible. Religion can be as much concerned with the public life of a society as it is with the private lives of individuals. Over a hundred years ago Fustel de Coulanges wrote, in *The Ancient City*: "One would have a very false idea of human nature to believe that this ancient religion was an imposture, and, so to speak, a comedy. Montesquieu pretends that the Romans adopted a worship only to restrain the people. A religion never had such an origin; and every religion that has come to sustain itself only from motives of public utility, has not stood long."[14]

One of the functions of religion is to relate institutions, roles, and the events of family and society to an ultimate reality, whether these events be the birth of a child, the crowning of a king, the eating of

13. Agnes Kirsopp Michels, review of Kurt Latte, *Römische Religionsgeschichte* (Munich, 1960), *American Journal of Philology* 83 (1962):434–44.

14. Numa Denis Fustel de Coulanges, *The Ancient City: A Study of the Religion, Laws, and Institutions of Greece and Rome* (New York: Doubleday Anchor Book, n.d.), 166–67.

food and the drinking of wine, the waging of war and the making of peace, or the coming of age of a young man or woman. Religion places the ordinary and extraordinary events of social and individual life within a sacred and cosmic frame of reference. The coins people use in transacting business, the statues one passes in the city square, the public buildings where one conducts business, triumphal arches and pillars, public holidays, literature and art and education—all these are vehicles through which religious feelings can be expressed, and were expressed, in the ancient world. Religion was at the heart of social and cultural life.

For most people, to have a good time with their friends involved some contact with a god who served as guest of honor, as master of ceremonies, or as host in the porticoes or flowering, shaded grounds of his own dwelling. For most people, meat was a thing never eaten and wine to surfeit never drunk save as some religious setting permitted. There existed—it is no great exaggeration to say it of all but the fairly rich—no formal social life in the world of the Apologists [second and third centuries] that was entirely secular. Small wonder, then, that Jews and Christians, holding themselves aloof from anything the gods touched, suffered under the reputation of misanthropy![15]

In his *Social Contract,* Jean Jacques Rousseau categorized such religion under the rubric of "civil religion." This religion is described as a "profession of faith which is purely civil" and whose first dogma is the belief in an "omnipotent, intelligent, benevolent divinity that foresees and provides." Public officials, kings, emperors, and governors concern themselves with this form of religion because it touches on moral attitudes and duties, what Rousseau calls "sentiments of sociability." Such sentiments would include attitudes toward one's fellow citizens, the law, justice, and the defense of the state. Besides belief in the gods, civil religion usually stresses moral responsibility and human immor-

15. MacMullen, 40. See also the perceptive remarks of William B. Schoedel, "Christian 'Atheism' and the Peace of the Roman Empire," *Church History* 42 (1973): 310–11.

tality, for without such beliefs the sanctity of the social contract is rup-
tured and "there is no bond to hold together and cement the life of
society."

To say, then, that Christianity is a superstition is not a matter of
simple bias or the result of ignorance; it expresses a distinct religious
sensibility. When Tacitus wrote that Christianity was the "enemy of
mankind," he did not simply mean he did not like Christians and
found them a nuisance (though this was surely true), but that they
were an affront to his social and religious world. When later critics
faulted Christians for not participating in civic affairs or in the military, the point of such criticism was as religious as it was social, although the specific acts mentioned do not appear to us to be religious.
"You do not go to our shows, you take no part in our processions,
you are not present at our public banquets, you shrink in horror from
our sacred games" (Minucius Felix, *Octavius* 12). Roman games were
religious events as well as shows for gladiators or gymnastic contests.
As one early Christian put it, thus reflecting the world in which he
lived, "What is a stage show without a god, a game without a sacrifice?" (Pseudo-Cyprian, *De spectaculis* 4).

The observations of Pliny, Tacitus, and Suetonius presaged the response of Romans to the Christian movement during the next several
hundred years. Stories about the new religion shocked them, and the
self-righteousness and arrogance of the martyrs offended them.
Though the popular culture of our society views the Romans as de-
generate and irreligious and delights in lurid portraits of the lives and
loves of lecherous and lascivious emperors, one could hardly find a
more upright and virtuous, at times even censorious, group than the
men from Pliny's class. Strange as the term *superstition* may sound to
modern Christian ears, the designation was apt. Perhaps the surest indication that the charge hit home was the seriousness with which the
early Christians took it. The apologists sought to present Christians as
pious and god-fearing by the standards of Greco-Roman society.

The earliest Christians did not use the term *piety* to describe their
faith, but it began to crop up in Christian literature at about the same
time that outsiders began taking notice of the new movement. The

word occurs only in the later writings of the New Testament, the pastoral epistles, 2 Peter, and once in the Book of Acts. By the middle of the second century, however, a Christian apologist such as Justin Martyr, who was well aware that Christianity was being viewed as a superstition, had begun to make the counterclaim. "We cultivate *piety*, justice, philanthropy, faith and hope." This passage could have been written by the Roman moralist and philosopher Seneca. From the side of philosophy, "religion never departs, nor *piety*, nor justice, nor any of the whole company of virtues which cling together in close-united fellowship" (*Ep.* 90.3).

IV GALEN: THE CURIOSITY
OF A PHILOSOPHER

THE CHRISTIANS WERE FORTUNATE, AFTER PLINY, TO have a philosopher as commentator on the new movement, the famous physician Galen, who lived in the latter part of the second century. In the interim, several writers mentioned Christianity—for example, Epictetus, the Stoic moralist; Apuleius, the North African author of the novel *The Golden Ass*; Lucian of Samosata, the Greek satirist; and, on occasion, other Christian authors referred to comments of pagans on the Christians. Justin Martyr, writing in the mid-second century, also mentions the Cynic philosopher Crescens, who called the Christians "atheistic" and "impious," echoing the charge of Pliny (2 *Apol.* 3). Furthermore, the emperor Hadrian (117–133 C.E.), Trajan's successor, issued an imperial rescript in response to accusations brought against the Christians in 121–22 C.E. But as we do not possess the text of the original inquiry by the proconsul Silvanus Granianus, it does not tell us much about the Christians. In contrast to the Pliny–Trajan correspondence, which gave us Pliny's view of the matter and provided an insight into how the Christians were viewed in the local community, Hadrian's rescript deals primarily with legal questions. It does show, however, that Hadrian, like his predecessor Trajan, insisted that the Christians be treated fairly, that the laws of the empire be respected, and that innocent people not be accused falsely. "If the inhabitants of the province can clearly sustain the petition against the Christians so as to give answer in a court of law, let them pursue this course alone, but let them not have resort to men's petitions and outcries. . . . But, by Hercules, if any one bring any accusation through mere calumny, decide in regard to his criminality, and see to it that you inflict punishment" (Eusebius, *Hist. Eccl.* 4.9.1–3).[1]

PHILOSOPHY AND MEDICINE

Galen was a native of the city of Pergamum, located in the fertile Caicus Valley in western Asia Minor some fifteen miles from the Aegean Sea. In 88 B.C.E. Pergamum had become free and was one of the leading cities in the province of Asia, though the citizens of Ephesus nearby, according to one of their own inscriptions, proclaimed Ephesus the "greatest and best" of the cities of Asia. Pergamum was nevertheless a major city. Its natural resources, particularly silver mines and agriculture, gave its citizens the means not only to make it one of the most beautiful cities in the empire but also to sustain a rich and diverse cultural life. Its library, second only to the famous one in Alexandria, contained 200,000 volumes. A spectacular shrine dedicated to the god of healing, Asclepius, was located there. This complex of buildings included a large temple, a circular structure with six apses adjoining the temple, a smaller temple, and a theater, as well as other buildings that served as guest houses and places of incubation. Asclepius's power to heal attracted people from all over the world, and in the second century the Asclepieion at Pergamum had become a destination of pilgrimage.

Galen, Pergamum's most famous native son, was born in ca. 130 C.E. on an estate outside the city. His family was wealthy and well educated and his father took an active role in Galen's upbringing and education. "It was my good fortune to have a father who was perfectly calm, just, serviceable and devoted." An architect by profession, Galen's father Nicon was formally educated in mathematics and the physical sciences, but he had a deep interest in literature, the arts, and philosophy. He insisted that Galen not only receive a liberal education

---

1. For a survey of pagan criticism of Christianity during this period, see Stephen Benko, "Pagan Criticism of Christianity during the First Two Centuries A.D.," in *Aufstieg und Niedergang der römischen Welt*, 23.2: 1054–1118.

but also develop a genuinely critical spirit toward all intellectual matters.

After Galen had spent his boyhood on his father's estate learning to read and write, his father encouraged him to study philosophy and even participated with him in this study. Galen recalled later in life that his father had not joined any one philosophical school, nor had he identified with one teacher. He insisted that his son, like himself, critically examine the various philosophical options of his day without adopting one view. First Galen studied with a Stoic by the name of Philopator; later he turned to a Platonist; then he studied with a Peripatetic (Aristotelian); and finally he took up with an Epicurean who had recently arrived from Athens. Never abandoning his critical approach, as a mature thinker Galen criticized all the philosophical schools for their dogmatism and unwillingness to entertain opinions different from their own. Even though he had a keen interest in philosophy, Galen never became an adherent of one school.

Once he had completed his philosophical studies, Galen shifted his interest to anatomy and medicine. He studied with Satyros, an anatomist teaching at Pergamum at the time, and on the death of his father he began to travel around the Mediterranean, learning from other anatomists and physicians. During these years he also produced his first book, a treatise on the movements of the lungs and thorax. At the same time he continued his interest in philosophy by going to hear the great Platonist philosopher Albinus, who was teaching at Smyrna.

To further his medical studies Galen moved to Alexandria in 152, but he also continued to dabble in philosophy and to pursue the other intellectual enticements offered by the diverse and varied environment of the great city. By the time he returned home to Pergamum five or six years later, he had been studying anatomy and medicine for twelve years. The chief priest of the Asclepeion, the shrine to the god Asclepius as well as the medical center of the cult, asked Galen to serve as one of its physicians. After several years, however, he again grew restless, and in 161–62 he set out for Rome just as the new emperor Marcus Aurelius was beginning his reign. In Rome, Galen met the emperor, and Marcus was so impressed with the young doctor that he asked him to become private physician to his son Commodus, the man who later would succeed his father in the imperial office. Until the end of the century, when he returned to Pergamum to spend his final years in his native city, Galen lived in Rome.

By the time Galen arrived in Rome a Christian community had existed there for over a hundred years. In relation to the size of the city and other religious groups there—for example, the Jews, or the followers of Isis—the Christian community (or communities) was not very large. It was, however, one of the most significant Christian groups in the empire and had already begun to achieve preeminence. It drew Christians, especially intellectuals, from various parts of the Roman world. Almost all of the outstanding Christian thinkers in the second century spent some time in Rome: Valentinus, the brilliant Gnostic teacher and author of the Gospel of Truth; Marcion, a radical Christian leader and biblical scholar who rejected the Old Testament and was a fanatic follower of Paul; Hegesippus, an early historian of the Christian movement who came to Rome to pursue research into the list of bishops in the Christian centers; and Justin Martyr, one of the earliest and most astute apologists, who wrote his two works to the "Greeks" as well as a defense of Christianity to the Jews, his *Dialogue with Trypho,* in Rome.

Galen was a prolific writer. The complete edition of his works, compiled in the nineteenth century, comprises twenty-two volumes. His writings range over many fields: medicine, anatomy, pharmacy, logic, philosophy. They include commentaries on philosophical treatises as well as works on philology and pathology. Like Pliny and Tacitus, Galen did not write a book or treatise on the Christians, but in the course of discussing other topics in several of his medical treatises he mentioned them. One passage on the Christians occurs in a treatise on the uses of the parts of the body. Though his observations are wedged in between these other concerns, he had clearly given thought to Christianity and made an attempt to understand the new movement and to place it within the context of his intellectual and social world. Galen was genuinely interested in new and unusual phenomena, both physical and social, and his observations on Christianity, reflecting a serious and critical mind, give us new insight into how the Christian movement was perceived in the middle of the second century C.E.

CHRISTIANITY AS A PHILOSOPHICAL SCHOOL

The first reference to Christianity in Galen's works occurs in a book on the pulse. In the course of the work Galen discusses the studies of a certain physician of his day, Archigenes. Galen thought his conclusions were faulty and imprecise because his approach to the pulse was not based on careful investigation and sound reasoning. With such people, says Galen, it is pointless to engage in serious discussion. It is, he continues, the same with Christians and Jews. "For one might more easily teach novelties to the followers of Moses and Christ than to the physicians and philosophers who cling fast to their schools. So in the end I decided that I should avoid unnecessary talk by having nothing to do with them at all, which is what I do at present and what I shall continue to do in the future" (*De pulsuum differentiis* 3.3). Later in the same work, again in a discussion of the defects of Archigenes' work, Galen criticized the latter's view that the pulse had eight qualities. This opinion, says Galen, was "commonly spoken of by the prominent people," but would it not be preferable to provide a "cogent demonstration" than to appeal to commonly held opinion? If one offers no reasons for one's views it would be "as if one had come into the school of Moses and Christ and heard talk of undemonstrated laws" (*De pulsuum differentiis* 2.4). In another fragment Galen, speaking of the opinions of certain physicians, says, "They compare those who practice medicine without scientific knowledge to Moses, who framed laws for the tribe of Israel, since it is his method in his books to write without offering proofs, saying 'God commanded, God spake'" (*On Hippocrates's Anatomy*).[2]

It is curious that Galen, writing in the middle of the second century, lumps together Jews and Christians. By this time Christianity had es-

2. Galen's references to Christianity are conveniently edited and translated into English in Richard Walzer, *Galen on Jews and Christians* (London, 1949). Texts discussed in this chapter can be found on pp. 10–16.

tablished itself as a movement independent of Judaism, and it is likely that even people who only knew Christians casually could tell the difference between Christians and Jews. Nevertheless, as we shall see in the following chapter, which discusses another pagan critic, Celsus, the informed observer recognized the intimate historical relation between Christianity and Judaism. This passage from Galen, however, is not concerned with the historical relation between Judaism and Christianity, or with the relation of Christ to Moses; it is concerned with the similarity in the way the two religions deal with the question of "faith and reason." The most obvious explanation for this conjunction is that Galen bases his criticism on the Mosaic account of creation in Genesis 1. He realized that both Christians and Jews considered the Book of Genesis authoritative. Hence, on the point that here interested Galen, there was no need to distinguish between the two.

Galen, in contrast to earlier observers, did not view Christianity as a superstitious sect or a foreign cult. Instead he dignified Christianity (and Judaism) with the term "school," by which he meant a philosophical school, and he offered philosophical criticism of Christian and Jewish beliefs. Even if Pliny had been interested in philosophy, it would have been pointless for him to offer philosophical criticisms of a group of fanatics. Galen, however, treated the Christians with respect. This is not to say that he agreed with Christian teaching, or even that he thought it philosophically interesting. It simply means that Galen treated Christianity on the same terms as other philosophical schools that were native to the Greek and Roman world, and that he criticized the Christian and Jewish schools for not living up to the intellectual ideal appropriate to philosophers.

Christians and Jews, however, were not the only schools that appealed to "faith" or to the authority of their teachers. By the second century of the Common Era the Greek philosophical tradition had splintered into many competing parties. The result was a plethora of schools whose names have become synonymous with the ancient world: Platonists, Peripatetics (Aristotelians), Stoics, Epicureans, Pythagoreans, Cynics, Skeptics. Each of these schools had its own intellectual tradition, exemplified in a succession of famous teachers, and adherents often came to resemble doctrinaire proponents of inherited views rather than inquiring philosophers. In some cases, members of a particular school exhibited an almost religious veneration of the founder, celebrating his memory with a festival that included religious sacrifices, a banquet, and readings from his works.

Philosophers became hucksters, salesmen marketing the ideas and beliefs of their respective schools. Addressing crowds on street corners and in the marketplace, they offered advice on how to live one's life and deal with personal problems. Appealing less to reason and logic than to emotion and feeling, philosophers appeared as traveling evangelists, directing their hearers to the wondrous accomplishments of the founder of the school, its venerable tradition, or the high regard in which many people viewed it. In his dialogue, *Philosophies for Sale,* Lucian, a second-century satirist and contemporary of Galen, offers a humorous account of the hawking of philosophy in the great cities of the Roman Empire.[3] The setting for the following dialogue is a slave market in a Greek-speaking city in the eastern Mediterranean.

Zeus: You arrange the benches and make the place ready for the men that are coming. You bring on the philosophies [literally "ways of life"] and put them in line: but first groom them up so that they will look well and will attract as many as possible. You, Hermes, be crier and call them together.

Hermes: Under the blessing of Heaven, let the buyers now appear at the sales-room. We shall put up for sale philosophies of every type and all manner of creeds; and if anyone is unable to pay cash, he is to name a surety and pay next year.

Hermes: Which do you want us to bring on first?

Zeus: This fellow with the long hair, the Ionian, for he seems to be someone of distinction.

Hermes: You Pythagorean, come forward and let yourself be looked over by the company.

3. Text and translation of Lucian's *Philosophies for Sale (Vitarum Auctio),* in A. M. Harmon, ed., *Lucian* (Cambridge: Loeb Classical Library, 1968), 2:449–511.

Zeus: Hawk him now.

Hermes: The noblest of philosophies for sale, the most distinguished; who'll buy? Who wants to be more than man? Who
wants to apprehend the music of the spheres and to be born
again?

A buyer steps up and asks the Pythagorean several questions about
his philosophy and the Pythagorean replies with a caricature of his
school. "If I buy you, asks the interested customer, what will you
teach me?" The Pythagorean answers. "I shall teach you nothing, but
make you remember" [i.e. all genuine learning is remembering]. Next
Lucian places a Cynic on the platform, and he is followed by a
Democritean and a Heraclitean. Then he puts up the Platonist.

Hermes: Come here, sir. We are putting up a righteous and intelligent philosophy. Who'll buy the height of sanctity?
Buyer: Tell us what you know best.
Platonist: I am a lover, and wise in matters of love.
Buyer: How am I to buy you, then? What I wanted was a tutor
for my son, who is handsome.
Platonist: But who would be more suitable than I to associate
with a handsome lad? It is not the body I love, it is the soul
that I hold beautiful. As a matter of fact, even if they lie be-
neath the same cloak with me, they will tell you that I have
done them no wrong.

Next comes the Stoic.

Zeus: Call another, the one over there with the cropped head,
the dismal fellow from the porch (stoa).
Hermes: Quite right; at all events it looks as if the men who fre-
quent the public square were writing for him in great numbers.
Sell virtue itself, the most perfect of philosophies. Who wants
to be the only one to know everything?
Buyer: What do you mean by that?
Hermes: That he is the only wise man, the only handsome man,

the only just man, brave man, king, orator, rich man, lawgiver, and everything else that there is.

Buyer: Come here, my good fellows, and tell your buyer what you are like, and first of all whether you are not displeased with being sold and living in slavery?

Stoic: Not at all for these things are not in our control and all that is not in our control is immaterial.

Lucian is, of course, poking fun at the philosophical schools, but his caricature has an element of truth in it. The appeal of a philosopher frequently had less to do with the teachings of his school than with how the philosopher dressed, what kind of success he could promise its adherents, and which philosophy was fashionable and highly regarded in influential circles. In another work, *Hermotimus*,[4] Lucian ridicules the intellectual arguments people offered for adhering to one school rather than another. One of the characters in the dialogue says: "Well, then, please teach me this first, how, right at the beginning, we can distinguish the best, the true philosophy, the one we must choose, leaving aside the others." To which Hermotimus answers: "I will tell you. I saw that most people look at this one [Stoicism] so I guessed it was the best" (*Hermotimus* 16). Although Hermotimus claimed to have reasonable grounds for choosing Stoicism, he explains his decision as follows. "I used to see the Stoics walking with dignity, decently dressed, always thoughtful, manly in looks, most of them close-cropped; there was nothing effeminate, none of that exaggerated indifference which stamps the genuine crazy Cynic" (*Hermotimus* 18).

Philosophers appealed to tradition to win people over to their way of life. "Believe those who have made the journey before you and you cannot go wrong" (*Hermotimus* 27). Often doctrinaire, they asked people to accept their beliefs on faith or on the authority of former teachers. Galen, no satirist like Lucian, makes the same point in sober, reasoned prose.

People admire this or that particular physician or philosopher without proper study of their subject and without a training in

4. Text and translation in Harmon, 6:260–415.

scientific demonstration, with the help of which they would be able to distinguish between false and true arguments; some do this because of their fathers, others because of their teachers, others because their friends were either empirics or dogmatics or methodics, or simply because a representative of a particular school was admired in their native city. The same applies to the philosophical schools; different people have for different reasons become Platonists, Aristotelians, Stoics, or Epicureans (*Libr. ord.*).[5]

As philosophy became more popular, the schools began to adapt to the personal inclinations of adherents and disciples. By the second century of the Common Era the philosophical schools were not simply intellectual schools of *thought* but *ways of life* (Lucian calls them *bioi*) similar to what we today would call religious movements. Then as now, people embraced a new way of life because they were impressed by an exemplary life, because someone in their family belonged to a particular school, because of ties of marriage or friendship, or similar reasons. Joining a philosophical school often had little to do with rational argument or appeals to empirical evidence.

THE PRACTICE OF PHILOSOPHY

Once it is recognized that what Galen says of the Christians could just as well be said of other schools, it must also be said that Christians had already developed a reputation among the Greeks and Romans for appealing to faith. Celsus, another critic of Christianity whom we will consider in the next chapter, complained that Christians sought out uneducated and gullible people because they were unable to give reasons or arguments for their beliefs. They asked people to accept what they said solely on faith (*c. Cels.* 1.9). What Galen and Celsus said about the Christian movement no doubt fitted the kind of Christianity that most people met with in the cities of the Roman Empire. Nevertheless, precisely at the time that Galen and Celsus were writing

5. Walzer, 19–20.

against Christian fideism a number of Christian thinkers had begun to revise and correct this view of Christianity. Among the defenders of the reasonableness of the Christian tradition were such early Christian apologists as Justin Martyr and Athenagoras, but there was another group of men, less known, who lived in Rome at the time and may have been directly influenced by Galen's criticism of Christianity and his approach to philosophical thinking. This group is described in a fascinating fragment, sometimes called the Little Labyrinth, preserved in Eusebius's *Ecclesiastical History*.

This text, sometimes attributed to the early Christian writer Hippolytus, describes in unfavorable terms a group of Christians who lived in Rome in the latter part of the second century (during the time of Bishop Victor, 187–89). According to the Little Labyrinth, their leader was a cobbler named Theodotus, and they admired the work of Galen and sought to set Christian belief on a rational foundation. "They have tampered with the Holy Scriptures without fear," writes the author.

> Instead of asking what Holy Scripture says, they strain every nerve to find a form of syllogism to bolster up their impiety [atheism]. If anyone challenges them with a text from divine Scripture, they examine it to see whether it can be turned into a conjunctive or disjunctive form of syllogism. They put aside the holy scriptures of God, and devote themselves to geometry, since they are from the earth and speak from the earth, and do not know the one who comes from above. Some of them give all their energies to the study of Euclidean geometry, they admire Aristotle and Theophrastus, and some of them almost worship Galen. When people avail themselves of the arts of unbelievers to lend color to their heretical views and with godless rascality corrupt the simple faith of the holy Scripture, it is obvious that they are nowhere near the faith. So it was that they laid hands unblushingly on the Holy Scriptures, claiming to have corrected them. [Eusebius, *Hist. Eccl.* 5.28.13–15]

Though the author of this passage was a well-educated person, his crabby attitude toward the use of Greek learning to interpret the Bible reflects the attitude of most Christians during the first two centuries. Only a few enterprising intellectuals, and only after more than one hundred years of Christian history, had begun to take the risk of expressing Christian beliefs within the philosophical ideas current in the Greco-Roman world. Most Christians were opposed to such attempts. As late as the third century, after the apologetic movement had introduced Greek ideas into Christian thinking, Christian preachers complained that the rank-and-file opposed such ideas. In the few places in early Christian sources where philosophy is mentioned up to the mid-second century, the term was always used pejoratively. It referred to pagan belief, never to Christian teaching or life.

As we have already observed, earlier critics had agreed in calling Christianity a superstition. That Galen does not use this term may be significant; yet what is more significant is that he chose a new term—namely, *philosophical school.* The term *superstition* accented that Christianity was a foreign cult whose origin and practices stood outside the accepted religious standards of the Greco-Roman world. Superstition, by definition, was opposed to genuine religious feelings. The philosophical schools, on the other hand, were part of the public life of the empire. There were times, as for example under the capricious emperor Domitian, when philosophers were sent into exile, but in general people respected the philosophical life, and some from the upper classes identified with particular philosophical schools. In Galen's time the emperor Marcus Aurelius had become a Stoic even though his tutor Fronto disapproved. Fronto, like Pliny, preferred rhetoric to philosophy. Marcus nevertheless went ahead with his plan. In calling Christianity a philosophical school, even one whose dialectical skill did not impress him, Galen gave Christianity a boost on the ladder of acceptance within the Roman world. From another of Galen's works it is clear that what led him to call it a philosophy was the success Christians had in leading men and women to a life of virtue.

Most people are unable to follow any demonstrative argument consecutively; hence they need parables, and benefit from them just as we now see the people called Christians drawing their faith from parables and miracles, and yet sometimes acting in the same

way as those who practice philosophy. For their contempt of
death and of its sequel is patent to us every day, and likewise their
restraint in cohabitation. For they include not only men but also
women who refrain from cohabiting all through their lives; and
they also number individuals who, in self-discipline and self-control in matters of food and drink, and in their keen pursuit of justice, have attained a pitch not inferior to that of genuine philosophers.[6]

Philosophy in Galen's day had become less a way of thinking than a
way of living. Although philosophers were the inheritors of intellectual traditions that dealt with the great metaphysical issues, and many
still wrote books on these topics, they had gone into the streets of the
cities to address the populace and to offer men and women advice on
how to live. As we have already seen in Lucian's account, the term
used to describe the philosophical schools was *bios* (way of life), and
the selling point of the various philosophies turned more on life-style
and ethics than on metaphysical or epistemological questions. Philosophy was a matter of moral discipline (*askēsis*), and its goal was a life of
virtue (*Hermotimus* 4,7). Marcus Aurelius described philosophy as a
moral ideal which contrasts with the vain and empty goals most men
pursue (*Meditations* 8.1; 10.1). Socrates was said to have risen above
his ordinary human instincts by the *practice* (not study) of philosophy.
"He would indeed have been such as all this implies [Socrates is being
criticized] so far as his natural bent had he not become better than this
through the practice (*askēsis*) of philosophy" (Alexander of Aphrodi-
sias *On Fate* 6). Another philosopher from this period, Musonius
Rufus, said that the task of philosophy is "to find out by discussion
what is fitting and proper and then to carry it out in action." In the
letter of Seneca already quoted, he writes that philosophy "shows us
what things are evil and what things are seemingly evil; she strips our
minds of vain illusion. She bestows upon us a greatness which is sub-
stantial, but she represses the greatness which is inflated and showy
but filled with emptiness" (90.28).

6. Ibid., 15.

This conception of the philosopher had worked its way into Greco-Roman funerary art. It was customary among the wealthy to bury members of one's family in stone sarcophagi, on which could be sculpted symbols and images reflecting the life and aspirations of the deceased. One of the more interesting types of sarcophagi from this period portrays a set of two figures: on one end a figure with hand uplifted in prayer, the so-called *orans*; on the other end, the figure of a young man carrying a sheep on his shoulder, the *chriophoros*. (Later Christian tradition came to identify this latter figure with the good shepherd of the Gospels.) The *orans* was a visible way of representing *pietas* toward the gods and the *chriophoros* was meant to represent philanthropy to one's fellows. The two figures represent the two chief characteristics of a virtuous man or woman, piety and respect toward the gods and philanthropy and justice toward one's fellow human beings.

On some sarcophagi the *orans* and the *chriophoros* appear together on either end, and between them sits a bearded man gazing at a book on his lap. When these sarcophagi are compared with similar figures on coins and with Greco-Roman statuary, as well as with literary allusions, it appears that they were designed to exemplify the philosophical life. The bearded figure in the center was a philosopher who lived in piety toward the gods and in philanthropy toward his fellows, and the person buried in the sarcophagus was thought to have striven during his or her lifetime to achieve such a philosophical life.[7]

In the early years of the Roman Empire philosophy had become a popular idea. The philosophical schools offered, writes A. D. Nock, not only "intelligible explanations of phenomena" but also "life with a scheme." They spoke about fear and friendship, about courage and peace of mind, about anxiety, love, freedom, about old age and death, about wealth and fame. In short, they preached to men and women about how to live amid the twists and turns of fate and fortune. The philosophers sought to set people on a firm and sure path. For this

7. Theodor Klauser, "Studien zur Entstehungsgeschichte der christlichen Kunst," *Jahrbuch für Antike und Christentum* (Münster, 1958–60), 1:20–51; 2:115–45; 3:112–33.

reason, when a man or woman turned from his or her former ways to embrace philosophy, he or she was sometimes said to be "converted."[8]

It is in this sense that Galen identified the early Christian movement as a philosophical school. Christians led people to embrace lives of discipline and self-control, to pursue justice, to overcome the fear of death. Though they did not provide men and women with intellectual foundations for their beliefs, they did achieve a way of life not inferior to that led by "those who are truly philosophers."

Not everyone shared Galen's positive evaluation of the Christian way of life. His contemporary, Marcus Aurelius, who had embraced Stoicism, seemed to think that the Christian attitude toward death, illustrated by the behavior of martyrs, was at odds with a genuinely philosophical life (*Meditations* 11.3).[9] To Marcus, the Christians appeared fanatical and foolish—one might even say superstitious. Their presumed lack of fear of death did not arise out of genuine self-control, or out of an understanding of the self, or out of free will, but from mere obstinacy based on irrational ideas. Another Stoic, Epictetus, made a passing reference to the Christians in a similar context (*Discourses* 4.7.6). Speaking of serenity in the face of death, Epictetus remarks that some people are able to face death fearlessly because of childish ignorance, others from madness, and others, for example, the Galileans, out of "habit," but without any appeal to reason or demonstration (*Discourses* 4.7.6). Christians, in spite of their vaunted bravery, do not offer a truly philosophical approach to life and death because their actions are not based on sound reasoning.

Galen's judgment, however, was the more prescient. For it was through their way of life, not simply their teachings, that Christians first caught the attention of the larger society, and the idea that Christianity was a philosophical school helped Christian apologists to pre-

---

8. A. D. Nock, *Conversion* (London, 1933), 167–80.

9. It is uncertain whether Marcus is actually referring to Christians. The text has the words "as the Christians," but the phrase seems to be an interpolation. It is possible, however, that here and in other passages Marcus had Christians in mind. See C. R. Hains, ed. and trans., *The Communings with Himself of Marcus Aurelius Antoninus* (New York: Loeb Classical Library, 1916), 382–83.

sent the person of Jesus and the Christian way of life intelligibly and persuasively to outsiders. In the middle of the second century, Melito, Bishop of Sardis in western Asia Minor, spoke of Christianity as "our philosophy" (*Frag*. 7), and Justin Martyr, another early Christian apologist writing about the same time, presented his conversion to Christianity as a conversion to philosophy. His *Dialogue with Trypho* began with an account of his examination of the differing philosophical schools of his day—Stoics, Peripatetics, Platonists, et al. It was not, however, until he met an old man who introduced him to the Hebrew prophets that a flame enkindled his heart and he found "this philosophy [Christianity] alone to be sure and profitable" (*Dial*. 8).

THE ARBITRARY GOD OF THE CHRISTIANS

Though it was the Christian way of life that made an impact on Galen, he knew that Christianity (and Judaism) also held certain distinctive teachings. These impressed him much less, and he wondered how Christians could be successful in leading men and women to lives of virtue when their philosophy was so deficient. Like others educated in the Greek intellectual tradition, he believed it was impossible to do good without knowing the truth. Knowledge and virtue complemented each other. *Sophos*, sage, was the term for the good person. A genuinely moral life began with a knowledge of the nature of things.

Galen's criticism of Jewish and Christian teachings appeared in his book *On the Usefulness of the Parts of the Body*, written in Rome in approximately 170 C.E.[10] The book is a study in anatomy, not philosophy, but the analysis of the various functions of the parts of the body—hands, feet, digestive organs, eyes, nerves, and so on—caused Galen to reflect on the harmony of nature as exhibited in the order and structure of the human body. Why, he asks, are certain muscles

---

10. This text mentions only Moses, not Christ; but because Galen deals with Christians and Jews together in other places it seems reasonable to see his philosophical criticism as also applying to Christian teaching. Christians also used the Book of Genesis, and it is the account in Genesis that Galen is criticizing here. Further, Christian writers in the next several decades responded to criticisms similar to those of Galen. For discussion of the text, see Walzer, 24–37.

larger than others and shaped differently, and why are the organs of
the body placed where they are? Is it a matter of chance or of design?
On the basis of his anatomical observations he sought to show the
"cause of these things," for "nature does nothing without a reason"
(11.5; 11.2.3).

In one discussion Galen asks why there is hair on the top of the
head and elsewhere on the face but none on the forehead. He gives
the obvious answer that if hair grew on the forehead one would have
to cut it continually in order to be able to see. This hair stays the same
length, whereas nature has caused the hair of the head and chin to
grow very long. But he wished to know *why* this hair does not grow
and other hair does, and in discussing this problem he departs from
his anatomical discussion to contrast the Greek view of creation with
the viewpoint of Moses in the book of Genesis.

> Did your demiurge [i.e., the creator in Genesis] simply enjoin
> this hair to preserve its length always equal, and does it strictly
> observe this order either from fear of its master's command, or
> from reverence for the God who gave this order, or is it because
> it itself believes it better to do this. Is not this Moses's way of
> treating nature and is it not superior to that of Epicurus? The
> best way, of course, is to follow neither of these but to maintain,
> like Moses, the principle of the demiurge as the origin of every
> created thing, but also adding to it the material principle [existing
> matter from which the world was made]. For our demiurge cre-
> ated it to preserve a constant length, because this was better.
> When he had determined to make it so, he set under part of it a
> hard body as a kind of cartilage, and under another part a hard
> skin attached to the cartilage through the eyebrows. For it was
> certainly not sufficient merely to will their becoming such; it
> would not have been possible for him to make a man out of a
> stone in an instant, by simply wishing so. [*De usu partium* 11.4].

Galen rejects the Epicurean view out of hand because it attributes
creation to "chance." He takes Moses more seriously but still finds
him deficient. Two points are important. From Galen's perspective,

the account in Genesis suggests that God brought things into being solely by the act of his will without regard to whether what was created was the best way for things to be. The Mosaic cosmogony has no place for reason in the act of creation. Second, Galen, like other Greeks, believed that God had fashioned the world from matter that already existed. He calls this the "material principle," and by it he means what Aristotle called the material cause, the matter in which a change is wrought. The Mosaic view implies that the world was created out of what did *not* already exist. Moses omits the material cause in his account and speaks only of the efficient cause, that by which the change is wrought. His account implies that matter came into existence only at the time of creation and did not exist prior to creation.

The classical Greek view of creation that lies behind Galen's criticism of Genesis was set forth by Plato in the *Timaeus*, an essay on cosmogony widely read and studied in the ancient world. Modern readers may find the *Republic* or the *Apology* the most attractive of Plato's dialogues, but the ancients loved the *Timaeus*. In it Plato describes God as the "fashioner" (*demiurgos*) of existing matter, a wise and providential craftsman who takes matter, as a potter takes clay, and fashions it into an object of form and beauty. The creator is the "maker" and "modeler." His task was to bring order out of disorder, to bring to rest what was in discordant motion, and to produce a world of harmony and proportion (*Timaeus* 302-c). By the use of reason the creator transforms unformed and chaotic matter into an intelligible universe.

Plato's account is much more expansive than the account in Genesis. It discusses in great detail how and why the various parts of the cosmos were fashioned, whereas Moses gives only a sketchy account punctuated with the refrain "And God said, 'Let there be' . . . and there was . . .". Plato explains the reason behind the creation. The cosmos does not have eyes because "outside of it there was nothing visible left over." Nor did it need respiratory organs because there was no air surrounding it. It did not need hands because there was nothing to grasp, nor feet because it did not move (*Ti.* 33c-d). Similarly, the demiurge constructed the human body with reason as his guide, giving every part its distinctive purpose and function and not making any useless organs or appendages. The head does not consist only of bare bone "because of the excessive variations of temperature in either direction, due to the seasons; nor yet was it possible to allow it to be shrouded up, and to become, in consequence, stupid and insensitive owing to its burdensome mass of flesh." Hence God covered it with skin and in some places added hair "to serve as a light roofing for the part about the brain for safety's sake, providing a sufficient shade and screen alike in summer and in winter, while proving no obstacle in the way of easy perception" (*Ti.* 75e–76d). The construction of the world as well as the human body can be ascribed to this type of "reasoning" (*Ti.* 72e). The result is a universe that is good, in which all the various parts have their purpose and function, and whose principle is order. "For God wishing that all things should be good and not evil insofar as it was possible, took over all that was visible, that which was not at rest but in a discordant and disordered motion, and brought order out of disorder, thinking that the one was better than the other" (*Ti.* 30a).

Viewed from the perspective of Plato's *Timaeus*, the Mosaic cosmogony appears to be the work of a capricious and unbridled deity who brought the world into being by an act of will without reference to the consequences of his actions. He simply spoke and things came to be. Because there is no mention of the reasons for creation, the account in Genesis suggested to the Greeks that if God had willed things to be another way he could, out of his unlimited power, have made them so. But this would place God completely beyond the cosmos and exempt him from the laws that govern the universe. In the Greek view, God is not above the laws of nature. He could not, for example, make a man out of a stone.

It is precisely this point [i.e., the idea that God could have made man out of a stone if he had wished to do so] in which our own opinion and that of Plato and of the other Greeks who follow the right method in the natural science differ from the position taken up by Moses. For the latter it seems enough to say that God simply willed the arrangement of matter and it was presently arranged in due order; for he believes everything to be possible with God, even should he wish to make a bull or a horse out of ashes. We, however, do not hold this; we say that certain things are impossible by nature and that God does not even attempt such things at all but that he chooses the best out of the possibilities of becoming. We say therefore that since *it was better* that the eyelashes should always be equal in length and number, it was not that he just willed and they were instantly there; for even if He should just will numberless times, they would never come into being in this manner out of a soft skin; and in particular, it was altogether impossible for them to stand erect unless fixed on something hard. We say thus that God is the cause both of the choice of the best in the products of creation themselves and of the selection of the matter. For since it was required, first that the eyelashes should stand erect and secondly that they should be kept equal in length and number, he planted them firmly in a cartilaginous body. If he had planted them in a soft and fleshy substance he would have suffered a worse failure not only than Moses but also than a bad general who plants a wall or a camp in marshy ground. [*De usu partium* 11.14].

Certain things are impossible by nature and God does not—indeed cannot—do such things. He chooses the best possible way, the way according to reason. It is not enough to decree that the eyelashes should always be equal in length and number, for were there not other conditions—namely, the presence of cartilage—it would be nonsense to speak of the eyelashes standing erect. The world of nature cannot be understood unless it is recognized that all things, including the creator, are governed by unalterable laws according to reason. These laws determine the way things are and always will be, not because God decided they should be this way, but because that is the best way for them to be. God is part of nature. He is, in the hymn of the Stoic Cleanthes, "leader of nature, governing all things by law."

Galen's criticism is directed at the account of creation in Genesis. It is unlikely that he had read any of the books of the New Testament, but his reading of Genesis may have been conditioned by what he had heard concerning Christian teaching about God. According to the Gospel of Matthew, Jesus said: "God is able from these stones to raise up children to Abraham" (*Matt.* 3 : 9). The Christian theologian Irenaeus, writing two decades after Galen's book *On the Usefulness of the Parts of the Body*, cited the words of Jesus, "What is impossible with men is possible with God" (Luke 18:27; Irenaeus, *Adversus haereses* 2.10.4) in a discussion of creation intended to show that God's way of creating was categorically different from human fashioning. The account in Genesis appeared to go against the grain of the Greek thinking.

At the time Galen wrote, Christian thinkers had given scant attention to the doctrine of creation. There had been some discussion in Jewish circles, notably in the writings of Philo, the Jewish philosopher from Alexandria, but Jewish thinking on this topic, as we know it from our meager sources, had not departed significantly from the Platonic cosmology. The Jewish book of 2 Maccabees includes a passage which says that God "did not make [the world] out of things that exist" (2 *Macc.* 7:28), and this has sometimes been taken to be early evidence of the later doctrine of creation out of nothing (*creatio ex nihilo*). However, it is seems unlikely, in light of recent studies,[11] that this passage can bear this philosophical sense. Philo followed the basic lines set down by Plato and made God the fashioner of already existing matter (*De opificio* 171). Similarly, the Christian philosopher Justin Martyr, a contemporary of Galen, explicitly draws the parallel between Plato and the Christian view (1 *Apol.* 20) and says that God "formed all things that are . . . out of unformed matter (1 *Apol.* 10; cf. 59).

The idea that God had created the world out of nothing—that is, out of matter which existed prior to the act of creation—began to be adumbrated in Christian circles shortly before Galen's time. The first Christian thinker to articulate the rudiments of a doctrine of *creatio ex nihilo* was the Gnostic theologian Basilides, who flourished in the second quarter of the second century. Basilides worked out an elaborate

11. G. Schuttermayr, "'Schöpfung aus dem Nichts' in 2 Makk. 7, 28?," *Biblische Zeitschrift*, n.f. 17 (1973): 203–28.

cosmogony as he sought to think through the implications of Christian teaching in light of the Platonic cosmogony. He rejected the analogy of the human maker, the craftsman who carves a piece of wood, as an anthropomorphism that severely limited the power of God. God, unlike mortals, created the world out of "nonexisting" matter. He first brought matter into being through the creation of "seeds," and it is this created stuff that is fashioned, according to his will, into the cosmos.[12]

Whether Basilides' ideas had any direct impact on other Christian thinkers we cannot say. What the fragments from his writings do indicate, however, is that Christians had begun to turn their attention to the doctrine of creation and to elaborate a new view at odds with the classical Greek cosmogony as set forth in the *Timaeus*. Somewhat later, about the time Galen was composing his work on the parts of the body, the bishop of Antioch, Theophilus, stated the new Christian view that God had created the world out of nothing. There would be nothing remarkable, he wrote, in God making the world out of "already existent matter." The power of God is revealed "by his making whatever he wishes out of what does not exist (*ex ouk ontōn*), just as the ability to give life and motion belongs to no one but God alone" (Theoph. *ad Autol.* 2.4). Like Basilides, Theophilus wished to preserve God's transcendence, his sole rule or sovereignty (*monarchia*). If matter was introduced as a principle alongside God, it would imply that matter had existed prior to the creation. Only God is eternal.

At the time Galen wrote there was no fixed interpretation of the doctrine of creation presented in Genesis. Genesis 1–2 could be taken to mean that God, like the Platonic demiurge, was the fashioner of already existing matter, but others had begun to suggest that Genesis taught that God created the world out of nothing. This was eventually to become *the* Christian teaching on the subject, and Galen was the first critic of Christianity to see the implications of the emerging Christian doctrine.

The idea that the world came into existence out of non-being was

12. Gerhard May, *Schöpfung aus dem Nichts. Die Entstehung der Lehre von der Creatio ex Nihilo*, Arbeiten zur Kirchengeschichte 48 (Berlin, 1978), 63–85.

abhorrent to the Greeks. For Aristotle, it was axiomatic that "nothing can come out of what does not exist" (*Physics* 187a 33–34). Greek thinkers in Galen's time took the same point of view. "The substance or matter out of which [the kosmos] has come into being did not come to be but was always available to the demiurge to whom it submitted itself for disposing and ordering, for the source of what comes into being is not what does not exist, but as in the case of a house and a garment and a statue, what is not in good and sufficient condition" (Plutarch, *De animae procreatione in Timaeo, Moralia* 1014b).

Another critic of Christianity, Celsus, offered a similar criticism of Christian teaching, though he was more concerned about the Christian belief in the resurrection of the dead than in the doctrine of creation. "What sort of body, after being entirely corrupted, could return to its original nature and that same condition which it had before it was dissolved? As they [the Christians] have nothing to say in reply, they escape to a most outrageous refuge by saying that 'anything is possible to God.' But, indeed neither can God do what is shameful nor does He desire what is contrary to nature. . . . He himself is the reason of everything that exists; therefore he is not able to do anything contrary to reason or to his own character" (*c. Cels.* 5.14). What is at issue, then, in this criticism of Christian teaching is not simply the idea of creation out of nothing but the Christian view that God is beyond the laws of nature and has sovereign power to deal with the world at will.

The Latin poet Lucretius, who lived in the first century B.C.E., expressed the classical point of view in his grand poem *On the Nature of Things*.

Nothing can ever be created by divine power out of nothing. The reason why all mortals are so gripped by fear is that they see all sorts of things happening on the earth and in the sky with no discernible cause, and these they attribute to the will of a god. Accordingly, when we have seen that nothing can be created out of nothing, we shall then have a clearer picture of the path ahead, the problem of how things are created and occasioned without

the aid of the gods. First then, if things were made out of nothing, any species could spring from any source and nothing would
require seed. Men could arise from the sea and scaly fish from the
earth, and birds could be hatched out of the sky. Cattle and other
domestic animals and every kind of wild beast, multiplying indiscriminately, would occupy cultivated and waste lands alike. The
same fruits would not grow constantly on the same trees, but
they would keep changing; any tree might bear any fruit. If each
species were not composed of its own generative bodies, why
should each be born always of the same kind of mother? Actually,
since each is formed out of specific seeds, it is born and emerges
into the sunlit world only from a place where there exists the right
material, the right kind of atoms. This is why everything cannot
be born of everything, but a specific power of generation inheres
in specific objects. [*De rerum natura* 1.160]

Lucretius was, of course, not speaking about Christianity, as he
wrote long before the Christian movement had begun. Yet when
Christianity did begin to appear in the cities of the Roman Empire
and came to the attention of Greek and Roman intellectuals, the
Christian view of God's will in creation offended Roman and Greek
sensibilities. God, in the Greek view, dwelt in a realm above the earth,
but he did not stand outside of the world, the *kosmos*. Earth and
heaven are part of the same cosmos, which has existed eternally. The
world is not the creation of a transcendent God. The cosmos has its
own laws, and all that exists—the physical world, animals, man, and
the gods—are subject to nature's laws. "Certain things are impossible
to nature," said Galen, and "God does not even attempt such things at
all." Rather, "he chooses the best out of the possibilities of becoming."

How sharply the Christian view diverges from the classical can be
seen in another Greek writer, this one an anonymous second-century
author of an essay on cosmology: "God is to us a law, evenly bal-
anced, receptive neither to correction nor change, and I think better
and more stable than those [laws] which are engraved on tablets. Under his motionless and harmonious rule the whole ordering of heaven

and earth is administered, extending over all created things through the seeds of life in each both to plants and to animals, according to genera and species." Summing up his view, he says: "God and nothing else is meant when we speak of necessity" (Pseudo Aristotle, *De mundo,* 401 a–b).

By the middle of the second century Christianity had begun to make an impact on some Greek and Roman intellectuals. The contrast between the comments of Pliny and those of Galen is a sign of this shift in outlook. Pliny had to deal with the Christians in the course of his work as governor of the province of Bithynia. His knowledge of Christianity came largely through hearsay, through the statements of a few uneducated Christians, and perhaps through trials that had been held in Rome. But he had no real interest in the Christian movement and made only a limited effort to understand what Christians believed and practiced. He certainly had not read any Christian writings.

By contrast, Galen seems to have been interested in the new movement and made an effort to understand how Christians lived, what they believed, and how the Christian way of life compared with other "philosophies" in the world of his time. Galen is, as Walzer observes, "the first pagan author who implicitly places Greek philosophy and the Christian religion on the same footing."[13] Galen was impressed that Christians were able to lead men and women to a life of virtue in the same fashion as the leading philosophical schools of the day. Through Christian practice, Christian morality, the early Christian movement made its first bid for acceptance within the Greco-Roman world.

Galen, however, found Christian (and Jewish) teaching objectionable. He considered Christians dogmatic and uncritical. They were unwilling to submit their beliefs to philosophical examination. They asked people to accept their doctrines solely on faith. This was, if not a fatal flaw to Galen, certainly a serious shortcoming. But his criticism of Christianity extended to specific points of Christian doctrine. He singled out a topic of major theological and philosophical significance in discussing the interaction between Christianity and classical culture.

13. Walzer, 43.

Even on the basis of his limited knowledge of Christianity, Galen sensed that the Christian and Jewish views had implications that were profoundly at odds with classical Greek conceptions of the relation of God to the world. To Galen the Christian God appeared capricious, arbitrary, even whimsical, subject to no laws other than his own will, and beyond the bounds of nature, a rule unto himself.

Even though Galen does not mention *creatio ex nihilo* and only deals explicitly with the Book of Genesis, he sets forth what would become a classical criticism of the Christian doctrine of God. In doing so he calls attention to the emergence of a new and distinctively Christian teaching. Already at this early stage in the history of Christian thought, the belief that God had created the world by an act of volition had begun to suggest the idea of creation out of nothing. Galen's contemporary, Theophilus, Bishop of Antioch, criticized Greek philosophers for deifying the universe through their view that God created the world out of existing matter. If God is "uncreated" and matter is also "uncreated," then the "sovereignty of God is not demonstrated." "What would be remarkable," he asks, "if God made the world out of pre-existent matter? Even a human artisan, when he obtains material from someone, makes whatever he wishes out of it. But the power of God is revealed by his making whatever he wishes out of the non-existent, just as the ability to give life and motion belongs to no-one but God alone" (*Ad Autol.* 2.4). It was not to be long before Christian writers began to make the doctrine of *creatio ex nihilo* central to Christian thinking. Though his knowledge of Christianity was limited, Galen had insight into certain characteristics of the new movement. His curiosity helped prepare the way for Christianity to be taken seriously in intellectual circles. The appearance of philosophical critics of the new religion was a momentous development for the history of Christian theology.

V CELSUS: A CONSERVATIVE INTELLECTUAL

UNTIL THE LAST HALF OF THE SECOND CENTURY ALL our information about Roman and Greek attitudes toward the Christians could be written in a few pages. But about the year 170 C.E. a Greek philosopher by the name of Celsus wrote a major book devoted solely to the Christians. This work, entitled the *True Doctrine,* is preserved for us only in fragments, but the fragments are so extensive that it is possible, with some confidence, to reconstruct the main outlines of the book. About eighty years after the publication of the *True Doctrine,* Origen, the famous Christian philosopher and theologian from Alexandria, wrote a massive reply to Celsus in eight books. In this work Origen cited Celsus's book at length, sometimes sentence by sentence, before offering his own views. Through the investigations of several generations of scholars it is possible today to construct not only the main ideas of Celsus's book but its actual wording. If one reads the passages of Celsus cited by Origen in their original context—that is, as a work of a pagan philosopher living in the second century—rather than in light of Origen's criticism, it is possible to see in some depth what educated persons were thinking about the Christian movement in the second half of the second century.

Unfortunately we know nothing about Celsus except for the information provided by Origen and the fragments of the work itself. Even in Origen's day nothing was known about Celsus except that he had been dead for a long time (*c. Cels.* Pref. 4). Origen at first thought that Celsus was an Epicurean philosopher, and in the beginning of his work *Contra Celsum* he interpreted Celsus's book as the product of

Epicurean thinking. But as Origen developed his own arguments against Celsus, he gradually changed this view and began to claim that Celsus was not really an Epicurean at all, or if he had been, that he had modified his views to conform to Platonism. It is possible that Origen simply wanted to pin the label "Epicurean" on Celsus to make his task of criticism easier. In Greco-Roman society, "Epicurean" was an epithet somewhat like "Communist" in the United States. Epicureans were thought to be atheists who undermined society. It was to Origen's advantage to portray a critic of Christianity as an Epicurean.

But Celsus was not an Epicurean. Close examination of the fragments of his book has shown that he cannot be identified with any of the major philosophical schools of his time.[1] He is closest to the Platonists, but his own philosophical stance was eclectic. He reflects popular beliefs and opinions that were not peculiar to any particular sect or school but were shared by intellectuals with differing philosophical or religious inclinations. I would characterize him as a conservative intellectual. He supports traditional values and defends accepted beliefs, but unlike Pliny, he is not a politician or civil official. He approaches the institutions and mores of society as an intellectual prepared to offer philosophical and religious arguments in support of the traditional political and social order. His philosophical and religious ideas are not simply theoretical convictions; they are interwoven with the institutions, social conventions, and political structures of the Greco-Roman world.

BEGGING PRIESTS OF CYBELE AND SOOTHSAYERS

Celsus obviously knew Christianity at first hand, and as a skilled polemicist his portrait of the Christian movement is detailed and concrete. He has a keen eye for Christianity's most vulnerable points and the wit to exploit them for a laugh. Even when he is poking fun at the

1. The most perceptive and thorough analysis of Celsus's *True Doctrine* is Carl Andresen, *Logos und Nomos. Die Polemik des Kelsos wider das Christentum* (Berlin, 1955). Citations of Celsus's *True Doctrine* from Origen's *Contra Celsum*, ed. Marcel Borret, S.J. *Origène. Contre Celse*, Sources Chrétiennes (Paris, 1967–). Translation by Henry Chadwick, *Origen: Contra Celsum* (Cambridge, 1953).

Christians the informed reader knows he has a point. His most humorous dig at Christian piety comes in book 6 where he discusses the Christian penchant to venerate the instruments of Jesus' death.

> Everywhere they speak in their writings of the tree of life and of resurrection of the flesh by the tree—I imagine because their master was nailed to a cross and was a carpenter by trade. So that if he had happened to be thrown off a cliff, or pushed into a pit, or suffocated by strangling, or if he had been a cobbler or stonemason or blacksmith, there would have been a cliff of life above the heavens, or a pit of resurrection, or a rope of immortality, or a blessed stone, or an iron of love, or a holy hide of leather. Would not an old woman who sings a story to lull a little child to sleep have been ashamed to whisper such tales as these. [*c. Cels.* 6:34]

Origen can at times be as satirical as Celsus (*c. Cels.* 4.67), but he failed to catch the humor in this passage.

In contrast to earlier critics who viewed Christianity from a single perspective, Celsus's portrait of the Christian movement is rich and varied. At times he draws on popular prejudice toward marginal groups in society; in other places he offers well-informed philosophical criticism based on a serious study of Christian writings and beliefs; elsewhere he draws on stock criticism of philosophical positions drawn from handbooks which circulated among intellectuals. One of his strategies was to compare Christianity to unpopular and arcane religious movements that offended the sensibilities of the Romans. Early in the work, for example, he compares the Christians to the "begging priests of Cybele and soothsayers, and to worshippers of Mithras and Sabazius, and whatever else one might meet, apparitions of Hecate or of some other daemon or daemons" (*c. Cels.* 1.9). In another place he compares Christian worship to the superstitious practices of the Egyptians and to "those in the Bacchic mysteries who introduce phantoms and terrors" (*c. Cels.* 3.17, 4.10). These comments, which are reminiscent of Pliny's, indicate that people still viewed the Christian movement as a foreign cult or superstition. Lucian, a Greek satirist writing about the same time, presents a similar portrait in his tract *The Passing of Peregrinus*. He speaks of the "wondrous lore of the Christians" that Peregrinus, a second-century charlatan and con-man, had learned by associating with their "priests and scribes in Palestine." The Christians, writes Lucian, "worshipped the man who was crucified in Palestine because he introduced this new *cult* into the world" (*Peregrinus* 11). Galen's notion that Christianity was a philosophical school appears to have been a minority view.

Celsus, however, does reiterate points made by Galen. He does not explicitly call Christianity a philosophical school, but there are passages where he seems to have this analogy in mind (*c. Cels.* 5.61–62), and like Galen he is sharply critical of Christian fideism. Celsus knew that the Christian scriptures provided justification for eschewing appeals to reason and argumentation. "Some [Christians]," says Celsus, "do not even want to give or to receive a reason for what they believe, and use such expressions as 'Do not ask questions; just believe' and 'Your faith will save you.' Others quote the apostle Paul. 'The wisdom in the world is evil and foolishness a good thing'" (1 Cor. 1 : 25–26; *c. Cels.* 1.9).

In another passage, Celsus makes a similar point by caricaturing Christian efforts at proselytizing.

In private houses also we see wool-workers, cobblers, laundry-workers, and the most illiterate and bucolic yokels, who would not dare to say anything at all in front of their elders and more intelligent masters. But whenever they get hold of children in private and some stupid women with them, they let out some astounding statements as, for example, that they must not pay any attention to their fathers and schoolteachers, but must obey them; they say that these talk nonsense and have no understanding, and that in reality they neither know nor are able to do anything good, but are taken up with mere empty chatter. But they alone, they say, know the right way to live, and if the children would believe them, they would become happy and make their home happy as well" (*c. Cels.* 3:55).

Celsus exaggerates, with an eye on the rhetorical tradition as much as on the Christians, but his characterization may not be far from the truth. Some Christians were arrogant and contemptuous of the opinions of others; they kept to themselves and appealed to people's fears or ignorance.

Just because many in the churches were uneducated and illiterate, Christians had the reputation of being gullible and credulous. The huckster Peregrinus became a member of the church for no other reason than to exploit simple Christians. The authorities finally caught up with him and had him imprisoned. But naive Christians still did not see through his deception. While he was in prison, they waited on him hand and foot, bringing him food and money and treating him as a hero. "The poor wretches," wrote Lucian, "have convinced themselves . . . that they are going to be immortal and live for all time. . . . They despise all things indiscriminately and consider them common property, receiving such doctrines traditionally without any definite evidence. So if any charlatan and trickster, able to profit by occasions, comes among them, he quickly acquires sudden wealth by imposing upon simple folk" (*Peregrinus* 13). Christians were an easy target for the racketeers of the Roman Empire.

Celsus is the first critic to call Jesus a magician and charge the Christians with practicing magic. It may be that this view was already adumbrated in Suetonius, who spoke of Christianity as a "new and criminal (*maleficus*) superstition." The term *maleficus* can mean "magical," and used as a noun it designated a magician.[2] If so, Suetonius foreshadows what later became a common charge.[3] Celsus is, however, explicit. "It was by magic that he [Jesus] was able to do the miracles which he appeared to have done" (*c. Cels.* 1.6). Further, he says that "Christians get the power which they seem to possess by pronouncing the names of certain daemons and incantations" (*c. Cels.* 1.6).

2. Morton Smith, *Clement of Alexandria and a Secret Gospel of Mark* (Cambridge, 1973), 234; also, *Jesus the Magician* (New York, 1978), 45–67.
3. See, for example, the writing of Hierocles, governor of Bithynia, comparing Jesus to Apollonius of Tyana. Hierocles's treatise is lost, but a good idea of the work can be gained from Eusebius's response. Text and English translation in F. C. Conybeare, *Philostratus: The Life of Apollonius of Tyana* (Cambridge: Loeb Classical Library, 1969), 2: 484–605.

The practice of magic was a criminal offense in the Roman Empire and the word *magician* a term of opprobrium and abuse. Apuleius, the author of a racy novel, *The Golden Ass*, was brought to trial for allegedly practicing magic. He married a woman named Pudentilla who had been betrothed to someone else. When the brother-in-law of the man she was supposed to marry heard of the marriage, he accused Apuleius of winning her love by the use of magical charms and potions. Though eventually acquitted, Apuleius was forced to stand trial and defend himself against the false charge.

Many of the things recorded about Jesus in the Gospels were similar to the things magicians did. In the Gospel of John, for example, Jesus is reported to have healed a man born blind by spitting on the ground, making clay out of the spittle and touching the man's eyes with the clay (John 9). A number of stories pictured Jesus as an exorcist who drove out evil demons (cf. Mark 1:23, 34; 3:11). Besides these obvious similarities to the work of magicians, there are other passages in the Gospels that closely parallel accounts of magicians in the Magical Papyri from the time: the stilling of storms (Mark 4:35), miraculous provision of food (Mark 6:35), making oneself invisible (John 8:59), knowledge of the thoughts of others (Mark 2:8).[4]

Not only did the Gospels present Jesus in the guise of a magician, that is, of one who does wonders, but Christians had begun to use the name of Jesus in spells and incantations. The practice of exorcising demons in the name of Jesus is one example. Celsus was familiar with certain Christian sects that openly practiced magic and he had seen Christian books "containing magical formulas" (*c. Cels.* 6.40). Furthermore, the earliest Christian apologists and propagandists, before the philosophical apologists such as Justin Martyr and Athenagoras, placed Jesus' wonders at the forefront of their efforts to persuade people of the truth of Christianity. Quadratus, an apologist during the reign of Hadrian (117–34 C.E.), urged people to believe in Jesus because the effect of his miracles continued up to the present—people had been cured and raised from the dead, and "some of them," he

4. Smith, *Clement of Alexandria*, 224–26.

wrote, "have survived even to our own day" (Eusebius, *Hist. Eccl.* 4.3.2). The miracles of Jesus were complemented by the miracles of the Apostles, as the apocryphal Acts of the Apostles testify. The view of the new breed of intellectuals that Jesus was chiefly a moral and philosophical teacher was a minority position in the early church, and one that was resisted by the rank and file.

Christians claimed that the miracles of Jesus proved he was the son of God. The most obvious way for Celsus to respond to such a claim was to deny that Jesus had performed the wonders attributed to him. But he did not take this approach. He was willing to grant that Jesus actually did the things the Gospels record, "cures or resurrections or a few loaves feeding many people, from which many fragments were left over, or any other monstrous tales . . . related by his disciples" (*c. Cels.* 1.68). Celsus did not dispute that Jesus performed miracles. What he wanted to know was: by whose power was he able to accomplish such wonders? From his reading of the Gospels he knew that Jesus was reported to have spent some time in Egypt. From this he concluded that Jesus "was brought up in secret and hired himself out as a workman in Egypt and after having tried his hand at certain magical powers he returned from there, and on account of those powers gave himself the title Son of God" (*c. Cels.* 1.38). Here Celsus raises a point that will become central to his attack on Christianity. Did Jesus' ability to work wonders mean that he was the son of God, or was he simply another successful magician like others who could be found in the cities and towns of the Roman Empire? To Celsus the answer was evident. Jesus belonged among the "sorcerers who profess to do wonderful miracles . . . who for a few obols make known their sacred lore in the middle of the market-place and drive daemons out of men and blow away diseases and invoke the souls of heroes" (*c. Cels.* 1.68).

Celsus's charge that Jesus was a magician was not separate from his overall criticism of the Christian movement.[5] He wished to show that Christians had no basis for claiming that Jesus was the son of God. He

5. See Eugene V. Gallagher, *Divine Man or Magician? Celsus and Origen on Jesus,* Society of Biblical Literature, Dissertation Series, no. 64 (Chico, CA: Scholars Press, 1982).

was not the only one to work wonders; others had similar power. The question was not whether Jesus had worked wonders, or whether his followers, by invoking his name, could do the same. The issue was: Is there any reason, on the basis of Jesus' miracles, to call him Son of God? To see how Celsus deals with the question we must now turn to a fuller examination of his presentation of Christian teaching.

THE DEFICIENCIES OF CHRISTIAN DOCTRINE

Celsus not only read Christian writings; he also understood what he read. He knew that Christianity originated as a movement within Judaism and that Christians continued to use the Jewish Scriptures; he knew that most Jews did not accept the new movement and that its relation to Judaism was an embarrassment to Christians; he was familiar with the gospel accounts of Jesus' life, his teaching, his suffering and death, and he realized the importance of the resurrection in Christian teaching; he had some familiarity with Christian worship and practice.

It is also likely that Celsus was acquainted with the first Christian apologetic writings, specifically the work of Justin Martyr, whose apologies had appeared approximately two decades before Celsus wrote his *True Doctrine*. Some scholars believe that Celsus wrote his book in response to Justin's work and that the specific form of his argument can be attributed to his familiarity with Justin.[6] Clearly Celsus has been able to sort out many of the things he had heard and read about Christians and to focus on the most significant, and vulnerable, points of Christian teaching. From his reading of Christian writings he knew that Christian intellectuals were sensitive to arguments from the Greek philosophical tradition and that they recognized the need to argue their case in the public forum of ideas. Though Celsus might make rhetorical points against Christian reliance on faith instead of reason, his more serious arguments assume that Christian thinkers wished to be judged by the same standards as others.

On an initial reading Celsus's book might suggest, as did Galen's

6. Andresen, *Logos und Nomos*, 308 ff.

comments on Christian doctrine, that Christianity offered little that was new, its teachings simply reflecting, in less sophisticated form, what others had said earlier. Celsus said as much when he observed that many of the things taught by Christians "have been better expressed among the Greeks, who refrained from making exalted claims and from asserting that they had been announced by a god or the son of a god" (c. Cels. 6.1). Later in the same book he mentions a number of teachings that fall into this category, for example, the notion of the highest good (c. Cels. 6.4–5), certain views about the origin of the world (6.49–50), and ideas about immortality. "Divinely inspired men of ancient times related that there is a happy life for fortunate souls. Some called it the Islands of the Blessed; others the Elysian Fields because they were there set free from the evils of the world. Thus Homer says: 'But immortals will send thee to the Elysian Fields / and the ends of the earth where life is very easy.' And Plato, who thinks the soul immortal, quite openly calls that region where the soul is sent a land . . ." (c. Cels. 7.28). However, it is clear from a closer reading of Celsus's work that he recognized, as did Galen, that Christianity had set forth some new and original religious teachings, and these are the chief target of his polemic.

I will discuss only three of the more important of his theological criticisms. The first is the Christian claim that God came down from the heavens to live on earth among men. This assertion, says Celsus, "is most shameful and no lengthy argument is required to refute it" (c. Cels. 4.2). God is not the kind of being who can undergo mutation or alteration. He cannot change from the purity and perfection of divinity to the blemished and tarnished state of humans. "God is good and beautiful and happy, and exists in a most beautiful state. If then he comes down to men, he must undergo a change, a change from good to bad, from beautiful to shameful, from happiness to misfortune, and from what is best to what is most wicked. . . . It is the nature only of a mortal being to under-go change and remoulding, whereas it is the nature of an immortal being to remain the same without alteration. Accordingly, God could not be capable of undergoing this change" (c. Cels. 4.14). What makes this observation telling is that Christians also claimed to believe that God was an immutable spiritual being who was "uncreated, eternal, invisible, impassible, incomprehensible, infinite, who . . . is encompassed by light, beauty, spirit, and indescribable power" (Athenagoras, *Leg. pro Christ.* 10). Christians claimed to have a conception of God similar to that of the most sophisticated of the pagan philosophers, including Celsus. In effect, then, Celsus asks: If you truly claim to believe in the same kind of God that we do, how can you assert that God has taken on human form? How can a deity who is by definition immutable undergo change and alteration to live as a human being?

If one grants that God is omnipotent and omniscient, and rules the world from a lofty throne in the heavens, asks Celsus, "What is the purpose of such a descent on the part of God? Was it in order to learn what was going on among humans" (*c. Cels.* 4.2)? Further, if God is all-powerful why did he need to come to earth to bring about a moral reformation in mankind? Was he not capable of doing this "by divine power" without such a descent (*c. Cels.* 4.3)? This point leads Celsus to an argument that was to recur in pagan polemics for the next several centuries. If Christians do insist that God appeared in human form at a specific time in history, what happened to the countless generations who lived before Jesus? "Is it only now after such a long age that God has remembered to judge the human race? Did he not care before" (*c. Cels.* 4.8)? How can God concern himself only with humans who live at a particular time in history? The Christian view presents an arbitrary and capricious God who acts willfully without regard to what is best for all creatures. Hence Celsus is led to the conclusion that Christians "babble about God impiously and impurely" and it is only people who do not know better who are drawn to Christian beliefs (*c. Cels.* 4.10). Those who are well informed on theological and philosophical questions can see the irrationality of Christian doctrine.

A second major criticism is a variant of Galen's argument against the notion that "all things are possible to God." Celsus, however, discusses the maxim in connection with the Christian belief in the resurrection of the dead. He has some sharp words against the account of creation in Genesis, specifically about a story that presents the "greatest God" creating "so much on one day and again so much more on the second, and so on with the third, fourth, fifth, and sixth" (6.60). His more serious criticism, however, is directed against the idea that God could reverse the natural process of the disintegration of the human body or that a body that had rotted could be restored again. "For what sort of body, after being entirely corrupted, could return to its original nature and that same condition which it had before it was dissolved? As they have nothing to say in reply, they escape to a most outrageous refuge by saying that 'anything is possible to God.' But, indeed neither can God do what is shameful nor does He desire what is contrary to nature" (c. Cels. 5.14).

The resurrection of the dead at the end of time and the resurrection of Jesus appear fairly frequently as topics in Celsus's work. As Origen observed, Celsus "often reproached us about the resurrection" (c. Cels. 8.49), suggesting that pagan critics realized that the resurrection was one of the central and distinctive Christian doctrines. Celsus located the theological difficulty of the resurrection in the Christian understanding of God, specifically in God's relation to the created order. Christians did not have a rational view of the deity. Instead of recognizing that God was subject to the laws of nature and reason, Christians believed in a God who stood completely above and beyond nature and was therefore capable of doing whatever he willed no matter how much it disrupted the order of the world. "As for the flesh, which is full of things which it is not even nice to mention," says Celsus, "God would neither desire nor be able to make it everlasting contrary to reason. For he himself is the reason of everything that exists; therefore He is not able to do anything contrary to reason, or to his own character" (c. Cels. 5.14). A God who is contrary to reason is not a fit object of devotion.

A third major criticism was also leveled at the Christian view of God, specifically, the consequences of the worship of Jesus for the idea that God is one. If the Christians "worshipped no other God but one, perhaps they would have had a valid argument against others. But in fact they worship to an extravagant degree this man who ap-

peared recently, and yet think it does not offend God if they also worship his servant" (*c. Cels.* 8.12). By the time that Celsus wrote it was
widely known that Jesus was not only the founder of the Christian association, but that he had become the object of worship and adoration. In a passage already cited, Lucian said that Christians "worship
the man who was crucified in Palestine" (*Peregrinus* 11), and Pliny
had said that Christians sing hymns to Christ "as to a god." Now
Celsus had no difficulty accepting the idea that a man who had performed wondrous works or distinguished himself by his life and teachings should be given adoration. Some of the Greek gods, for instance,
Heracles and Orpheus, were known to have once been men. Some
men, called heroes by the Greeks, had been translated to divine status.
"In the same manner," says Plutarch, "in which water is seen to be
generated from earth, air from water, and fire from air, as their substance is borne upward, even so from men into heroes and from heroes into daimones the better souls obtain their transmutation. But
from the daimones a few souls still in the long reach of time because
of supreme excellence, come, after being purified, to share completely
in divine qualities" (*De def. or.* 415c).

In principle, then, Celsus had no objection to the elevation of a
man, even Jesus, to divine status. But was Jesus really deserving of
such honor? Were Christians justified in ranking Jesus with such men
as Heracles, Asclepius, or Orpheus? Some of the other men Christians
(and Jews) revered were more deserving than Jesus. "A far more suitable person for you than Jesus would have been Jonah with his gourd,
or Daniel who escaped from wild beasts, or those of whom stories yet
more incredible than these are told" (*c. Cels.* 7.53). Jesus was a low-
grade magician, not a great hero like the men of old.

Celsus's criticism of the elevation of Jesus to divine status, however,
has another dimension. By offering such adoration to Jesus, Christians
make him a rival of the one high God, the God above the heavens, as
Celsus calls him. If Christians taught that "God is father of all and that
we really ought to worship him alone" there would be no quarrel. But
Christians make Jesus almost equal to God, "not because they are
paying very great reverence to God but because they are exalting Jesus

excessively" (*c. Cels.* 8.14). When Origen read Celsus's statement that Christians set up Jesus as equal to, or even greater than, the one high God, he said that Celsus had obviously got things wrong because we "do not hold that the son is mightier than the Father, but inferior" (*c. Cels.* 8.15)! For Origen, Jesus is clearly subordinate to God the Father.

Celsus, however, has a point, and it is central to his case against Christianity. Christians threatened the hard-won view that there was only one God, a conviction shared by many pagan intellectuals in the early empire, and which was thought to be distinctly superior to the polytheism and anthropomorphism of popular religion. Celsus presents his views as an interpretation of a stock quotation from Homer's *Iliad* (*Iliad* 2.205). "Let there be one king, him to whom the son of crafty Kronos gave the power." This line was taken to mean that there is one God who is king and father of all, a spiritual being who transcends the world and who is the source and origin of all that is. Another second-century pagan philosopher said:

> God being one yet has many names, being called after all the various conditions which he himself inaugurates. We call him Zen and Zeus, using the two names in the same sense. . . . He is called the son of Kronos and of Time. . . . He is the God of Lightning and Thunder. . . . Moreover, after the fruits he is called the Fruitful of God, after cities the City-God; he is God of Birth, God of the house-court, God of kindred and God of our fathers. . . . He is . . . in very truth the Savior and God of Freedom, and to complete the tale of his titles, God of heavens, and of the world below, deriving his names from all natural phenomena and conditions, inasmuch as he is himself the cause of all things." [Ps.-Aristotle, *De mundo*, 401a]

Celsus expresses the same sentiment. "It makes no difference if one invokes the highest God or Zeus or Adonai or Sabaoth or Amoun, as the Egyptians do, or Papaios, as the Scythians do" (*c. Cels.* 5.41).

Belief in the one god of many names did not mean that the one god was the only god. There were also many lesser deities: the stars and heavenly bodies; the Olympian gods, Zeus, Hera, Poseidon, et al.; the Capitoline gods, Jupiter, Juno, Minerva; the daimones who stood between earth and the higher gods; and, on the lowest level, heroes, outstanding men who had been raised to divine status. The one high God stood at the pinnacle of a host of deities who ruled the world with him. "In the midst of such contention, strife, and disagreement [on other matters]," wrote Maximus of Tyre, a second-century pagan intellectual, "you would see in all the earth one harmonious law and principle that there is one God, king and father of all, and many gods, sons of God, fellow rulers with God. The Greek says this, and the barbarian says it, the mainlander and the seafarer, the wise and the unwise" (*Or.* 11.5; ed. Holbein). When a person worshipped these lesser gods, it was assumed that he or she was also worshipping the one high god. Such worship did not detract from the honor shown the highest god, nor did it, in the view of the ancients, threaten the belief that God was one.

To pagan observers schooled in these religions, the Christian worship of Jesus, however, seemed to compromise belief in the oneness of God. This was a significant insight into the character of the Christian tradition, for though Christian thinking was a long way from the time when Christ would be declared "of the same substance" (*homoousios*) as God, and eventually one with the Father, the seeds of that development were apparent to pagan observers in the middle of the second century, a hundred and fifty years before the Council of Nicaea (325 C.E.), when the view that Jesus was equal to God the Father was proclaimed.

Excessive adoration of Jesus robbed the one high God of his proper due and discouraged devotion to other divine beings. Celsus argued that the "worship of God [the one high God] becomes more perfect by going through them all [the lesser gods]" (8.66), but he knew that Christians rejected this viewpoint. Even Lucian realized that the reverence which simple Christians showed to the huckster Peregrinus, "reverence as a god" as he put it, was different from the honor given Jesus. Peregrinus was "next after that other"—namely, after Jesus (*Peregrinus* 11). The singular emphasis on Jesus implied that there were two supreme objects of worship, thereby destroying the most fundamental principle of the philosophical view of God. If there are two high gods, there is no longer a single source of all things. The two gods are really secondary gods who derive their existence from a more transcendent source, a yet higher God.

For Celsus these philosophical ideas were intimately linked to the political structure of the Roman Empire ruled by one emperor. In the passage in which he cites the line from Homer, "Let there be one king" [i.e., one God] he says: "For if you overthrow this doctrine, it is probable that the emperor will punish you. If everyone were to do the same as you, there would be nothing to prevent him from being abandoned, alone and deserted, while earthly things would come into the power of the most lawless and savage barbarians, and nothing would be heard among men either of your worship or of the true wisdom" (*c. Cels*. 8.68). So Christian worship of Jesus set up a rival God whose followers created an independent and factious group within the body politic. Here I wish only to call attention to the theological dimension of Celsus's defense of monotheism (more precisely henotheism, belief in one god without excluding belief in other lesser gods) against the Christian exaltation of Jesus. Later in the chapter I shall discuss the political and social dimensions of this aspect of his criticism.

DEMYTHOLOGIZING THE STORY OF JESUS

Celsus was the first critic of Christianity to give careful attention to the figure of Jesus. All of the earlier observers recognized that Jesus was the founder of the Christian movement, and several had begun to realize that he had also become an object of adoration among Christians, but the few comments we possess on Christianity up to the time of Galen were concerned more with Christians than with Jesus. No doubt part of the explanation for this omission is that earlier critics learned about Christianity by firsthand contact with Christians, but had little knowledge of the Christian scriptures, including the Gospels, whereas Celsus had studied the Gospels, and devoted a significant part of his book to an analysis of the accounts of Jesus' life retold there.[7] He realized, as earlier observers had not, that his attack on Christianity would be ineffective if he dwelt only on Christian behavior or doctrine. Christian assertions about the truth of their way of life rested finally on the credibility of their claims concerning Jesus.

Celsus's discussion of Jesus' life centered on the following points: the virgin birth, the baptism in the river Jordan by John, his death and resurrection from the dead, his miracles and his teachings. His arguments concerning the virgin birth, the baptism, and the resurrection are chiefly literary and historical. He attempts to show that there is insufficient evidence to verify the accounts recorded in the scriptures. But as he develops his case, it becomes clear that his historical criticism is secondary to another interest—namely, to show that Jesus' miracles prove he was a sorcerer, not a true sage.

Of Celsus's several historical discussions the one on the virgin birth is the least interesting, but it is worth noting because it allows him to make the larger point about Jesus' reliance on magic. According to Celsus, it was Jesus himself who "fabricated the story of his birth from a virgin" (c. Cels. 1.28). Jesus had come from a Jewish village where he had been born of a "poor country woman who earned her living by spinning." This woman became pregnant by another man, a soldier named Panthera, and "was driven out by her husband, who was a carpenter by trade, since she was convicted of adultery" (c. Cels. 1.32). While she was wandering about in disgrace she secretly gave birth to Jesus. When Jesus grew up he went to Egypt, and because he was poor, hired himself out as a workman and "there tried his hand at certain magical powers on which the Egyptians pride themselves; he returned full of conceit because of the powers, and on account of them gave himself the title Son of God" (c. Cels. 1.28).

Where Celsus would have gotten this story is uncertain.[8] Though some of the details are similar to the accounts in the Gospels, there is

7. For a discussion of literary and historical criticism of the Gospels in the second century, see Robert M. Grant, *The Earliest Lives of Jesus* (New York, 1961).
8. Chadwick, 31.

clearly more here. For example, he provides a name for the man who impregnated Mary, Panthera. It is possible that this story was circulating in the empire, perhaps in Jewish circles. Celsus presents his criticism of Jesus not as his own but as that of a Jew, and there are some references in Jewish literature to a Jesus ben Panthera, Jesus son of Panthera. Also, the name Panthera is close to the Greek term for virgin, *parthenos*.

Celsus was certainly aware that he had gone beyond the text of the Gospels, but his point is clear. The Gospels are based only on hearsay. Why should one give greater credibility to what is written in them than to other stories about Jesus? The accounts in the Gospels were written solely by Christians and passed on in Christian circles. Should the legends there be taken with greater seriousness than the many legends in Greek literature? The Christian Gospels offer no reliable basis on which to establish the truth of the accounts about Jesus. The baptism of Jesus is a good illustration.

Celsus imagines Jesus having a conversation about his baptism with a Jew. "When," says the Jew, "you were bathing near John, you say that you saw what appeared to be a bird fly towards you out of the air. . . . What trustworthy witness saw this apparition, or who heard a voice from heaven adopting you as son of God? There is no proof except for your word and the evidence which you may produce of one of the men who were punished with you" (*c. Cels.* 1.41). Here the question centers wholly on historical verifiability. How does one substantiate that a certain event took place? What are the criteria by which one evaluates the veracity of a document claiming to record a historical event? (Origen read Celsus's discussion in this way. He discusses in elaborate detail the problem of historical verification, for example, the difficulty of establishing the historicity of events such as the war in Troy between Greeks and Trojans, the story about Oedipus and Jocasta, and so on.) Celsus said that any informed person knows there are countless legends told about men and heroes, and the stories told about Jesus have no greater claim on historical truth than other legends. The only reasonable way to verify an account is to test the reliability of the witness. Since the account of the baptism of Jesus comes only from Jesus and his followers, one should be suspicious. Like other stories, it was concocted by the hero's followers to glorify his deeds.

A similar argument occurs with respect to the accounts of Jesus' resurrection from the dead.

How many others produce wonders like this to convince simple hearers whom they exploit by deceit? They say that Zalmoxis, the slave of Pythagoras, also did this among the Scythians, and Pythagoras himself in Italy, and Rhampsinitus in Egypt. The last-named played dice with Demeter in Hades and returned bearing a gift from her, a golden napkin. Moreover, they say that Orpheus did this among the Odrysians, and Protesilaus in Thessaly, and Heracles at Taenarum, and Theseus. But we must examine this question whether anyone who really died ever rose again with the same body. Or do you think that the stories of these others really are the legends which they appear to be, and yet that the ending of your tragedy is to be regarded as noble and convincing—his cry from the cross when he expired, and the earthquake and the darkness? While he was alive he did not help himself, but after death he rose again and showed the marks of his punishment and how his hands had been pierced. But who say this? A hysterical female, as you say, and perhaps some other one of those who were deluded by the same sorcery, who either dreamt in a certain state of mind and through wishful thinking had a hallucination due to some mistaken notion (an experience which has happened to thousands), or, which is more likely, wanted to impress the others by telling this fantastic tale, and so by this cock-and-bull story to provide a chance for other beggars. [2.55]

Christians cannot produce reliable witnesses to the events they claim took place. Celsus evokes parallels from Greek religion and mythology to show that the stories about Jesus are not unique. Many of the things that were said about him were said about other gods and heroic figures in Greek history. Resurrection from the dead, one of the points that Christians vigorously insisted on, had been attributed to other divine figures in the ancient world. He also makes the further suggestion that the stories of Jesus' resurrection can be explained by dreams or hallucinations. What his followers said is not a report of what actually happened but what in their enthusiasm and ecstasy over their leader they *wished* had happened. This wish became the basis of the later claim that Jesus was a divine figure and not an ordinary mortal.

Celsus's concern with historical verification, like other points discussed in this chapter, helps one understand not only the nature of the conflict between Christianity and pagan intellectuals, but also gives us insight into the developing character of the Christian tradition. As is clear from Origen's response, the questions of whether the gospel accounts of Jesus are reliable, and whether Christian theological claims are based on the kind of person Jesus was and the life he lived, were matters of great import for Christian thinkers. As late as the early fifth century, Christian thinkers were still troubled about the trustworthiness of the gospel accounts of Jesus, as the discussion of Augustine's book *Harmony of the Gospels* (in chapter 6) will show. The question of the mythological and legendary character of the Gospels did not first arise in modern times. The historical reliability of the accounts of Jesus' life was already an issue for Christian thinkers in the second century.

AN APOSTASY FROM JUDAISM

The Roman historian Suetonius had identified Jesus as an instigator among the Jews (*Claudius* 25) and Galen had discussed common points of agreement between Jewish and Christian doctrines. Anyone who knew anything about Christianity knew that the movement had begun in Palestine among the Jews and that Christians appealed to Jewish writings, specifically the Jewish Scriptures (the Christian Old Testament). But not until Celsus had a pagan critic seen the significance of the relation between Christianity and Judaism for criticizing the Christian movement. Some people knew that "Christians and Jews quarrel with each other" (*c. Cels.* 3.1), but Celsus's observations on

Christianity and Judaism cut deeper than that. He charged that Christians deserted the Jewish Law even though Jesus, the founder of Christianity, was a Jew and Christians claimed to be faithful to the Jewish heritage. Celsus puts this criticism into the mouth of a Jewish interlocutor. "Why do you [Christians] take your origin from our religion [Judaism], and then, as if you are progressing in knowledge, despise these things, although you cannot name any other origin for your doctrine than our law" (*c. Cels.* 2.4)?

To understand the force of this criticism one must recall that Judaism was a thriving religious movement within the Roman Empire in the second century C.E. The Christian movement had to make its way alongside of, and sometimes in opposition to, well-established Jewish communities, many of which had existed for centuries in the cities of the Roman Empire. This fact is seldom appreciated in the writing of the history of this period. In the conventional account of early Christianity, the Jews played a major role *before* the beginning of Christianity and during the first generations of it. All serious study of the New Testament, for example, begins with an examination of the Jewish background of Christianity. However, due to the Christian interpretation of history that dates the beginning of a new era from the birth of Christ (and hence divides all history, sacred and secular, into A.D., "in the year of our Lord," and B.C., "before Christ"), it appears that *after* the rise of Christianity the Jews became peripheral to the main story, the emergence and establishment of the Christian church.[9]

The Jews were a significant minority within the Roman Empire, numbering four to six million people out of a population of approximately sixty million. In the provinces where Christianity first established itself—Palestine, Syria, Egypt, and Asia Minor—the Jews comprised a larger percentage of the populace. Although the Jews in Palestine suffered because of the war with the Romans in 69–70 C.E. and the uprising in Cyrene and Egypt in 115–17 C.E., as well as the Bar Kochba revolt in 132–35 C.E. which caused many casualties, the overall number of Jews did not decrease dramatically. The events in

9. See Robert L. Wilken, *John Chrysostom and the Jews* (Berkeley, 1983), especially chapter 2.

Palestine had little impact on the actual life of the Jewish communities in other provinces, and even in Palestine, by the second century Jewish life was prospering. In many cities in this period, Palestine as well as elsewhere, Jews served on the city councils; some held posts in the Roman provincial administration; and Jews actively participated in the educational, cultural, and economic life of the cities.

In this milieu, where Christianity was a tiny unknown movement that had only recently originated and was only beginning to come to the attention of people, it perplexed pagans that Christians claimed to be inheritors of the Jewish tradition while at the same time rejecting the Jewish community and its customs and laws. It is obvious that Jews were justified in criticizing Christians for deserting the Jewish tradition yet claiming to be faithful to Jewish origins. In his *Dialogue with Trypho,* a debate between a Christian and a Jew, Justin Martyr quotes the Jew Trypho as follows: "But you [Christians] openly despising this covenant, neglect the [laws] which follow from it, and you attempt to persuade yourselves that you know God, even though you perform none of those things that those [Jews] who fear God do" (*Dial.* 10). But that such criticism would come from a pagan critic is another matter, especially when one considers that Celsus is also critical of the Jews: "The Jews were Egyptian by race, and left Egypt after revolting against the Egyptian community and despising the religious customs of Egypt" (*c. Cels.* 3.5).

Celsus knew that the truth of the Christian teaching depended on Christianity's relation to Judaism, because Christians claimed to be the rightful inheritors of the Jewish tradition. Justin, for example, said that he was converted to Christianity by reading the prophetic writings of the Jews (*Dial.* 7). The actual practice of the Christians, however, ignored Jewish customs, and the continuing existence of Jewish communities that kept the ancient Jewish traditions called into question Christian assertions. By continuing to observe the Jewish Law—circumcision, the food laws, celebration of Jewish festivals—the Jews preserved continuity with earlier Jewish tradition and showed they were faithful to the laws of Moses. The Christians, on the other hand, who claimed to be inheritors of this tradition, observed none of the

Jewish laws. Hence Celsus has his Jewish interlocutor ask: "What was wrong with you [Christians] that you left the law of our fathers, and being deluded by that man [Jesus] whom we were addressing just now, were quite ludicrously deceived and have deserted us for another name and another life?" (c. Cels. 2.1).

Had there not been visible Jewish communities in the cities of the empire, the contention that Christianity had apostasized from Judaism would have been unpersuasive, even unintelligible. In such a situation Christians could have claimed that they were indeed the rightful inheritors of the Jewish tradition. Who would gainsay their claims? But the existence of another religious group, and one that was well known and well established in the cities, made the Christian assertion implausible in the extreme. Why, asks Celsus, did God "give contradictory laws to this man from Nazareth, his son"? Jesus taught many different things than Moses taught. "Who is wrong? Moses or Jesus? Or when the Father sent Jesus had he forgotten what commands he gave to Moses? Or did he condemn his own laws and change his mind, and send his messenger for quite the opposite purposes" (7.18)?

Celsus also knew that the Jews did not recognize Jesus as the Messiah. "Why is he not recognized by people who had been long expecting him?" asks Celsus. How does it happen, asks Celsus's Jew, that Christians take their "origin from our religion" yet despise the very things that the Jewish Scriptures teach (c. Cels. 2.4)? Christians claimed that the facts of Jesus' life were proclaimed beforehand in the Jewish prophecies, but in fact the "prophecies could be applied to thousands of others far more plausibly than to Jesus" (2.28). If the Christian claims about Jesus cannot be supported by an appeal to the Jewish Scriptures, Christians cannot hide under the umbrella of Judaism. "Deluded by Jesus, they have left the law of their fathers, and have been quite ludicrously deceived, and have deserted to another name and another life" (c. Cels. 2.11).

Celsus respected the many traditional ways of worship within the various "nations" of the Roman world. Indeed, as we shall see in the next section, Celsus's own religious outlook linked the "true teaching" to the "ancient teaching." If a practice was traditional, Celsus thought it was true and worth perpetuating. The Christians, however, had no tradition of their own. "I will ask them where they have come from, or who is the author of their traditional law. Nobody, they will say. In fact, they themselves originated from Judaism, and they cannot name any other source for their teacher and chorus-leader. Nevertheless they rebelled against the Jews." Though Celsus had little admiration for the Jews, at least their way of life was old and venerable and should not be rejected out of hand. "They observe a worship which may be very peculiar, but it is at least traditional" (*c. Cels.* 5.25).

One of Celsus's chief arguments, then, was that the Christian repudiation of its origin proved the illegitimacy of the new movement. In a revealing comment, Origen said: "What sort of objection is it to Christianity that John who baptized Jesus was a Jew?" (*c. Cels.* 2.4). The answer obviously is that it was a fundamental objection because the Christians, though claiming to be the inheritors of Judaism, were not recognizable as Jews nor acknowledged by them. The very existence of Jewish communities that continued to observe the Jewish customs was a decisive argument against the legitimacy of Christian claims. Two centuries later the emperor Julian made the apostasy from Judaism a fundamental objection to Christianity.

The significance of Celsus's argument that Christianity was an apostasy from Judaism has seldom been recognized in discussions of pagan criticism of Christianity or of early Christian apologetics. The persistence of this theme among critics suggests that the debate between Christianity and Hellenism was not simply a two-way debate, as has been assumed for generations. Most scholars, following Adolf von Harnack, the great nineteenth-century historian, have interpreted the history of early Christianity almost wholly in relation to Greco-Roman culture. The relation to Judaism is, however, very significant to understanding the development of Christianity in the Roman world. In many cases the Jews participated actively in the debate; but in other cases, as with Celsus's *True Doctrine,* the simple fact that the Jews were part of the social world changed the terms of the discussion. As long as there were active Jewish communities living alongside the emerging Christian ones, critics such as Celsus could argue that Christianity was patently false because, contrary to its own claims, it had deserted Jewish ways. Christians may have claimed to have the correct interpretation of the Jewish Scriptures, but on those points which were clearly set forth in the Scriptures—such as circumcision and the keeping of the Sabbath, the festivals, and the food laws—Christians wantonly disregarded the meaning of the very books they claimed as their own. Christian apologists had to deal not only with the philosophical objections of pagans, but with scriptural and historical arguments offered by pagans (and by Jews) that were supported by a rival tradition of interpretation and of practice. In any effort to understand the response of pagan critics to Christianity in the Roman world, the continuing presence of the Jews is a major factor. Christianity's claimed relation to Judaism was perceived as one of its most vulnerable points.

RELIGION AND THE SOCIAL ORDER

On the basis of what has been said thus far, it may appear that Celsus's *True Doctrine* consisted chiefly of ad hoc criticism of particularly vulnerable aspects of Christian doctrine or practice. His work, however, was not a "planless polemic" (Andresen). He writes from a consistent point of view, and his rejection of the Christian movement arises out of his views about the society in which he lives, the intellectual and spiritual traditions that animated this society, and the religious convictions on which it was based. Earlier in the chapter I briefly touched on these matters when discussing Celsus's views about belief in one God, but now it is time to look more closely at the social and political dimensions of his attack on Christianity.

Toward the end of the *True Doctrine* Celsus had urged Christians "to help the emperor with all [their] power, and cooperate with him in what is right, and fight for him, and be fellow-soldiers if he presses for this, and fellow-generals with him" (*c. Cels.* 8.73). Celsus, however, knew that most Christians refused military service and hence were unwilling to do their part in protecting the empire. Origen, writing seventy years later, confirms this. Christians do more for the good of the empire, he says, by forming an "army of piety" that prays for the well-being of the emperor and the safety of the empire.

In the next fragment quoted by Origen, Celsus says that Christians ought to "accept public office in our country . . . for the sake of the preservation of the laws of piety" (*c. Cels.* 8.75). The point of Celsus's comments is not that Christians are pacifists, but that they refuse to participate *in any way* in the public and civil life of the cities of the Roman Empire. As another critic put it, Christians "do not understand their civic duty" (Minucius, *Octavius* 12).

On the face of it, Celsus's comments about Christian refusal to assume civic responsibilities appear similar to the charge, reported in Tacitus, that Christians were punished by Nero because of their "hatred of the human race," their aloofness and disdain for the ways of others. Celsus cites the words of Jesus, "It is impossible for the same man to serve several masters" (Matt. 6 : 24) and calls it a "seditious word" [or "word of revolution"] of "people who wall themselves off and break away from the rest of mankind" (*c. Cels.* 8.2). However, there was more at issue than the presumed antisociality and exclusiveness of Christians. Celsus is concerned about the theoretical basis of Christian factionalism. In human affairs, he says, one cannot serve two masters because one who has pledged loyalty to one person cannot do the same to another. But "where God is concerned it is irrational to avoid worshipping several gods," for the "man who worships several gods, because he worships some one of those which belong to the great God, even by this very action does that which is loved by him." Hence Celsus concludes, "Anyone who honors and worships all those who belong to God does not hurt him since they are all his" (*c. Cels.* 8.2).

The term *revolution* or *sedition* occurs several times in the *True Doctrine* to describe the Christian movement. As we have already noted, Celsus criticized Christians because they apostasized from Judaism. "A revolt against the [Jewish] community led to the introduction of new ideas." But in the passage cited above from book 8, Celsus is speaking about a revolt against the institutions of the Greco-Roman world, against the customs and traditions of the cities, against the wisdom which had been handed down for generations by wise men of old. Christians had contempt for these ancient and hallowed ways. They would have nothing to do with "temples and altars and images," even though they did not take the trouble to understand why men built temples and worshipped images. They claimed that an image of stone or wood or bronze or gold could not be a god. But such "wisdom is ludicrous. Who but an utter infant imagines that these things are gods and not votive offerings and images of Gods" (7.62). They also refused to give proper adoration to the *daimones*, the intermediate beings which stood between humans and God (8.63); and they refused to serve the emperor.

The Christian movement was revolutionary not because it had the men and resources to mount a war against the laws of the Roman Empire, but because it created a social group that promoted its own laws and its own patterns of behavior. The life and teachings of Jesus led to the formation of a new community of people called "the church." Christianity had begun to look like a separate people or nation, but without its own land or traditions to legitimate its unusual customs. Like the Jews, Christians held profane what the Romans held sacred, and permitted what others thought reprehensible. But in contrast to the Jews, Christians had introduced a new feature into their cult—namely, the worship of a man, Jesus—and in giving adoration to Jesus, they had turned men and women away from true devotion to God.

If you taught them [the Christians] that Jesus is not [God's] Son, but that God is father of all, and that we really ought to worship him alone, they would no longer be willing to listen to you unless you included Jesus as well, who is the author of their sedition. Indeed, when they call him Son of God, it is not because they are paying very great reverence to God, but because they are exalting Jesus greatly." [*c. Cels.* 8.14]

Celsus sees the worship of Jesus lurking behind the saying in the Gospels against serving two masters (Matt. 6 : 24). By making Jesus the central object of worship in their new association, Christians turned people away from service to the one high God. Devotion to this God, however, did not mean that this was the only God, but that God stood at the pinnacle of a hierarchy of gods. These deities were

God's emissaries and helpers in ruling the world. Accordingly, it was proper to worship these lesser gods *and* the one high God as long as one did not make one of these emissaries—Jesus, for example—the sole object of worship *to the exclusion of* the high God and his other emissaries. A king rules over others like himself. Like a king who rules over fellow humans, not animals, God, the monarch of all, rules over other gods. "The man who worships several gods, because he worships some one of those which belong to the great God, even by this very action does that which is loved by him" (*c. Cels.* 8.2).

Celsus was ready to acknowledge Jesus as divine if Christians could bring forth sufficient proof that he deserved such honor. His own view was that Jesus did not deserve it because he accomplished his wonders through magic and sorcery. The Christians, however, made even more extravagant claims: they said that Jesus was unique among the gods and that he should be worshipped to the exclusion of all other gods. To Celsus such excessive adoration set up Jesus as a rival to God and undercut the worship of the one God. "If these men [Christians] worshipped no other God but one, perhaps they would have had a valid argument against others. But in fact they worship to an extravagant degree this man who appeared recently, and yet think it is not inconsistent with belief in god if they also worship his servant" (*c. Cels.* 8.12). Christians created a revolutionary society whose object was not the worship of God, nor of the daimones, God's emissaries, but of a "corpse" (*c. Cels.* 7.68). That they refused to frequent the temples, to venerate images and statues, and to participate in the public religious rites was a sign that they were an "obscure and secret society" (*c. Cels.* 8.17).

Celsus was convinced that if an association of this sort attracted too many adherents it could disrupt the cohesion and stability of society. The Christian movement was beginning to create a "counterculture" that shifted people's loyalties and drained their energies away from the larger society. At the time Celsus was writing it is unlikely that Christians were numerous enough to offer such a threat, but Celsus was uneasy with the social implications of the Christian movement. For whoever makes the god or gods of one's own association equal to the God of all, thereby robbing the one God of his proper devotion, throws into fundamental question the established order. In the most profound sense, then, the Christian movement appeared seditious. By transgressing the *Nomos* (structure or law) of Judaism, the tradition from which it sprang, Christianity exposed Hellenism to acute peril. For the revolt against Judaism injected a poison into the society that would eventually destroy the traditions of Hellenism. Christianity "encourages the dissolution of the religious *Nomos*. The cause of its destructive influence lies finally in its unfaithfulness to that historical inheritance with which the various people have been entrusted in their *Nomos*."[10]

Nomos in Celsus's vocabulary refers to the accumulated wisdom and practices of a particular culture. Disregard for tradition could only lead to error and social anarchy. Celsus's arguments against Christianity have two faces. On the one hand, he offers logical and philosophical reasons why Christian beliefs cannot be accepted. Many of these arguments have a timeless character. The argument that God cannot do the impossible would fall into this category. On the other hand, he offers another line of criticism, linked to his view of *Nomos*, and peculiar to his own time and culture. He believed that truth and antiquity were one and that what was handed down by the ancients was true *because* it was old. "It was because men of ancient times were touched by the spirit that they proclaimed many excellent doctrines." Christians ignored these sages and set forth supposedly new and better teachings.

Who were these sages? Most were nameless men of hoary antiquity whose wisdom could be learned from the moral maxims, the customs, the inherited beliefs, and the religious practices that were to be found among the various peoples who inhabited the Roman world. The authority of these teachings and customs derived from their antiquity. The "true doctrine" (*alethēs logos*) was identified with the "ancient doctrine" (*palaios logos*). One of these venerable sages was Plato. In an extended discussion of Plato's *Crito*, a dialogue dealing with the prob-

10. Andresen, *Logos und Nomos*, 223–24.

lem of justice, Celsus shows that the Christian injunction to turn the other cheek when struck (Luke 6:29) is an imitation of a teaching already found in Plato. "They [the Christians] have a precept to this effect—that you must not resist a man who insults you. Even . . . if someone strikes you on the cheek, yet you should offer the other one as well. This too is old stuff, and was better said before them. But they expressed it in more vulgar terms" (*c. Cels.* 7.58). Then he cites the *Crito* to show that Plato taught that even if one suffers harm one should not do harm in return. The views of Plato, however, were "set forth still earlier by divinely inspired men" (7.58). Elsewhere he charges Christians with misunderstanding the teachings of the ancients (*c. Cels.* 6.15).

Celsus's appeal to the wisdom of the ancients was directed against the kinds of claims Christians were making to defend their teachings. The early apologists appealed to the prophets of the Jews to substantiate Christian teaching (Justin Martyr *Apol.* 1.30–52). Moses was thought to have lived earlier than the ancient Greek sages (*Apol.* 1.54). Even before the rise of Christianity Jews had argued for the truth of their tradition by showing its antiquity. Josephus, the Jewish historian and apologist, entitled one of his works the *Antiquities of the Jews*.

But there was a deeper reason why Celsus appealed to the wisdom of antiquity. Unlike our culture, which seems to thrive on the new and up-to-date, Greco-Roman society revered the past. The older something was, the better it was thought to be. This was especially true in matters of religion, because the men and women of earlier times, especially those who lived very long ago, were thought to have been closer to the gods. In his *Laws,* a work dealing with the customs and traditions of Rome, Cicero writes: "The preservation of the rites of the family and of our ancestors means preserving the religious rites which, we can almost say, were handed down to us by the gods themselves, since ancient times were closest to the gods" (*Leg.* 2.10.27). Cicero was simply echoing the words of Plato: "The ancients are better than we for they dwelled nearer to the gods" (*Phil.* 16c). Tradition was the test of truth.

In this sense, Celsus is a profoundly conservative thinker. "There is an ancient doctrine (*logos*) which has existed from the beginning that has always been maintained by the wisest nations and cities and wise men." Among the nations he mentions the Egyptians, Assyrians, Indians, Persians, Odrysians, Samothracians, and Eleusinians. Yet Celsus was not authoritarian or dogmatic. He was intelligent enough to know that the beliefs and practices of these varied peoples were dissimilar and could not be reduced to one ancient teaching (*c. Cels.* 1.14). Though he appeals to a teaching or *logos* which had been expressed by the sages of old, this teaching has little specific content, nor does it take the same form in every "nation." In another sense, Celsus is extremely "relativistic," a point which Origen saw and roundly attacked (*c. Cels.* 5.27). His appeal is less to a specific "doctrine" than it is to established ways whatever these may be. One should observe the "laws" of the various nations, he writes, "because it is necessary to preserve the established social conventions" and because the various nations were handed over by God to different overseers who established differing practices. As long as one observes the traditional ways, the "overseers" will be pleased. "It is impious to abandon the customs which have existed in each locality from the beginning" (*c. Cels.* 5.26).

Celsus can praise the Jews even though he despises their particular customs. The Jews became an individual nation, he says, and "made laws according to the custom of their country; and they maintain these laws among themselves at the present day, and observe a worship which may be very peculiar but is at least traditional. In this respect they behave like the rest of mankind, because each nation follows its traditional customs, whatever kind may happen to be established" (*c. Cels.* 5.25). Because they have maintained their customs over the centuries up to the present time, the Jews have a claim on the ancient and true doctrines. But Christians can make no such claim, for their sect came into existence only recently; hence the force of the charge that Christians are apostates. Their attempt to appeal to the antiquity of the Jews is easily refuted. Christians can only point to a shallow and inconsequential past going back a little over a hundred years. If I ask them "where they have come from or who is the author of their traditional laws," they will say: "Nobody. In fact they themselves originated from Judaism, and they cannot name any other source for their teacher and chorus-leader. Nevertheless they rebelled against the Jews" (*c. Cels.* 5.33).

Celsus's standard, then, for judging the Christian movement was custom and tradition, or to use his term, the *Nomos* which had been handed down from antiquity. He does not defend a particular set of religious beliefs. Indeed, he is quite willing to tolerate wide diversity in practice as long as the practices are traditional.

> There is nothing wrong if each people observes its own laws of worship. Actually we will find that the difference between each nation is very considerable and nevertheless each one of them appears to think its own by far the best. The Ethiopians who live at Meroe worship only Zeus and Dionysus. The Arabians worship only Ourania and Dionysus. The Egyptians all worship Osiris and Isis. . . . Some abstain from sheep, reverencing them as sacred, others from goats, others from crocodiles." [*c. Cels.* 5.35]

There is another dimension to this exchange between Celsus and the Christians. It is not simply a debate between paganism and Christianity, but a debate about a new concept of religion. Celsus sensed that Christians had severed the traditional bond between religion and a "nation" or people. The ancients took for granted that religion was indissolubly linked to a particular city or people. Indeed, there was no term for *religion* in the sense we now use it to refer to the beliefs and practices of a specific group of people of a voluntary association divorced from ethnic or national identity. The term "could speak of a particular system of rites (a cult or an initiation), or a particular set of beliefs (doctrines or opinions), or a legal code, or a body of national customs and traditions; but for the peculiar synthesis of all those which we call a 'religion' the one Hellenistic word which came the closest was 'philosophy.'"[11] The idea of an association of people bound together by a religious allegiance with its own traditions and beliefs, its own history, and its own way of life independent of a par-

11. Morton Smith, "Palestinian Judaism in the First Century," in Moshe Davis, *Israel: Its Role in Civilization* (New York, 1956), 79.

ticular city or nation was foreign to the ancients. Religion belonged to a *people,* and it was bestowed on an individual by the people or nation from which one came or in which one lived. "Piety lay in a calm performance of traditional rites and in a faithful observance of traditional standards."[12]

Celsus opposed the "sectarian" tendencies at work in the Christian movement because he saw in Christianity a "privatizing" of religion, the transferral of religious values from the public sphere to a private association. Christians not only refused military service but they would not accept public office nor assume any responsibility for the governing of the cities. It was, however, not simply that Christians subverted the cities by refusing to participate in civic life, but that they undermined the foundations of the societies in which they lived. By elevating the founder of their society to divine status, they set up a rival to the one high God who watched over the empire. If you overthrow the teaching that there is one king, says Celsus, there is "nothing to prevent the emperor from being abandoned, alone and deserted, while earthly things would come into the power of the most lawless and savage barbarians" (*c. Cels.* 8.68).

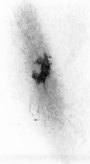

12. A. D. Nock, *Conversion* (Oxford, 1933), 18.

VI PORPHYRY: THE MOST
LEARNED CRITIC OF ALL

OF ALL THE CRITICS OF CHRISTIANITY IN ANTIQUITY, Porphyry, the biographer of the great Neoplatonic philosopher Plotinus and editor of his *Enneads*, was the most learned and astute. Though Plotinus towers over Porphyry in the history of philosophy, Porphyry was a man of genuine intellectual stature, whose broad learning and philosophical acumen made him a formidable foe indeed. Celsus's work against the Christians merited the response of one apologist, Origen, but Porphyry's writings claimed the attention of several generations of Christian intellectuals, among whom were Eusebius, the church historian; Methodius, an early proponent of virginity; Apollinarius, an innovative theologian from Syria; Jerome the biblical scholar; and Augustine, who was still wrestling with Porphyry's arguments against Christianity late in life, when he wrote the *City of God*. Even the emperor Constantine sought to still Porphyry's voice, not by composing another treatise against him, but by putting his writings to the torch, a precedent that was followed a century later by another emperor, Theodosius II, in 448 C.E. "The vigor, scope and sheer size of [Porphyry's] attack must have stunned the Christian communities," wrote Robert Grant.[1]

Although Porphyry's critics were many, they have unfortunately preserved for us little of his work, and what fragments are extant are scattered through a half-dozen authors, often with no sure indication that they derive from Porphyry himself. Consequently, we are uncer-

1. Robert M. Grant, "Porphyry among the Early Christians," in *Romanitas et Christianitas,* ed. W. den Boer et al. (Amsterdam, 1973), 182.

tain not only about what he actually wrote, but in what form, and whether he wrote one book or several against the Christian movement. What we do know is that his attack on Christianity made a deep impression on Christians; that it drew on wide learning in history, philosophy, religion, chronography, and literary criticism; and that it subjected both Jewish and Christian Scriptures to thorough and detailed criticism. Augustine, no mean scholar, called him the "most learned of philosophers," and even Eusebius, himself a polymath, was intimidated by Porphyry. It was hard for Christian intellectuals to be comfortable with an opponent who knew the Bible almost as well as they knew it themselves.

Celsus wrote at a time when little was known about the Christian movement, when Christianity was a small sect gaining public attention for the first time. By the time Porphyry wrote, in the second half of the third century, Christianity had become a significant force within the Roman Empire. Indeed, it is likely that its growing influence among the educated and its broad appeal to the lower classes not only prompted Porphyry to write against Christianity but also suggested to him the approach he would take. Celsus had certainly taken Christianity seriously, but he believed that its baneful influence could be retarded if its claims were shown to be false. Porphyry had no such illusion; he sensed that Christianity was here to stay and he sought, within the framework of the religious traditions of the Roman Empire, to find a way of accommodating the new creed. This is why he was so threatening to the Christians of antiquity and is so fascinating to us.

We know the figure of Celsus only through his opposition to Christianity, but Porphyry was much more than a critic of Christianity. He was a philosopher in his own right trying to preserve the intellectual tradition of Greek antiquity and a religious thinker who sought to reconcile the religious heritage of the Greco-Roman world with philosophical reason. He defended, for example, the religious value of the traditional practice of animal sacrifice. His philosophical writings, particularly his work on Aristotle, have had a continuing influence on Western philosophy since the time of Boethius. In the medieval curriculum his introduction to and commentary on Aristotle's *Categoriae* (*Isagoge*) became the first treatise a student of philosophy was asked to master. He belonged to an intellectual tradition, Platonism, that was very much alive in the third century, yet he was a man of traditional piety. In a letter addressed to his wife, whom he married in his old age, he wrote, "The greatest fruit of piety is to worship God according to the tradition of one's fathers" (*Marc.* 18). In contrast to Plotinus, whose piety was intellectual and spiritual, Porphyry found a place in his thinking for ritual, animal sacrifices, and the public ceremonies in the cities. He recognized the importance of religion for philosophy. "Neoplatonism grew up not only as an academic institution of the Empire, but as a spiritual movement in an age of religions. . . . What is new is the attitude of academic philosophers to religion. From having viewed religion with varying degrees of respect as morally valuable, Platonists came to accept it as aspiring to the same end as philosophy."[2]

IN DEFENSE OF PLATO

Porphyry was born and raised in the city of Tyre in Phoenicia on the Mediterranean coast north of Palestine. The date of his birth is uncertain, but it was probably 233 C.E. His father's name was Malchos, the Syriac word for king, and from it came the Greek name *Porphyrios,* the term for purple, the traditional color of royalty. That his family had any royal blood is doubtful, but his parents were sufficiently well off to provide him with a thorough education, which meant a rhetorical and literary one. Though his native language was Syriac, Tyre was a Hellenized city and all of Porphyry's education was in Greek. It was possible he knew some Hebrew, and he devoted a good part of his attack on Christianity to the Jewish Scriptures, but nowhere does he show that he knew the language.

Tyre, a trading and commercial center situated at a strategic point on the eastern Mediterranean, was a meeting point of East and West.

2. A. D. Lloyd, in *The Cambridge History of Later Greek and Early Medieval Philosophy* (Cambridge, 1967), p. 277.

It boasted a splendid harbor and a large purple-dyeing industry. Some of its citizens maintained permanent residences in Rome and Puteoli (present-day Pozzuoli) for business purposes. Situated where it was, Tyre attracted and nurtured diverse religions, and here Porphyry had his first experience with the variety of religious practices in the ancient world and developed his tolerance for differing religious beliefs. It was also in Tyre that he had his first contact with Christianity and Judaism, and it is possible that his interpretation of the Jewish Book of Daniel, which played a role in his polemic against the Christians and caused later Christian commentators much anguish, was learned in Tyre.[3]

As a young man Porphyry traveled from Tyre down the Mediterranean coast to Caesarea to hear the Christian thinker, Origen, lecture. At the time, Origen, the most original intellect Christianity had produced during its first two centuries, was at the height of his powers and had recently produced his massive defense of Christianity to the pagans, his *Contra Celsum*. Porphyry, however, was not impressed by Origen. He was put off by the "absurdity" of Origen's efforts to reconcile the Greek intellectual tradition with the new religion that had arisen in Palestine. Comparing Origen to another contemporary Greek philosopher, Ammonius, Porphyry said:

> Ammonius was a Christian brought up in Christian ways by his parents, but when he began to think philosophically he promptly changed to a law-abiding way of life. Origen on the other hand, a Greek schooled in Greek thought, plunged headlong into un-Greek recklessness; immersed in this, he peddled himself and his skill in argument. In his way of life he behaved like a Christian, defying the law; in his metaphysical and theological ideas he played the Greek, giving a Greek twist to foreign tales. [Eusebius, *Hist. Eccl.* 6.19]

Because of Porphyry's acquaintance with Origen, some Christians later thought that he had once been a Christian who had apostasized

3. P. M. Casey, "Porphyry and the Origin of the Book of Daniel," *Journal of Theological Studies*, n.s. 27 (1976): 15–33.

to Hellenism. This is most unlikely, but it is easy to see how such an idea could arise. To Christians it was inconceivable that a man of Porphyry's stature would not have fallen under the spell of Origen's powerful mind and ascetic spirituality, especially a man who himself was an ascetic. Nevertheless, even the great Origen could not work his magic on Porphyry. His initial contact with a Christian intellectual had large consequences, however, because from Origen Porphyry learned the importance of the Bible to Christian thinking, and he may even have learned the art of biblical criticism from him. Robert Grant writes:

> When he [Porphyry] encountered the Stromateis [a book on exegetical difficulties] of Origen, with their criticism of the Bible and their subsequent allegorizations, he presumably found that a good deal of his anti-Christian tasks had been done for him. All he had to do was accept Origen's negative statements (although in many instances he went further along this line) and reject the deeper spiritual meanings which Origen sought to find. In this regard the critical work of Origen provided a *praeparatio Neoplatonica* for the work of Porphyry.[4]

Porphyry was to make the Bible more central to his attack on Christianity than any critic before or after him.

Porphyry's education, like that of other privileged men of his day, was chiefly rhetorical and literary. In many respects it was similar to the education received by Pliny, except that its vehicle was Greek rather than Latin and the writers he studied were Homer, Euripides, Menander, and Demosthenes, not Virgil, Terence, Sallust, and Cicero. Porphyry, however, did not seek a career in law or in the civil service. Instead, he left Tyre for Athens to study philosophy. In the third century Athens was still a major intellectual center, and there he met his first master, Longinus, by profession a philosopher and rhetorician, but by inclination and temperament a literary critic and pedant. Porphyry's biographer, Eunapius, called Longinus a "living library and a walking Museion" (*VS* 456); Plotinus said he was a "scholar but cer-

---

4. Robert M. Grant, "The Stromateis of Origen," in *Epektasis. Mélanges patristiques offerts au Cardinal Jean Daniélou* (Paris, 1972), 292.

tainly not a philosopher" (*Vita Plotini* 14). In Athens Porphyry studied philosophy, but his chief preoccupation seems to have been philology and literary criticism.

A glimpse of the concerns of Longinus's school can be found in a passage from Porphyry describing the way the school celebrated Plato's birthday. It was the custom among philosophical schools to commemorate the founder by a banquet followed by conversation, and on this particular occasion the topic was plagiarism. With much erudition, the members of the school tried to outdo each other by citing even more obscure authors or showing how even the best and most respected writers had plagiarized sections of their writings. Castrius, one of the members of the group, began by showing that Ephorus borrowed as many as three thousand lines from other writers, to which Apollonius replied that, in his history of Philip, Theopompus copied word for word from the *Areopagiticus* of Isocrates. After debating this point, Apollonius said that even the great Menander was guilty of the same fault, though people have generally overlooked it, but Latinus exposed his borrowings in a work known only to a few. And so the discussion continued—salon talk, after-dinner conversation, the idle moments of the overeducated. Porphyry thrived in this setting, and through this door he entered the great world of Greek thought. From Longinus he also learned the tools and the skills to deal critically with literary and historical works—skills that would make him one of the most learned and respected men of his age.

Under Longinus's influence Porphyry published his first books. One of these, the *Homeric Questions,* was a textual and literary analysis of the Homeric poems. He discussed difficulties with the text, summarizing the views of earlier scholars and proffering his own solutions. He analyzed the etymology and meaning of words, discussed grammatical problems and historical allusions. What is absent from the work is any interest in philosophical questions or any concern with the allegorical meaning of the text. In a later work, however, *De Antro Nympharum (Cave of the Nymphs)* Porphyry showed that he was quite familiar with the tradition of allegorical interpretation. In this work, an interpretation of the Cave of the Nymphs in the *Odyssey* (13.102–12), Porphyry argues that the poet is speaking of "higher things." The

Cave of the Nymphs is a symbol of the cosmos and the dwelling place for the soul.

After spending some years under Longinus's tutelage, Porphyry grew restless. Plotinus's fame had reached the East and Porphyry decided to move to Rome and study with him. Longinus was disappointed that Porphyry would seek a new master, but Porphyry had learned all he could from Longinus. The encounter with Plotinus was to change his intellectual direction as well as the course of his life. For the rest of his life Porphyry lived in Rome, studying Plotinus's ideas and eventually taking over the responsibility of transcribing his lectures and editing his writings. When he moved to Rome in 262–63 C.E., Porphyry was thirty years old and Plotinus was fifty-nine. Porphyry lived in Rome for forty years. After the superficial aestheticism of Longinus, Plotinus opened up new philosophical and spiritual horizons.

To become an adherent of Plotinus's school required a break with the world. Philosophy, as we saw in the chapter on Galen, was not simply an intellectual pursuit; it demanded a change of life, a moral commitment to a new and higher way. Porphyry describes the change in the life of a well-known senator who joined the school.

There was also Rogatianus, a senator, who advanced so far in renunciation of public life that he gave up all his property, dismissed all his servants, and resigned his rank. When he was on the point of appearing in public as praetor and the lictors were already there, he refused to appear to have any thing to do with the office. He would not even keep his own house to live in, but went the round of his friends and acquaintances, dining at one house and sleeping at another (but he only ate every other day). As a result of this renunciation and indifference to the needs of life, though he had been so gouty that he had to be carried in a chair, he regained his health, and, though he had not been able to stretch out his hands, he became able to use them much more easily than professional handicraftsmen. Plotinus regarded him with great favor and praised him highly and frequently held him up as an example to all who practiced philosophy. [*Vita Plotini* 7]

In this environment Porphyry blossomed and soon came to be Plotinus's favorite student. Once, when he read a poem on Plato's birthday, expounding his "mystic doctrine," some of Plotinus's disciples said he "had gone mad," but Plotinus praised him. "You have shown yourself at once poet, philosopher and hierophant" (*Vita Plotini* 15).

Though it is difficult to date many of Porphyry's writings because they are philosophical treatises unrelated to the course of external events, it is assumed that his commentaries on philosophical works come from the years after he came to Rome. He wrote, as already noted, a commentary on Aristotle's logic, but he also wrote commentaries on other works of Aristotle, for example, the *Physics* and the section in the *Metaphysics* dealing with the Platonic theory of ideas, as well as works on Plato and other earlier philosophers. Few of these works are extant, but they do give an important clue to the interest of the Plotinian school. Plotinus considered himself an exponent of the classical philosophical tradition, particularly Plato, and he took upon himself the responsibility of examining this tradition critically and presenting it in its most compelling and persuasive form. Consequently, one of the tasks of this school was to show how others had corrupted the Platonic tradition and departed from its teachings. Plotinus and his students produced treatises defending the ancient philosophy which had been abandoned by Christians and others (*Vita Plotini* 16). Among Plotinus's extant writings is an essay against the Gnostics.

The years with Plotinus were emotionally exhausting as well as intellectually productive for Porphyry. Sometime in his mid-thirties he began to experience a growing depression that forced him to give up his work. The depression was so severe that he contemplated suicide (*Plot.* 11). However, Plotinus stepped in, gave him sound counsel, and, according to Porphyry's account, showed him the irrationality of taking his own life. Instead, Plotinus recommended that he go on an extended trip. Taking the advice, he set sail for Sicily, where he remained for several years. During his stay there, he was restored to health and he began to write once again. Unfortunately, however, Plotinus died during Porphyry's absence. When Longinus heard of Plotinus's death, he encouraged Porphyry to come back to Syria where he was now living, but Porphyry decided to return to Rome.

Porphyry died early in the fourth century, perhaps as late as 305 C.E. We know few details of his life after his return to Rome until his death, but it seems likely that during this period he devoted a good deal of his time to putting together an edition of Plotinus's writings. Plotinus had written little until he was fifty years old, and what he produced after that was chiefly a series of philosophical essays on beauty, the immortality of the soul, destiny, the good or the one, virtue, and so on, designed for circulation among his students. These essays were collected by Porphyry and arranged according to topics in six *Enneads*, or groups of nine.

From this long period in Porphyry's life we know of only two events, but both are interesting. The one was his marriage to Marcella, a widow with seven children, when he was almost seventy years old. Porphyry had never married, and he is somewhat apologetic that he eventually did, especially in light of his ascetic life. Asceticism was thought to promote a genuinely philosophical life. In a long letter to his wife, Porphyry defended his decision to marry, reminding Marcella that they were not marrying to have children: their union would only produce those who could be reared in the "correct philosophy." His letter is filled with moral exhortation, and many of the maxims he cites were also used by Christians. More than anything else he wrote, this letter shows that Porphyry and his Christian opponents shared many moral and religious values.

In this same letter to Marcella, Porphyry also mentions that he had undertaken the trip—it was a genuine letter not a literary fiction— because of a "need of the Greeks" (*Marc.* 4). Neither Porphyry's destination nor the purpose of the trip is stated, and the phrase "need of the Greeks" has puzzled scholars. The trip occurred just at the time when Diocletian was initiating a new persecution against the Christians. Henry Chadwick has made the intriguing suggestion that Porphyry had been requested by the emperor to prepare a defense of the traditional religion which could be used as a justification for repressing Christianity. The Christian writer Lactantius said that at this time a man living in Constantinople, the capital of the empire, whom he calls the "priest of philosophy" (*Div. Inst.* 5.2) had written a work against the Christians. The phrase "priest of philosophy" fits Porphyry, and it is possible that his trip because of a "need of the Greeks" was undertaken in order to prepare a frontal attack on the Christian movement.[5]

In the twentieth century, scholars have disputed the form and content of Porphyry's writings against the Christians. That he wrote against Christianity is without doubt; many later writers testify to his work, and a number of these wrote refutations of it. The response of Apollinarius included thirty books. Consideration of Porphyry as a critic of Christianity has focused almost entirely on a work entitled *Against the Christians,* though this title is first mentioned only ca. 1000 C.E. and is not used by Porphyry's critics in the fourth and fifth centuries. Most scholars, however have assumed that such a work did exist and they have attempted, on the basis of citations of Porphyry from later writers, to reconstruct its content and structure. But every effort to reconstruct the work founders because the number of genuine fragments is very small. Early in the century Adolf von Harnack published those which were thought to be from Porphyry, and this collection, which included ninety-seven fragments, has usually served as the basis for any discussion of Porphyry's anti-Christian work. Yet fully half of the fragments which allegedly come from *Against the Christians* were taken from a relatively obscure work, the *Apocriticus* of Macarius Magnes, a fourth-century Christian apologist. It is thought that Macarius excerpted his material from Porphyry, but he does not say this, and there is no way to establish that what he presents is actually drawn from this source. Ten years ago the historian Timothy

5. Henry Chadwick, *The Sentences of Sextus,* Texts and Studies, 5 (Cambridge, 1959), 66.

Barnes showed that the Macarian fragments could not, with confidence, be used to reconstruct Porphyry's lost work.[6] Without them, however, our knowledge of *Against the Christians* is extremely sketchy. Another dimension of Porphyry's attack on Christianity can be found in his lost work, *Philosophy from Oracles*. From this work we do have a number of genuine fragments, and on the basis of these we can construct a rough outline of the book. Furthermore, this book is cited by name by Christian authors, and it is clear from references to it that it was considered by Christians to be an anti-Christian work. Nevertheless, it has seldom been used to understand and assess Porphyry's case against Christianity. It is possible that this was the work written by Porphyry late in life at the request of the emperor.[7] The work mentioned by Lactantius and authored by the "priest of philosophy" had three books, and so did the *Philosophy from Oracles*.

The *Philosophy from Oracles* is not a work on Christianity as such, but a positive statement of the traditional religion of the Roman world. Porphyry presents an elaborate discussion of the theology of the various ancient peoples—Greeks, Romans, Egyptians, Chaldeans, even the Hebrews—to show that these ancient beliefs were similar to the philosophical religion accepted by many educated people in the third century. He does this by showing that the "oracles" of the traditional religions could be used as a source for belief in the One Supreme Being. His strategy was to provide a way to incorporate Christianity, which also claimed to believe in the one high God, into the religious framework of the Roman world.

In the discussion of Porphyry's attack on Christianity which fol-

---

6. T. D. Barnes, "Porphyry against the Christians: Date and the Attribution of Fragments," *Journal of Theological Studies*, n.s. 24 (1973): 424–42. For a more positive assessment of the value of Macarius for establishing the content of Porphyry's criticism of Christianity, see Robert Waelkens, *L'Economie, thème, apologétique et principe herméneutique dans l'Apocriticos de Macarios Magnes*, Recueil de Travaux d'Histoire et de Philologie, Université de Louvain, ser. 6, no. 4 (Louvain, 1974). I have used Macarius only when his reports are confirmed by other sources.

7. For the interpretation of Porphyry's *Philosophy from Oracles* presented here, see Robert L. Wilken, "Pagan Criticism of Christianity: Greek Religion and Christian Faith," in *Early Christian Literature and the Classical Intellectual Tradition*, ed. W. R. Schoedel and R. L. Wilken (Paris, 1979), 117–34.

lows, I will draw both on the fragments that may come from the work usually known as *Against the Christians* as well as from his *Philosophy from Oracles*. In the main, the material from *Against the Christians* deals with exegetical questions and literary problems in the Jewish and Christian Scriptures, whereas the material from the *Philosophy from Oracles* deals with the figure of Jesus, belief in the one God, and the apostasy of Christianity from the traditional religion.

THE JEWISH SCRIPTURES

On the basis of the fragments remaining from *Against the Christians,* we know that Porphyry devoted a major part of his book to the Jewish Scriptures, the Christian Old Testament.[8] A fifth-century Christian apologist who knew Porphyry's work said that he "spent much time with them" (i.e., the writings of Moses and the Prophets) in his "writing against us" (Theodoret of Cyrus, *Affect.* 7.36), and Eusebius said that what incensed Porphyry about Origen was that he used allegory to "explain away" the difficulties in the Jewish Scriptures (*Hist. Eccl.* 6.19.2). However, except for two fragments dealing with the historical problem of the date of Moses (the question is whether the Hebrew religion was older than other religions), all of the extant fragments from Porphyry's criticism of the Jewish Scriptures deal with the Book of Daniel. In itself this is significant because earlier critics had not discussed this book. Celsus mentioned the story of Daniel in the lion's den, but he was interested only in the heroic figure of Daniel, who was often pictured in early Christian art, not in the book itself.

By the time Porphyry wrote, however, the Book of Daniel had begun to play a major role in attempts to articulate a Christian view of history. Porphyry responded directly to this new development by arguing that Daniel could not be read as a prophecy of the future, as

8. For a general discussion of Porphyry's *Against the Christians,* see Anthony Meredith, "Porphyry and Julian against the Christians," in *Aufstieg und Niedergang der römischen Welt* (Berlin, 1980), 23.2: 1119–49. Fragments from Porphyry's work in Adolf von Harnack, *Porphyrius Gegen die Christen, 15 Bücher, Zeugnisse und Referate,* Abhandlungen der koen. preuss. Akademie d. Wissenschaft, phil.-hist. Klasse 1 (Berlin, 1916).

Christians were inclined to interpret it, but as a history of events in the author's own time. What Porphyry wrote about Daniel was so revolutionary, and so disturbing to Christian interpreters, that his critics sought to refute him in detail and at length. "The position of the neoplatonist philosopher Porphyry in this debate has been remarkable. Centuries before the advent of modern biblical criticism, Porphyry already knew that the book of Daniel was a Maccabean pseudepigraph."[9] Eusebius devoted three books to Daniel in his work in response to Porphyry, Methodius gave it close attention, and Apollinarius allowed it one large book. After all these scholars had written their responses, Jerome wrote an entire commentary on the Book of Daniel in defense of the traditional Christian interpretation. He mentions Porphyry's work on the first page and cites him at length in the commentary, responding verse by verse to his interpretation. Indeed, it is Jerome's commentary that is our chief source for Porphyry's interpretation of Daniel.

Why should Porphyry devote such attention to the Book of Daniel and why should his views cause such consternation among Christian thinkers? Daniel is a book of legends about a faithful Jew and his three friends, Shadrach, Meshach, and Abednego, who were captives when the Jews were in exile in the sixth century B.C.E. under the king of Babylon, Nebuchadnezzar. The first six chapters of the book comprise stories about Daniel and his dealings with the king; the remaining six chapters are made up of Daniel's visions about the ultimate vindication of the saints of God over the king and rulers of the world. The book presents the stories about Daniel and his friends as taking place in the sixth century, and the visions as prophecies of what was to happen in the future and at the end of time. Daniel became popular among early Christians because it was a collection of dramatic stories about deliverance from the persecution of a wicked ruler. The scenes of Daniel in the lion's den and of the three young men in the fiery furnace were among the earliest, and most frequent, representations of biblical stories to appear on the walls of early Christian catacombs.

9. Casey, 15.

The Book of Daniel was seen as a fertile source of prophecies about the coming of Christ and the destruction of the Temple in Jerusalem, a topic which assumed a major role in early Christian views of history, as we shall see more fully when discussing Julian in the following chapter. From the beginning of the Christian movement the appeal to prophecy was used to legitimate Christian claims about Jesus to Jews. When Christianity moved out of the Jewish context to present its case to the educated men and women of the Roman Empire, its apologists continued to rely on an appeal to prophecy. Justin Martyr wrote: "But lest someone should argue against us, 'What excludes the supposition that this person whom you call Christ was a man, of human origin, and did these miracles you speak of by magic arts, and so appeared to be God's son?' We will bring forward our demonstration. We do not trust in mere hearsay, but are forced to believe those who prophesied before [the events] happened, because we actually see things that have happened and are happening as was predicted" (*Apol.* 1.30).

Daniel was the quintessential prophet because, as Josephus, the Jewish historian, observed, he "not only prophesied of future events but also determined the *time* of their fulfillment" (*AJ* 10.267). Hence Christians turned to Daniel to support their claim that Jesus was the awaited Messiah, and it is noteworthy that the first full-length verse-by-verse exposition of a book from the Jewish Bible was written early in the third century by Hippolytus, a Greek-speaking theologian living in Rome. In this commentary Hippolytus argued, on the basis of chronographical considerations, that the predictions in Daniel about the Messiah fitted exactly the time Jesus was born.

In the third century a number of Christian thinkers had begun to study history and chronology in the hope of answering pagan critics. Their efforts eventually led to a Christian scheme for world history. The same Hippolytus wrote a chronicle of world history, an account of the major historical events from the beginning of time to the present, and he had been preceded by Julius Africanus, whose *Chronographiai* (Chronicles) was a history of the world to 217 C.E. in five books. Africanus's work was known and used by Origen as well as by Porphyry. Eusebius consulted it in writing his *Chronicle,* which began with Abraham's birth (2016/15 B.C.E.) and ended in 303 C.E. Euse-bius wished to show that Christianity was the legitimate continuation of the Jewish tradition. Of all these works the chronology in the Book of Daniel, and particularly his prophecy of the birth of Christ, was an integral part.

Porphyry was no stranger to the science of chronology. Sometime around 270 C.E. he came to know the work of Callinicus, who had written a history of the Ptolemies, the Hellenistic rulers of Egypt be-tween the time of Alexander the Great in the late fourth century B.C.E. and the Romans in the first century B.C.E. Using the work of Cal-linicus and others, Porphyry prepared his own chronicle of world his-tory, beginning with the fall of Troy and ending with the emperor Claudius, who ruled 268–70 C.E..[10] Armed with these skills as well as the literary techniques learned from Longinus, Porphyry turned his attention to the Book of Daniel.

In the traditional view of Christians and Jews, the Book of Daniel was thought to be written in the sixth century B.C.E. and to refer pro-phetically to later events—for example, the kingdoms of Persia and Greece, and the persecution of Jews under Antiochus IV (175–64 B.C.E.), king of the Seleucid Empire. Porphyry, on the other hand, came to the conclusion that Daniel was written in the second century B.C.E. to encourage Jewish perseverance in the face of Antiochus's re-pressive rule. Jerome summarizes his opinion in the prologue to his commentary on Daniel.

> Porphyry wrote his twelfth book against the prophecy of Daniel, denying that it was composed by the person to whom it is as-cribed in its title, but rather by some individual living in Judaea at the time of Antiochus who was surnamed Epiphanes. He further-more alleged that Daniel did not foretell the future so much as he related the past, and lastly that whatever he spoke of up till the time of Antiochus contained authentic history, whereas anything

10. Recently doubts have been raised as to whether Porphyry actually wrote a Chron-icle. His chronological studies may have been undertaken in connection with his work *Against the Christians*, and perhaps later in his life. See Brian Croke, "Porphyry's Anti-Christian Chronology," *Journal of Theological Studies* 34 (1983): 168–85.

he may have conjectured beyond that point was false, inasmuch as he would not have foreknown the future.

Porphyry undermined the whole structure of historical interpretation that Christians had constructed on the basis of Daniel. If Porphyry was correct, the apologetic value of the prophecies of Christ's birth was destroyed and the claim that Daniel had predicted the final destruction of the Jewish Temple—another weapon in the Christian armory—was invalidated.

Porphyry was too much of a scholar to be content simply with the general argument that Daniel was written four hundred years later than had been supposed. He went through the book section by section demonstrating, on the basis of a detailed analysis of the text, that a historical, as distinct from a prophetical, interpretation was the only one consistent with the statements of the book itself. In his view the book outlined in detail, from the perspective of one who had lived through the period, the actual course of events under the Seleucid king Antiochus Epiphanes in the first half of the second century. That the Book of Daniel (or at least part of the book) described events under Antiochus was not a matter of dispute between Christians and Porphyry. The issue was whether the author spoke as a prophet (from the perspective of the sixth century) or whether he was writing history. "Because Porphyry saw that all these things had been fulfilled and could not deny that they had taken place, he overcame this evidence of historical accuracy by taking refuge in this evasion, contending that whatever is foretold concerning Antichrist at the end of the world was actually fulfilled in the reign of Antiochus Epiphanes, because of certain similarities to things which took place at this time" (Jerome, prologue, *Comm. in Danielem*).

But the issue was not simply whether Daniel spoke prophetically or historically. Even if the Christian view that Daniel prophesied future events was accepted, there was a further difficulty. Christians took the prophet to be referring to two different sets of events, those things which happened in the second century B.C.E. during the reign of Antiochus, and those which took place at the time of Christ. Commenting on Daniel 11 : 20ff., "Then shall arise in his place one who shall send an exactor of tribute through the glory of the kingdom," Jerome writes: "Up to this point the historical order has been followed, and there has been no point of controversy between Porphyry and us. But the rest of the text from here on to the end of the book he interprets as applying to the person of Antiochus who was surnamed Epiphanes, the brother of Seleucus and the son of Antiochus the Great" (*Comm. in Dan.* 11.24). Porphyry claimed that the entire book was historical and was forced to interpret the later chapters in the same way. On this point, the character of the later chapters, Jerome had the better of the argument, because from chapter 11 to the end Daniel does actually prophesy (according to modern scholars) about the end of history. On the central point, however, whether the first part of the book was historical or prophetical, Porphyry had the stronger case. He was able to show that the author, on the basis of firsthand experience, described contemporary, not future, events.

One section of the Book of Daniel that played an important role in Christian apologetics was curiously—indeed suspiciously—absent from Jerome's commentary. I am referring to the famous section in chapter 9 which was thought to prophesy the permanent destruction of the second Jewish Temple in 70 c.e. "There will be an abomination of desolation in the holy place until the end of time" (Dan. 9 : 27 [LXX]). In his discussion of Daniel 9 : 24–27, Jerome reports in detail on the views of earlier commentators such as Apollinarius of Laodicea, Eusebius, Hippolytus, Clement of Alexandria, and Origen, but he says nothing about Porphyry. The omission is particularly striking, because in his commentary on Matthew (24 : 16ff.), where this passage from Daniel is cited, Jerome says that Porphyry discussed this verse from Daniel in detail (*Comm. in Matt.* 24 : 16). Furthermore, the passage from Daniel, as well as the prophecy of Jesus in Matthew 24 : 1–2, had long become familiar apologetic topics in Christian writings. Daniel and Matthew were interpreted together to mean that the Jewish Temple which had been destroyed in 70 c.e. would never again be rebuilt, and "sacrifice and offering will cease until the consummation of the age," as Jerome puts it (*Comm. in Dan.*

9.24–27). The end of sacrifices in Jerusalem was taken to mean that the Jewish religion had lost its legitimacy.

It is surprising, especially in light of Jerome's observation in his commentary on Matthew 24, that Porphyry would have overlooked this opportunity to show the falsity of the Christian view of Daniel 9. Jerome, however, avoids any mention of Porphyry in his discussion of Daniel 9, even though he cites many Christian commentators on the passage. It is possible that Jerome deliberately suppressed this section of Porphyry's work. This would be quite understandable, because chapter 9 of Daniel as well as Jesus' prophecy about the temple had become matters for heated debate late in the fourth century, after the emperor Julian's effort to rebuild the Temple in Jerusalem, thus restoring sacrificial worship to Jerusalem.[11] Jerome's *Commentary on Daniel* was written early in the fifth century.

Porphyry's criticism of the Old Testament was not limited to the Book of Daniel. I have already mentioned his discussion of the date of Moses. Unfortunately, what else he had to say is lost or has become part of a common stock of criticism of the Old Testament. Augustine, for example, said that pagans made fun of the story of Jonah and the whale. But Augustine, who thought such criticism puerile, was unwilling to attribute it to Porphyry, for whom he had high respect. Yet there is no reason to think that the comment could not have come from Porphyry. Augustine reports the objection as follows: "What are we supposed to think about Jonah who is said to have been in the belly of a whale for three days? It is improbable and incredible that a man should have been swallowed up with his clothing on in the inside of a fish; or if this is meant figuratively, you ought to have the courtesy of explaining it. Further, what does it mean that after Jonah had been vomited up, a gourd vine had sprung up over him? What reason was there for it to spring up?" (*Ep.* 102 *ad Deogratiam*). Porphyry also seems to have made fun of the Book of Hosea, for in it God commanded the prophet to marry a whore and have children by her (Jerome *Comm. in Osee* 1.2).

11. Robert L. Wilken, "The Jews and Christian Apologetics after Theodosius I *Cunctos Populos*," *Harvard Theological Review* 73 (1980): 451–71.

THE CHRISTIAN NEW TESTAMENT

Porphyry's *Against the Christians* must have included a major section on the Christian Scriptures, the New Testament. We are, however, poorly informed about this aspect of Porphyry's criticism, because Christian writers who do report pagan criticism of the New Testament seldom mention Porphyry as their source. It has been assumed, as mentioned above, that the *Apocriticus* of Macarius Magnes, a fourth-century Christian apologist, was based on material drawn from Porphyry's work, but there is no way one can be certain of this. There is, however, another Christian writing on the New Testament that does use Porphyry. This is Augustine's *On the Harmony of the Gospels (De consensu Evangelistarum)*. When this work is compared with the few presumably genuine fragments we do possess (not from Macarius), we can gain at least a general impression of Porphyry's approach to the New Testament.

On the Harmony of the Gospels was divided into four main sections. The first deals with the charge that the disciples invented the portrait of Christ presented in the Gospels. According to Augustine, some pagan critics had argued that Christ was a wise man, not a divine being as the writers of the New Testament claimed, and that he, like other sages, taught men and women to worship the one high God. His disciples, however, had made Christ into an object of worship, thereby detracting from the honor due to the one supreme God. The second and third sections of the book discussed disagreements and contradictions between the four Gospels, particularly those passages in Matthew which have parallels in Mark, Luke, and John. In the fourth section Augustine discussed texts from the Gospels of Mark, Luke, and John that have no parallels in Matthew.

Augustine had written the book because certain persons assailed the writers of the Gospels "with calumnies" and called into question "the veracity of their account" (*De consensu Evangelistarum* 1.10). Chief among their objections was that the Evangelists were "not in harmony with each other." Augustine wished to show that the writers of the Gospels based their view of Christ "on the most reliable information and the most trustworthy testimonies" (*De cons.* 1.1). In his view, two of the Evangelists, Matthew and John, were eyewitnesses and the other two, Mark and Luke, received their information through the "trustworthy" accounts of the former.

In the first section of the book *On the Harmony of the Gospels,* Augustine mentions Porphyry several times and intimates that he was the source of this type of criticism of the Gospels. One of the reasons, says Augustine, that pagan critics subjected the Gospels to examination was to show that the disciples had fabricated the stories about Jesus and

> claimed more for their master than he really was; so much more indeed that they even called him the son of God, and the word of God, by whom all things were made, and affirmed that he and God are one. And in the same way they [pagan critics] dispose of all other kindred passages in the epistles of the apostles, in the light of which we have been taught that he is to be worshipped as one God with the Father. For they are of the opinion that he is certainly to be honored as the wisest of men; but they deny that he is to be worshipped as God. [*De cons.* 1.11]

These comments seem to describe Porphyry.

Much of the *On the Harmony of the Gospels* is concerned with obvious discrepancies therein. Augustine discusses the apparent contradictions between the genealogical list given in Matthew and the one given in Luke, the discrepancy in the account of Christ's infancy in these same two Gospels, the variants in the account of the baptism of Jesus (only Matthew records a conversation between Jesus and John the Baptizer), the differences in the various accounts of the Last Supper, the fact that Matthew (27 : 3–10) cites a passage from Jeremiah which actually comes from the Book of Zechariah, the discrepancy in the accounts of Jesus' death (whether he died at the third or the sixth hour), the various statements made by Jesus on the cross, and many others.

It is doubtful that everything to be found in Augustine's *Harmony of the Gospels* was drawn from Porphyry's work *Against the Christians;*

but the general approach is similar to what we learn about Porphyry from other writers. Jerome said, for example, that Porphyry (along with Celsus and Julian) had charged the Evangelists with falsity (Jerome, *Ep. 57 ad Pammach*.9). In another passage Jerome reports that Porphyry thought the disciples were inexperienced in dealing with historical questions and were even ignorant of the Jewish Scriptures. Porphyry observed that the Gospel of Mark cited a verse from Malachi and assigned it to Isaiah (Mark 1 : 2; Frag. 9). In another place (Matt. 13 : 35), Porphyry pointed out that Matthew attributes to Isaiah a passage which in fact came from Psalm 77 (*Frag.* 10). Elsewhere he criticized the genealogy in Matthew and the discrepancies between the infancy narratives of Matthew and Luke (*Frag.* 11).

Even though this type of literary and historical criticism must have comprised a large part of Porphyry's analysis of the Christian Scriptures, it seems likely that he also dealt with other types of contradictions and inconsistencies, and that he may even have discussed the behavior and character of Jesus' disciples. Porphyry noticed passages in the New Testament that described strife between the disciples or in which they appear foolish. One example is the conflict between Paul and Peter presented in the opening chapters of the Epistle to the Galatians. When Paul and Peter clashed over the matter of circumcision, Paul, according to his own word, "opposed Peter to his face." Porphyry takes this incident to prove that Peter was in error (Frag. 21b), and this supported the view that the Apostles, to whom awesome authority was attributed by Christians, were not reliable men. This incident also showed Paul's "impudence" in claiming that he had received a special revelation from the Lord (Gal. 1 : 16), boasting that he did not have to confer with "flesh and blood" to learn what he should teach. All of which goes to show, according to Porphyry, that the disciples were not united in their teaching and that from the beginning there was strife and division within the church. This scene of conflict between Paul and Peter must have troubled Christians considerably, as Jerome discussed it at length and in a number of different places.

No doubt, in Porphyry's book there was much more of this kind of criticism as well as exposure of contradictions within the writings of

Paul, but unfortunately there is little else that we can attribute to Porphyry with confidence. The *Apocriticus* of Marcarius Magnes enumerates many other criticisms, especially of Paul, whose choleric outbursts and paradoxical language, inconsistency, and irrationality were offensive to a man like Porphyry, but there is no way we can say with certainty that these criticisms originated with him.

It is clear, however, on the basis of the meager information we do have concerning Porphyry's attack on Christianity, that the Christian and Jewish Scriptures were of special interest to him and that he was particularly adept at offering literary and historical criticism of the Bible. As we saw in an earlier chapter, Celsus also criticized the biblical text, but he did not know the Scriptures as well nor was he as skillful a literary critic as Porphyry. Porphyry also had the benefit of Origen's exegesis, which helped him to see where the problems lay.

It is, I think, important for understanding pagan criticism of Christianity in antiquity, as well as the development of Christian apologetics, to emphasize that historical and literary criticism of the Scriptures played a part in the conflict between Hellenism and Christianity.[12] The central issue, as stated by Porphyry and reiterated by Augustine in his defense of the Scriptures, was whether the Gospels provided a reliable account of the history of Jesus. Pagan critics realized that the Christian claims about Jesus could not be based simply on the unexamined statements of Christians, whether these statements be from the first disciples or from those who at a later time simply imputed authority to the earliest texts. If Christians were to make claims about the person and work of Jesus, they could not be based on faith or on the community's own memory and self-understanding; they had to be substantiated by an appeal to the same criteria used in establishing any document as reliable or any event as historical. The question of faith and history, so much a part of modern theological discourse since the Enlightenment, was also a significant part of the debate between pagans and Christians in the ancient world.

12. On the importance of the historical argument in Porphyry's criticism of Christianity, see V. den Boer, "A Pagan Historian and His Enemies: Porphyry against the Christians," *Classical Philology* 69 (1974): 198–208.

PHILOSOPHY FROM ORACLES

If all that was known of Porphyry's attack on Christianity were what we have discussed thus far, it would be hard to imagine why his work was so feared by Christians. This is precisely the conclusion to which a recent writer on Porphyry's *Against the Christians* has come. "That its burning should have been thought necessary as late as 448 is sufficient evidence of its power to move men's minds. Yet when we look at the undoubtedly genuine fragments it is difficult to see why such a fear existed if they are indeed characteristic of the whole."[13] There was, however, more to Porphyry's interpretation of the Christian movement than what is provided by the few fragments remaining from *Against the Christians*. Porphyry was feared because he also wrote another book, the *Philosophy from Oracles*, and this work sets forth more fundamental criticism of Christianity. In it Porphyry provided a sympathetic account and a defense of the traditional religions of the Greco-Roman world, and he sought to make a place within this scheme for the new religion founded by Jesus of Nazareth.

Porphyry's *Philosophy from Oracles* was a book about the worship of the gods. To appreciate his approach, however, it is necessary to say a few things about how men and women of this time conceived of the gods, and how they understood the relation between the many gods and the one supreme God who ruled over all. We are inclined to think of God as one, single and solitary, and to conceive of the category of divinity as having only one member, the one God. To the ancients, however, there were many different forms of divinity, and, as observed in the previous chapter, sophisticated thinkers such as Porphyry or Celsus believed that though there was one supreme God this did not prevent people from believing in other lesser gods. The term *divine* designated a category of being stretching from the one high God down through the Olympian gods, the visible gods (e.g., the stars), the daimones, and finally to heroes or deified men. The supreme God presided over a company of gods.

13. Meredith, 1136.

Each type of god required a different form of worship. To the one supreme God only spiritual worship of the mind and heart was thought appropriate, whereas to other gods it was proper to bring sacrifices. Long ago, said Porphyry, men "consecrated temples, shrines and altars to the Olympian gods, to terrestrial deities and heroes sacrificial hearths, and to the gods of the underworld ritual pits and trenches . . . and to the cosmos they dedicated caves and grottoes" (*De Antro Nympharum* 6). In his work *On Abstinence from Animal Food,* in which Porphyry defends vegetarianism, he outlines the different types of worship suitable to the various deities. "The first God is incorporeal, immoveable, and invisible and is in need of nothing external to himself." Hence, to this god "who is above all things, one sacrifices neither with incense, nor dedicates anything sensible to him. . . . Neither is vocal language nor internal speech adapted to the highest god . . . but we should venerate him in profound silence with a pure soul, and with pure conceptions about him" (*Abst.* 2.37, 34). To his "progeny," however, "hymns, recited orally, are to be offered." To other gods, like the stars, sacrifices of inanimate objects are fitting, whereas to lower gods, religious observances and other sacrifices should be offered. The daimones, for example, love the smell of burning flesh (*Abst.* 2.42).

The various categories of the divine are not firmly fixed. It is possible for certain deities to ascend or descend in the hierarchy of divinity. This can be seen particularly in the case of heroes, for heroes were once outstanding men who in the course of time were elevated to divine status because of the character of their lives or the wondrous works they performed. In the chapter on Celsus, I cited a passage from Plutarch that illustrates this point, and it may be helpful to cite it again. He says that some heroes are borne upward, "from men into heroes and from heroes into daimones. . . . But from the daimones a few souls still, in the long reach of time, because of supreme excellence, come, after being purified, to share completely in divine qualities" (*De def. or.* 415c).

Porphyry's *Philosophy from Oracles* differed from his other theological works in that it drew upon oracles which had been handed down among the Greeks and other ancient peoples. Instead of simply providing philosophical reasons for his beliefs, he sought to root his views in traditional (and authoritative) texts.

Sure, then, and steadfast is he who draws his hopes of salvation from this as from the only sure source, and to such you will impart information without any reserve. For I myself call the gods to witness, that I have neither added anything, nor taken away from the sense of the oracles, except where I have corrected an erroneous phrase, or made a change for greater clarity, or completed the metre when defective, or struck out anything that did not fit the purpose; so that I preserved the sense of what was spoken untouched, guarding against the impiety of such changes, rather than against the avenging justice that follows from sacrilege. And our present collection will contain a record of many philosophical doctrines according as the gods through oracles declared the truth to be."[14]

By drawing on oracles Porphyry sought to establish a link between the religious beliefs of philosophers and the beliefs of the men and women in the street who did not philosophize about the gods but worshipped them at home or participated in public rites.

The *Philosophy from Oracles* contained three books, and its outline, as it can be constructed from the fragments, conforms to the general theological outlook sketched above. The first book dealt with the worship of the gods in the proper sense of the term: the one high God, the Olympian deities (Hera, Apollo, Hermes, Poseidon, Artemis), the stars and heavenly beings (the visible gods); and it discussed the various forms in which these deities appeared, what sacrifices were appropriate to them, and the meaning of piety toward them. The second book dealt with the daimones, who also received their own forms of religious observance and honor. Book 3 dealt with heroes or divine men—for example, figures such as Heracles, the Dioscuri, Orpheus,

---

14. Fragments of Porphyry's *Philosophy from Oracles*, ed. G. Wolff, *Porphyrii de philosophia ex oraculis haurienda* (Berlin, 1856), 42–43. This passage is taken from Eusebius, *Praep. Evang.* 4.5.

Pythagoras, and so on. Porphyry placed Jesus in book 3 among the heroes, as a human being, a sage who had been elevated to divinity after his death.

To understand the significance of Porphyry's treatment of Jesus it may be helpful to outline briefly the intellectual tradition within Christianity to which he was responding. For over a century, since the time when the Apologists first began to offer a reasoned and philosophical presentation of Christianity to pagan intellectuals, Christian thinkers had claimed that they worshipped the same God honored by the Greeks and Romans, in other words, the deity adored by other reasonable men and women. Indeed, Christians adopted precisely the same language to describe God as did pagan intellectuals. The Christian apologist Theophilus of Antioch described God as "ineffable . . . inexpressible . . . uncontainable . . . incomprehensible . . . inconceivable . . . incomparable . . . unteachable . . . immutable . . . inexpressible . . . without beginning because he was uncreated, immutable because he is immortal" (*Ad Autol.* 1.3–4). This view, that God was an immaterial, timeless, and impassible divine being, who is known through the mind alone, became a keystone of Christian apologetics, for it served to establish a decisive link to the Greek spiritual and intellectual tradition. As late as the fifth century, in Augustine's *City of God* and Theodoret of Cyrus's apology, *The Curing of Greek Maladies,* apologists continued to argue that Christians and pagans worshipped the same supreme being. Porphyry's strategy was to sever the link between Christianity and Hellenism by showing that Christians had abandoned worship of this God in favor of the worship of Christ.

The nucleus of his argument can be deduced from a series of citations in Augustine's *City of God.* Throughout the work Augustine defends the worship of the one true God, and in book 19 he cites Porphyry in his support. In answer to the question, who is the God you worship, Augustine says: the god we worship "is the God whom Porphyry, the most learned of philosophers, although the fiercest enemy of the Christians, acknowledges to be a great God, even on the evidence of the oracles of those whom he supposes to be gods. For Porphyry produced a book entitled *Philosophy from Oracles,* a description

and compilation of responses [i.e., oracles], ostensibly divine, on matters of philosophical interest" (*Civ. Dei* 19.22–23). Augustine then
goes on to cite several oracles from the *Philosophy from Oracles* in which
the Jews are praised for their belief in the one God and the Christians
are denigrated. As an example of such an oracle, Augustine mentions
one quoted by Porphyry from Apollo: "In God, the begetter and the
king before all things, at whom heaven trembles, and earth and sea
and the hidden depths of the underworld and the very divinities shudder in dread; their law is the Father whom the holy Hebrews greatly
honor."

Then Augustine cites another section from the *Philosophy from Oracles* in which Porphyry praises Jesus: "What I am going to say [says
Porphyry] may certainly appear startling to some. I mean the fact that
the gods have pronounced Christ to have been extremely devout, and
have said that he has become immortal, and that they mention him in
terms of commendation; whereas the Christians, by their account, are
polluted and contaminated and entangled in error; and there are many
other such slanders they issue against them." As confirmation, Porphyry cites an oracle of Hecate: "To those who asked whether Christ
was God, Hecate replied, 'You know that the immortal soul goes on
its way after it leaves the body; whereas when it is cut off from wisdom it wanders forever. That soul belongs to a man of outstanding piety [i.e., Jesus]; this they worship because truth is a stranger to
them.'"

The point of these admittedly somewhat obscure oracles was that
genuinely religious men and women worshipped the one high God,
the "great God," who is above all, the beginning and source of all
things, an immaterial and changeless being, and that Jesus belonged
among the devout men and women who worshipped this one God.
Porphyry cites one oracle from Hecate that described Jesus as a "very
pious man" and another which said: "The wise men of the Hebrews
(and this Jesus was also one of them, as you have heard from the oracles of Apollo, quoted above) warned religious men against these evil
demons and lesser spirits, and forbade them to pay attention to them,
telling their hearers rather to venerate the gods of heaven, but above

all to worship God the Father. But this is what the gods also teach; and we have shown above how they advise us to turn our thoughts to God, and everywhere bid us worship him . . ." (*Civ. Dei* 19.23).

To summarize Porphyry's argument: There is one God whom all men worship, and Jesus, like other pious men, worshipped this God and taught others to venerate him. By his teaching Jesus directed men's attention to the one God, but his disciples fell into error and taught men to worship Jesus. "Thus Hecate said that he (Jesus) was a most devout man, and that his soul, like the souls of the other devout men, was endowed after death with the immortality it deserved; and that Christians in their ignorance worship this soul" (*Civ. Dei* 19.23).

Earlier in this chapter I discussed Augustine's work *On the Harmony of the Gospels* as a source for Porphyry's criticism of the Gospels. This same work also includes material from Porphyry dealing with Jesus and the worship of the one God. Some pagans, said Augustine, criticize Jesus because he wrote no books and spread his fame abroad by the use of magic. Others, however, attribute "superior wisdom" (*sapientia*) to Jesus, but "only as a man." They say that his disciples were responsible for teaching people that he was the son of God and promulgating the idea that he was the one through whom all things are made (John 1 : 1). These critics of Christianity believe that Jesus should be "honored as a very wise man, but they deny that he should be worshipped as God" (*De cons.* 1.7.11). Why pagans should honor Christ can be seen from some of their philosophers—for example, Porphyry—who "consulted their gods to discover what they should respond about Christ and were compelled by their own oracles to praise him" (*De cons.* 1.15.23).

These same pagan philosophers, continues Augustine, criticize the disciples of Jesus because, in abandoning the teaching of Jesus, they apostasized from the traditional worship and advocated the "destruction of temples, the ceasing of animal sacrifice, and the shattering of idols." Jesus cannot be blamed for the refusal of Christians to worship the gods, for the disciples "taught something different from what he taught" (*De cons.* 1.16.24). They began a revolutionary movement whose teaching was contrary to what they had learned from Christ, and Christianity as it has been known and practiced since then is not the religion inaugurated by Jesus but a new system of beliefs initiated by his disciples. The new religion focuses on Jesus, whereas the religion of Jesus centered on the supreme God of all. Porphyry's criticism has a curiously modern ring to it.

On the basis of Augustine's writings, Porphyry's discussion of Christianity in the *Philosophy from Oracles* included the following: (1) praise for Jesus as a good and pious man who ranks among the other sages or divine men, for example, Pythagoras or Heracles, venerated by the Greeks and Romans; (2) criticism of the disciples, and of those who follow their teaching, because they misrepresented Jesus and inaugurated a new form of worship; (3) defense of the worship of the one high God; (4) praise of the Jews for worshipping this one God.

Besides Augustine, two other Latin apologists, Arnobius and Lactantius, both of whom wrote early in the fourth century (i.e., shortly after Porphyry), give us further information about Porphyry's treatment of Christianity in the *Philosophy from Oracles*. In his *Adversus Nationes* written in 311 C.E., Arnobius says that he is at a loss to explain why the pagans attack and the gods are hostile to the Christians. "We have," he writes, "one common religion with you and join with you in worshipping the one true God. To which the pagans reply: 'The gods are hostile to you because you maintain that a man, born of a human being . . . was God and you believe that he still exists and you worship him in daily prayers'" (*Adv. Nat.* 1.36).

Arnobius does not mention Porphyry by name but his *Adversus Nationes* certainly had Porphyry in mind,[15] and the views he attacks are precisely the same as those outlined by Augustine. Christians are presented as worshipping the same God as the pagans; where they differ is in their view of Jesus. This worship, which marks Christian belief and practice, has led Christians to abandon the traditional worship. "You [i.e., Porphyry] charge us with turning away from the religion of earlier times" (*Adv. Nat.* 2.67).

15. Ernest Fortin, "The Viri Novi of Arnobius," in *The Heritage of the Early Church*, Orientalia Christiana Analecta, no. 195 (Rome, 1973), 197–226.

The other Latin apologist, Lactantius, who wrote approximately ten years before Arnobius, also seems to have had the *Philosophy from Oracles* in mind when he wrote his *Divine Institutions* in 303 C.E. Lactantius, as was observed earlier, mentions a "priest of philosophy" who was living in the capital and who wrote a work in three books against the Christians. In *Divine Institutions*, Lactantius cited part of the same oracle of Apollo quoted by Augustine in the *City of God*. This oracle, says Lactantius, speaks the truth when it praises Jesus for his wisdom and his wondrous works, but it errs in "denying that he was God." For if "Jesus is wise, then his system of instruction is wise and they are wise who follow it," why are we considered "foolish, visionary, senseless, who follow a master who is wise even by the confession of the gods themselves" (*Div. Inst.* 4.13)? Pagans "cast in our teeth" the suffering of Jesus because they say we "worship a man and one who was visited and tormented with remarkable punishment" (*Div. Inst.* 4.16). Without mentioning Porphyry by name, Lactantius seems to be summarizing the main arguments of his *Philosophy from Oracles*. The same motifs appear here as in Augustine: praise for Jesus as a wise man and criticism of his followers for their folly in worshipping him as God.

Eusebius the church historian, also writing at the beginning of the fourth century shortly after Porphyry's death, had also studied the *Philosophy from Oracles* carefully. In his *Evangelical Preparation*, a massive apology for Christianity, he cited Porphyry's writings in almost one hundred places. The only author to be quoted more often than Porphyry is Plato. One of the chief purposes of the *Evangelical Preparation* was to prove to pagan critics of Christianity that the revolt of Christianity ("our revolt" says Eusebius) from the traditional religion is "reasonable" (book 2, preface).

In a long passage in the first book of the *Evangelical Preparation*, Eusebius summarized the argument against the Christians, and this passage has been thought to derive from Porphyry, who is not named but is identified as "one of the Greeks." Porphyry, according to Eusebius's summary, wrote:

How can men not be in every way impious and atheistic who have apostasized from the customs of our fathers, through which every nation and city is sustained? What good can reasonably be hoped for from those who stand as enemies and warriors against their benefactors? What else are they than fighters against God? What types of pardon will they be worthy of who have turned away from those recognized as Gods from the earliest times among all Greeks and Barbarians, both in cities and in the country, with all types of sacrifices, and mysteries and initiations by all, kings and lawgivers and philosophers, and have rather chosen what is impious and atheistic among men . . . ? They have not adhered to the God who is honored among the Jews . . . but cut out for themselves a new way. . . . [*Praep. Evang.* 1.2.1–4]

Though the argument of this passage is similar to what was reported by Augustine and the Latin apologists, the emphasis on apostasy from the traditional religion is more pronounced. It is clear from this passage how Porphyry's writings could have been used as a religious defense of persecution, for this fragment states the case against Christianity in terms of the public piety that was necessary to sustain the cities of the empire. In a more sophisticated form, Porphyry has restated the same arguments that were implicit in the early second century, when Christianity was called a superstition.

THE RELIGION OF THE EMPEROR

Porphyry's words here about Christianity are not simply the idle musings of a solitary philosopher. Similar attitudes were shared by imperial officials, as can be seen in several official documents from the reign of Maximin Daia (310–13 C.E.), one of the last persecutors of the Christians. Of all the Roman emperors who persecuted them, Maximin was the most self-consciously religious.[16] All we know of his life

16. Robert M. Grant, "The Religion of Emperor Maximin Daia," in Jacob Neusner, ed., *Christianity and Other Greco-Roman Cults* (Leiden, 1974), 4:143–66.

and brief reign indicates that he took seriously the public piety of the Roman Empire. We are fortunate to possess a copy of a petition addressed to the emperor by a number of cities in Asia Minor, as well as Maximin's response to one sent by the city of Tyre. Both the petition and the response reflect Maximin's views, as it seems likely that the petitions were initiated by the emperor. The petition from Lycia and Pamphylia (provinces in southwestern Asia Minor) was discovered on a marble stele in 1892 in the village of Aruf (ancient Arykanda in Lycia) and can be seen today in the National Museum in Istanbul. It reads in part:

> To the masters of every nation and people, the emperors and Caesars Galerius Valerius Maximinus and Valerius Licinianus Licnius, from the nation of the Lycians and Pamphylians, a petition and supplication. Since the gods your kinsmen have demonstrated to all their love of mankind, oh most divine kings, who are concerned with worship of them on behalf of the eternal security of yourselves, we considered it would be well to take refuge with your eternal majesty and make petition that the Christians, long suffering from madness, and even now maintaining the same disease, should at length be made to cease and not give offense by some ill-omened new cult to the worship due to the gods.

In his response to this petition the emperor acknowledged that the world is "governed and kept secure by the benevolent providence of the immortal gods," and he thanked the city for its petition, which shows what sort of "devotion and piety (*theosebeia*) you displayed toward the immortal gods." He described Christians as those who "persist in that accursed folly" and encouraged the citizens to worship "Jupiter the best and greatest, the guardian of your most glorious city." Those who persist in the folly of shunning the traditional worship are to be "driven from your city . . . so that it may be purged of all contamination and impiety (*asebeia*) and in pursuit of its set purpose may with due reverence give itself to the regular worship of the immortal gods." Maximin concludes by expressing once again his wish that the citizens of Tyre continue to display evidence of their "piety towards the immortal gods" (Eusebius, *Hist. Eccl.* 9.7.3–15).

The language of his rescript is remarkably close to the sentiments expressed in Porphyry's *Philosophy from Oracles*. By the beginning of the fourth century, the official response to Christianity on the part of the emperor and the attitudes of some intellectuals were similar. Christianity had now become a powerful force within the life of the empire. Its numbers had increased significantly and its leaders were well-educated and influential. Yet Christians, in thought if not always in action, remained a people apart. They contributed little to the public life of society and by their fixation on Jesus undermined the religious foundations of the cities in which they lived.

Porphyry issued his great challenge to the Christians just as the emperors were seeking one more time to halt the advance of the Christian movement through persecution. The issue between pagans and Christians centered on what Eusebius called "political theology" —that is, the religious and theological beliefs that are integral to the life of a people or a city. Pagans bring this charge against us, writes Eusebius, that we do not honor the divinities of the cities and we are thought guilty of "the greatest impiety in taking no account of such manifest and beneficent powers, but rather openly break the laws, which require that each venerate the ancestral customs and not disturb what is inviolable, and do not follow in the footsteps of the piety (*eusebeia*) of the forefathers and are meddlesome through a love of innovation." Our opponents, concludes Eusebius, believe that punishment by death is a fitting penalty for such transgression of the laws (*Praep. Evang.* 4.1.3).

Although Porphyry's *Philosophy from Oracles* was a philosophical treatise in defense of the traditional religion, it may well have had a subsidiary purpose in providing a rationale for the persecution of Christians; for it revived the ancient charge that Christians, in forming a new religion devoted to the worship of Jesus, not only turned men away from the worship of the one supreme God, whose worship Christians claimed to share with others, but also undercut traditional piety. The emperors who were responsible for overseeing and protecting the traditional worship, and the philosopher Porphyry who assumed the intellectual task of defending this religion, acted in concert. Porphyry became the theoretician for the ideas implicit in the actions of Roman officials beginning with Pliny early in the second century.

JESUS NOT A MAGICIAN

Before concluding this section on Porphyry's *Philosophy from Oracles* a final point needs discussion. As we saw in the previous chapter, one of the charges brought against Jesus was that he was a magician and that he accomplished his wonders by the use of magical arts. This charge was still alive among pagans at the time Porphyry was writing. Eusebius, for example, wrote a little treatise against a certain Hierocles who had written a book comparing Jesus with Apollonius of Tyana, a popular wonder-worker, sage, and healer who was revered by many Greeks. Hierocles argued that Apollonius had been a true wise man and philosopher whereas Jesus was a magician and sorcerer (*Hierocl.* 1–2). Arnobius also mentioned the charge that Jesus was a magician who made use of incantations, formulas, and other magical arts to perform his wondrous works (*Adv. Nat.* 1.43). Lactantius reported a similar charge (*Div. Inst.* 5.3), and it is likely that he had Hierocles in mind.

Porphyry, however, did not accuse Jesus of practicing magic. Instead he praised him as a "wise man" and disassociated himself from such criticisms so that Jesus could be integrated into his portrait of the traditional religion. The *Evangelical Demonstration,* another long apologetic work written by Eusebius at about the same time he was writing the *Evangelical Preparation,* discussed the charge that Jesus was a magician. To defend Jesus against this attack, Eusebius appealed to the "oracles of your [pagan] gods," and cited an oracle to show that Jesus was not a "sorcerer but pious and wise and has access to the heavens." What could be a more convincing testimony, he says, "than the writing of our enemy against us which he entitled *Philosophy from*

Oracles where he says in the third book word for word: 'What I am about to say may seem surprising to some, namely that the gods have proclaimed Christ to be most pious and immortal, and that they remember him in a laudatory way'" (*Demon.* 3.6.39–3.7.1). This is the same passage cited by Augustine in the *City of God* and summarized by Lactantius in his *Divine Institutes*. By relying on Porphyry's positive appraisal of Jesus, Eusebius used Porphyry to criticize Hierocles, thus playing one pagan critic off against the other. Porphyry refuted those who say Jesus was a magician and sorcerer, for he showed, by appealing to oracles, that Jesus was "pious and most just and wise and an inhabitant of the vaults of the heavens."

Christians feared Porphyry's *Philosophy from Oracles* because it was the first work to give a positive appraisal of Jesus within the framework of pagan religion. Precisely at the time Porphyry was writing his book, Christian leaders were on the verge of a major dispute about the status of Christ. Shortly afterward, the Arian controversy exploded and Christian bishops became engaged in a far-reaching debate about whether Jesus was fully divine and equal to the one supreme God. It would be stretching the point to say that some of the Christian bishops would have agreed with Porphyry's view of Christ. But many of them, among whom was Eusebius of Caesarea, were very reluctant to consider Jesus as divine in the same sense that God the creator was divine. Indeed, the controversy, which was to divide the Christian world for several generations, centered precisely on that issue: Was Jesus to be thought of as fully God, equal to the one high God? Or was he a lesser deity, who, though sharing an intimate relation to God the Father, was nevertheless in the second rank? To place Jesus among the Greek heroes was, in the minds of the pagans, to give him a lofty place indeed, for this put him in a class with Heracles or Pythagoras. But to those Christians who were beginning to claim that Jesus was equal to the one high God, it was a stinging rebuttal.

AN UNREASONING FAITH

As I have indicated in the previous sections, I think that Porphyry's *Philosophy from Oracles* sets forth his most important criticism of the

Christian movement. Before concluding this chapter, however, a few words should be said about several of Porphyry's other points against Christianity, because they help us to see how thoroughly he had analyzed the new religion and also indicate that some of the criticisms offered earlier, chiefly by Celsus but also by Galen, continued to inform pagan critics. Some of these were to be repeated by Julian the Apostate several generations later.

Like Galen and Celsus, Porphyry charged Christians with promulgating an "unreasoning faith" (Eusebius, *Praep. Evang.* 1.3.1). In a recently uncovered fragment from Porphyry discovered in a work of Didymus the Blind, a fourth-century Christian exegete from Alexandria, Porphyry discussed the Christian doctrine that "all things are possible with God." Basing his comments on the passage in Job 10 : 13, "I know that you can do all things. Nothing is impossible for you," he objected, like Galen, to the idea that God is omnipotent. If God can do all things, then he can do things that are contrary to nature. If this is so, how can one claim to have a reasonable view of God?

A number of other objections concern specific items of Christian teaching. He raises questions about the resurrection of the dead at the end of time. Will the resurrection of all men and women be like the resurrection of Lazarus or the resurrection of Christ? asks Porphyry. "If it conforms to that of Christ how can the resurrection of the one who was born without any intervention of seed accord with that of the sons of his seed? And if it conforms to the resurrection of Lazarus, this does not seem appropriate, because the resurrection of Lazarus was accomplished with a body not yet corrupted, with that same body in which he was recognized as Lazarus, whereas our bodies will be raised after having been scattered for many centuries" (*Frag.* 92). Further, what will the resurrected body be like? If it is raised to a state of blessedness, impervious to suffering and not subject to hunger, why did Christ show his wounds and eat after his resurrection? Objections such as these were taken quite seriously by Christians. Augustine wrote a long letter responding to the inquiries of a friend who was troubled by such questions (*Ep.* 102). Similar issues lie behind the later books of the *City of God*, where Augustine discusses the resurrection of the dead and the life to come.

Porphyry also formulates anew a topic raised by Celsus—namely, the difficulties of believing in a historical revelation. Celsus had criticized Christians for their belief that God had appeared to humankind in a particular place and time in history (*c. Cels.* 4.7). Porphyry was struck by the passage in the Gospel of John: "I am the way, and the truth, and the life; no one comes to the Father but by me" (John 14 : 6). "If," asks Porphyry, "Christ says he is the way, the grace, and the truth, and claims that only in himself can believing souls find a way to God, what did the people who lived in the many centuries before Christ do . . . ? What became of the innumerable souls, who can in no way be faulted, if he in whom they were supposed to believe had not yet appeared among humankind? . . . Why did he who is called the Savior hide himself for so many ages?" It is arrogant for Christians to think that only since the coming of Christ have men and women had access to God. Realizing that Christians answered this objection by appealing to the antiquity of Jewish tradition, he says

> let them not say that the human race was saved by the ancient Jewish law, since the Jewish law appeared and flourished in a small part of Syria, a long time after [the ancient cults in Italy], and only later made its way into the Italian lands, after the reign of Gaius Caesar, or probably during his reign. What, then, became of the souls of Romans or Latins who were deprived of the grace of Christ which had not yet come until the time of the Caesars? [Augustine, *Ep.* 102.8]

This criticism is particularly significant because it touches the very center of the Christian understanding of God's relation to the world, and it will come up again in the writings of Julian and Symmachus, a Roman senator who defended the ancient religion against the bishop Ambrose later in the century. Porphyry's argument is at once historical and theological. He had not been able to discover a universal way among the many peoples of the world, though he had studied the matter intensively. "No doctrine has yet been established to form the teaching of a philosophical sect which offers a universal way for the liberation of the soul; no such way has been produced by any philosophy (in the truest sense of the word), nor by the moral teachings and disciplines of the Indians, nor by the magical spells of the Chaldaeans, nor in any other way" (Augustine *Civ. D.* 10.32). All of the various ways to salvation were concrete and particular, suitable for one people or nation, and it is illegitimate to think that the way of one people can be imposed upon all other peoples. As Symmachus, writing in the later fourth century, puts it in his little treatise defending the altar of Victory in the senate house against Christian efforts to have it removed, "We cannot attain to so great a mystery by one way" (*Relat.* 10).

Although Porphyry had not yet been able to discover a universal way, he did believe that one existed. Christianity, however, could not claim to offer such a way because of the very nature of the Christian view of revelation. By its insistence that no one can come to God except through a man who lived at a specific time and place, Christianity excludes those who have gone before and those who have no knowledge of Jesus of Nazareth.

VII JULIAN THE APOSTATE: JEWISH LAW AND CHRISTIAN TRUTH

FEW FIGURES FROM THE ANCIENT WORLD CONTINUE TO fascinate us as does Julian, the Roman emperor who reigned for nineteen short months in 361–63 C.E. A little over a decade ago he was the subject of a best-selling novel by Gore Vidal; earlier in the century he was the basis for a series of graceful and provocative poems by the modern Greek poet, C. P. Cavafy. Within the last several years two new biographies of him have appeared in English, one by the British historian Robert Browning and the other by the Princeton classicist Glenn Bowersock. In the historical tradition of the West, shaped as it has been by Christianity, Julian earned the name *Apostata*, the Apostate, for he committed the unpardonable sin: raised as a Christian, he later forsook his hereditary piety, as one Christian put it, to embrace paganism with enthusiasm. To some, however, Julian was a noble and tragic figure, one of the last ensigns of classical culture, cut down by cruel fate at the age of thirty-one as he fought to vanquish the armies of Persia.

His contemporaries were equally divided. His one-time friend, Gregory Nazianzus, poet, rhetor, and Christian bishop, composed two bitter invectives against him. "Hear you nation, tribes, tongues," begins the first,

> every kind of man from every age, as many as now are and as many as shall be . . . every power of heaven. Hear you angels, whose deed was the putting down of the tyrant, you who have not overthrown Sihon, king of the Amorites, nor Og, king of Bashan—insignificant princes injuring but a small part of the

land of Israel, but the dragon, the apostate, the great mind, the Assyrian, the public and private enemy of all in common, him who has madly raged and threatened much upon earth, and has proclaimed such unrighteousness against heaven. [*Or.* 4.1]

Another contemporary, the great pagan rhetor Libanius, teacher of both Gregory and Julian, in a lament over Julian, matches Gregory's excesses with his own hyperbole, not to vilify but to mourn his passing.

Alas, great indeed is the grief that has beset not just the land of Achaia but the whole empire where the laws of Rome hold sway. It is perhaps the greater in that part where the Greeks live . . . but the blow that smote and harrowed our souls with the thought that life is a mockery for the good man who wants to lead a good life, has . . . smitten the whole length and breadth of the world. Gone is the glory of the good; the company of the wicked and the licentious is uplifted. [*Or.* 17.1–2]

Julian lived in a still divided world. Since 313, when Christianity was recognized as a licit cult by the Roman government and Constantine had embraced the Christian religion, the emperors had been Christian. But the Roman Empire had not become a Christian state overnight, much less a Christian society. It was not until 380 C.E., seventeen years after Julian's death, that the emperor Theodosius I proclaimed Christianity the official religion of the Roman world, and it would be several generations after Theodosius before it was in a position to dominate the life of society. In the piety and practices of millions of people and in the thinking of intellectuals paganism remained very much alive. Nevertheless, it came as a shock to Christians when the young son of Julius Constantius, half brother of Constantine, who had been raised as a Christian and served as lector in the church, became emperor, disowned the Christian tradition, and fervently embraced the gods of Greece and Rome.

Julian, however, was not content simply to return to the old religion and tolerate the innovations of the Christians. He initiated a frontal attack on the Christian movement, using the law to restrict Christian influence and the power and prestige of his office to promote the practice of the traditional pagan rites. Julian was also a man of letters and a philosopher. He wrote a book on Christianity entitled *Against the Galilaeans,* which revived the tradition of pagan criticism of Christianity reaching back to the second century. Like the books of Celsus and Porphyry, Julian's work was destroyed, but much of it can be recovered from a fifth-century refutation written by Cyril, bishop of Alexandria from 412–44 C.E. In Cyril's *Contra Julianum,* Julian's book is cited extensively, and from it we can gain a clear idea of the character and content of the work. Further, information about Julian's reign from contemporary sources, as well as his own letters and essays, provide us with a rather full picture of the man and his views on Christianity. Julian's attack on Christianity, because he was a statesman and politician, a man of action and not simply of words, must also be linked to other events in his reign, among which the most important was the attempt to rebuild the Jewish Temple in Jerusalem.

THE EMPEROR'S PIETY

Julian was born in 331 C.E. the son of Julius Constantius, half brother of Constantine, and Basilina, a wealthy woman from Bithynia. He spent his earliest years in the capital, Constantinople, until this world was shattered by the death of Constantine in 337 C.E. Constantine's three sons came to power, Constantius, Constans, and Constantine II. Constantius, who was the strongest and the man destined to reign until 361, the year Julian became emperor, proceeded to murder Julian's father and eight of his relatives. Only Julian and his half brother Gallus were spared.

When he was only six years old, Julian was sent to Nicomedia, sixty miles from Constantinople, and was put in the charge of his maternal grandmother and the Christian bishop Eusebius. There he was given his first instruction in the Greek classics, Homer and Hesiod, and through Eusebius was introduced to Christian learning. It was customary for the sons of the wealthy to study both the Greek classics and the

Christian Scriptures, but in Julian's case pagan literature made the greater impression. When he was ten or eleven years old he was transferred, with his half brother Gallus, to an imperial estate in Cappadocia, and he lived there in complete isolation from society for the next six years. Most of his time was spent reading and studying works of rhetoric and philosophy. When he was approximately eighteen he was allowed to begin rhetorical studies with two rhetors, Nicocles, a pagan, and Hecebolius, a Christian. After studying with these two men, he moved to Nicomedia, where he became, in spite of Hecebolius's protestations, a disciple of the great fourth-century pagan rhetor, Libanius of Antioch.

His rhetorical studies completed, he became interested in philosophy and began to seek out the best teachers in Asia Minor. He went first to Pergamum to study with Aedesius, a disciple of Iamblichus, who had been a disciple of Porphyry. Aedesius emphasized the religious and ritualistic elements of the Neoplatonic school, and this attracted Julian. Iamblichus, who lived early in the fourth century, had been instrumental in transforming the philosophical religion of the Platonists into an experiential religion nurtured by religious rites and theurgy. Theurgy is the belief that the divine can be approached through "magical" acts, the use of salves and ointments, herbs and roots. It is not "thinking" that links men with the gods, said Iamblichus; union is attained "by the efficacy of the unspeakable acts performed in the appropriate manner, acts which are beyond all comprehension, and by the potency of the unutterable symbols which are comprehended only by the gods. . . . Without intellectual effort on our part these tokens accomplish their proper work by their own virtue" (*Myst.* 2.11).

One way of effecting union with the gods was through the practice of animating statues in order to extract oracles from them. By the use of incense, herbs, scents, and accompanying chants, the devotee sought to induce a statue to smile, nod, or in some other way respond to one's entreaty. Each god had its sympathetic representation in the animal, vegetable, or mineral world, and if the theurgist properly manipulated its representation, the deity would presumably respond.

One of the most famous theurgic feats in Julian's day was the causing of torches in the hands of the goddess Hecate to burst into flames. Another technique was to evoke the presence of the god in a human being by creating a trance or an altered state of consciousness. The intermediary was first purified with fire and water, dressed in a special girdle appropriate to the deity, adorned with a garland, and his or her eyes smeared with drugs. Then the god would appear as a luminous apparition.

When Julian was a young man studying philosophy, he heard of such experiences, and through a student of Aedesius, Eusebius, he learned of a philosopher named Maximus of Ephesus who could accomplish such feats. Against Eusebius's protestations Julian immediately sought him out. "Stick to your books," Julian said to Eusebius. "You have shown me the man I want."

Before long Julian had begun to experiment with theurgic practices and longed to be initiated. As soon as Maximus thought he was prepared, he took him into an underground crypt where Julian was initiated into the cult of Cybele, an experience that was to mark his religious outlook for the rest of his life. Later he was initiated into the cult of Mithras. This initiation took place in an underground chamber with incense, fire, and chanting. One of Cavafy's poems captures (with some Christian editorializing) Julian's fascination with the strange rites and his apprehension, at this time in his life, in the presence of the pagan gods.

> But when he found himself in darkness
> in the earth's awful depths,
> with a group of unholy Greeks,
> and bodiless figures appeared before him
> with haloes of light,
> the young Julian for a moment lost his nerve:
> an impulse from his pious years came back
> and he crossed himself.
> The figures vanished at once;
> the haloes faded away, the lights went out.

The Greeks glanced at each other.
The young man said: "Did you see the miracle?
I'm frightened, friends. I want to leave.
Didn't you see how the demons vanished
the second they saw me make the holy sign of the cross?"
The Greeks chuckled scornfully:
"Shame on you, Shame, to talk that way
to us sophists and philosophers!
If you want to say things like that,
say them to the Bishop of Nicomedia and his priests.
The greatest gods of our glorious Greece
appeared before you.
And if they left, don't think for a minute
that they were frightened by a gesture.
It was just that when they saw you
making that vile, that crude sign,
their noble nature was disgusted
and they left you in contempt."
This is what they said to him, and the fool
recovered from his holy, blessed fear,
convinced by the unholy words of the Greeks.[1]

Julian dates his conversion to this period in his life. He was twenty years old. The philosopher Maximus of Ephesus was instrumental in leading Julian away from Christianity to the ancient gods of Greece and Rome. "Upon your arrival in Ionia," Libanius later wrote to Julian, "you beheld a man wise both in repute and in reality [Maximus], heard of the gods who fashioned and maintain this whole universe, gazed upon the beauty of philosophy and tasted of its sweetest springs. Then you quickly cast off your error and, lionlike, burst your bonds, released yourself from darkness, and grasped truth instead of ignorance, the real instead of the false, our old gods instead of this recent intruder and his baneful rites" (*Or.* 13.12). Julian, of course,

1. C. P. Cavafy, *Collected Poems*, trans. Edmund Keeley and Philip Sherrard, ed. George Savidis (Princeton, 1975), 171.

could not announce openly that he had abandoned Christianity, as his cousin, the emperor Constantius, was a Christian (though an Arian), and it was assumed that all members of the imperial family were Christians. So for ten years he continued to hide his new faith and to go through the motions of Christian ritual. On occasion he even served as lector in the church.

Julian now entered a new stage. The emperor Constantius was having increasing difficulty with the German tribes who lived on the northern and western frontier and he summoned Julian to Gaul. Constantius named him Caesar, a second-level emperor under the supreme ruler, the Augustus, and put him in charge of the Roman armies in the West. For the next six years Julian lived in Gaul and in spite of his bookish ways won fame as a military leader.

In a series of campaigns, Julian reduced the power of the Franks and Germans and restored security to the Rhine frontier. As he moved from one success to another, Constantius began to have misgivings about his mounting power and ordered him to send some of his troops east. The army, however, refused to obey the order, and instead proclaimed Julian Augustus in Paris in February 360. Interpreting this acclamation as a sign from the gods, Julian accepted the honor. Constantius was enraged but helpless, and when Julian began to march east to confront his adversary and claim his new status as co-emperor, there was nothing Constantius could do. But as Julian was marching with his army to meet him, Constantius died. The date was 3 November 361.

Julian was now sole emperor. No longer need he pretend to worship the god of the Christians. To his former teacher Maximus he wrote, "We worship the gods openly, and most of the troops who are returning with me worship the gods. We sacrifice oxen in public. We have offered to the gods many hecatombs as thank-offerings. The gods command me to purify everything as far as possible, and I obey them enthusiastically" (*Ep.* 8).[2] In this letter Julian not only ex-

2. Text and English translation of Julian's orations and letters, as well as of the fragments of his *Against the Galilaeans*, in Wilmer Cave Wright, *The Works of the Emperor Julian*, 3 vols. (Cambridge: Loeb Classical Library, 1959–62).

presses jubilation that he can now practice his religion openly, but he also hints at his intention to restore and renew the traditional worship. Now that he had become emperor, the "mask was removed," as Bowersock writes. "With the elimination of the Christian Augustus (Constantius) Julian felt that the gods had rewarded his long years of secret piety and devotion. Just as he had given up shaving and stripped away the pretence of respect toward Constantius, so now he stripped away the pretence of being a Christian. The deferential Christian Caesar vanished, and in his place stood the pagan Augustus."[3]

GREEK EDUCATION AND CHRISTIAN VALUES

In contrast to all the earlier critics of Christianity Julian was raised a Christian and chose, consciously, with much thought and deliberation, to embrace the traditional gods. Indeed, he might rightly be called the first "convert" to paganism. He was not an "old-fashioned" Hellenist like Libanius, or a cultural defender of the traditional gods, as was Symmachus, the Roman senator who was his contemporary. For Libanius and Symmachus the chief function of religion was social and cultural. The worship of the gods and the preservation of the cultural heritage of Greece were akin to each other, said Libanius (*Or.* 62.8). The gods were the "protectors of the city" and religion consisted in preserving ancient traditions, in transmitting Greek literature and language, in cultivating traditional values. "Belief in the city as the essential form of social organization, and in the values of the cults of the city, are different aspects of the same attitude of cultural conservatism."[4] Religious institutions were to be nurtured because they were part of the cultural heritage. The proper observance of religious rites insured the stability and well-being of the cities.

Julian, too, was a lover of Greek antiquity, and he believed that the traditional religion and the cultural heritage of Greece went hand in hand. But Julian's attitude toward the traditional religion was not sim-

---

3. Glenn Bowersock, *Julian the Apostate* (Cambridge, 1978), 61.
4. J. H. W. G. Liebeschutz, *Antioch: City and Imperial Administration in the Later Roman Empire* (Oxford, 1972), 12–13.

ply cultural and intellectual; it was also passionate and emotional. "The mind of Julian was penetrated with sincere, deep, and unalterable enthusiasm," wrote Edward Gibbon in his *History of the Decline and Fall of the Roman Empire*.[5] Although Julian spoke the language of the cultural religion, and certainly believed in the public and civil function of religion, he also exhibited all the signs of an exuberant convert—acquiescence in the face of a reality larger than himself, obedience to the will of the gods, a fervor—even fanaticism—about his new faith. His was a private and particular faith. He lamented that sacrifices were chiefly public occasions without opportunity for meditation. "Things that are sacred to the gods and holy ought to be performed away from the beaten track in peace and quiet" (*Ep.* 58). He speaks of persuading people to adopt his religion, of convincing the weak-hearted. To a group of senators in Syria he says that when they heard his arguments they "applauded," but "few were converted by them" (*Ep.* 58). Speaking of the Jews, he praised their "fervid piety that they would choose to die for their belief" (*Ep.* 20). This is strange talk for a Greek intellectual. The contrast with Libanius, a more representative exponent of traditional Hellenism, is striking. On public holidays, when a sacrifice was being performed in front of a temple, Libanius was content to stay home and read a book. Julian, on the other hand, loved to sacrifice, and even while on a military campaign he regularly offered sacrifices. "I sacrificed in the evening and again at early dawn as I am in the habit of doing practically every day" (*Ep.* 58).

If we are to understand Julian's attitude toward Christianity we must bear in mind both his commitment to the traditional culture and his intense personal piety, especially his love of sacrifices. It was said of the emperor that if he succeeded in his Persian campaign the empire would not have enough bulls to satisfy his desire for sacrifices. But we must also remember that Julian was raised a Christian and that he had received a thorough education in the Scriptures and in Christian literature. His knowledge of the Christian tradition gave him an

5. Chapters 22 and 23 of Gibbon's *Decline and Fall* are still worth reading today. This citation is from chapter 23.

insight into those points of Christian belief that were most vulnerable to criticism. This can be seen in his approach to Greek language and culture and in his use of Judaism as a weapon against the Christians. Little more than six months after he became sole emperor Julian issued the following rescript:

> Schoolmasters and teachers should excel in morality, in the first place, and second, in eloquence. But since I cannot be present myself in each city, I order that whoever wishes to teach should not rush hastily or uncircumspectly into this profession, but should be approved by the judgment of the council and obtain a decree of the curials, by common agreement and consent of the best men. For this decree will be referred to me to deal with, so that they may take up their posts in the city schools with my approval as a kind of higher commendation.[6]

To modern ears there seems to be nothing exceptional in this decree, and even to the ancients it included, at least on the surface, nothing new. The cities had traditionally overseen education, particularly the appointment of teachers, and the laws allowed teachers certain immunities from taxation. Legislation from the period indicates that the city councils, acting on behalf of the emperor, took responsibility for the appointment of teachers. What is new in this law is that teachers are to be evaluated not only on their competence in language and literature ("eloquence") but also on their "character." By "character" Julian did not mean that teachers should exhibit the generally accepted virtues of integrity, uprightness, honesty, and so on, but that they should believe in the specific religious and moral values that were transmitted through Greek literature.

The literature of Greek antiquity, and the school tradition by which it was handed on, was not a neutral body of classical writings studied simply for aesthetic or literary purposes. This literature was the bearer of the values cherished by society, and its study was intended to form

---

6. Text of Julian's rescript can be found in *Codex Theodosianus* 13.3.5.

the student's character and outlook on life. Since those values were not divorced from religion, the educational system instilled belief in the traditional gods who figure large in ancient poetry and drama: Zeus, Hera, Apollo, Ares, Artemis, Aphrodite, and the rest.

Julian's seemingly innocuous rescript on education was the first salvo in his attack on the Christians. Its publication troubled Christian leaders and angered Christian parents, whose children would be affected by it. Even the historian Ammianus Marcellinus called the law "inhumane" and said it "ought to be buried in eternal silence" (22.10.7). It became evident several months later that Christians were not mistaken in their feeling that the edict was directed against them. Julian writes:

> I do not on this account call on them [teachers] to change their beliefs. I give them rather the choice either not to teach what they do not believe, or if they do teach, to do so honestly, and not to praise the ancients while condemning their religious beliefs. Since they live by *their* writings, it would be an admission that they will do anything for a few drachmae. Hitherto there were many reasons for not going to the temples, and secrecy about one's beliefs was excusable. But now that the gods have granted us freedom it seems to me absurd for men to teach what they disapprove. If they are real interpreters of the ancient classics, let them first imitate the ancients' piety towards the gods. If they think the classics wrong in this respect, then let them go and teach Matthew and Luke in the church. [*Ep.* 36]

Competence in the teaching of grammar and literature in the schools was now to be a matter of religious allegiance. The teacher had the responsibility to instill in the young the beliefs and values embodied in the literature, and if he believed in other gods and other values, says Julian, he could hardly be expected to be an effective teacher of the young. This law incensed Gregory Nazianzus, a Christian bishop, who like many other bishops had been educated in the Greek rhetorical tradition. Julian acted, wrote Gregory, as though "the Greek language belonged to religion exclusively and not to the tongue

. . . declaring that in using the Greek language we are stealing what belongs to others" (*Or.* 4.5).

For two centuries Christian intellectuals had been forging a link between Christianity and the classical tradition, and with one swift stroke Julian sought to sever that link. Julian's law, however, did not only concern intellectuals, for a rhetorical education was absolutely necessary for anyone who wished to advance in society. Christian parents, especially the wealthy, insisted that their sons receive the rhetorical education, and it now appeared as though Julian were limiting this to pagans.

Familiarity with classical literature and ability to express oneself not merely in classicizing literary language, but in terms of a classical framework of reference and allusion was essential for any youth who wished to pursue a career in the law or in the higher civil service, or to take an active part in the public affairs of his city or province. It was also a mark of social distinction, the sign of belonging to a class. The man who had not a classical literary education lacked prestige and influence in his local community. He was excluded from the network of correspondence and recommendation that we find exemplified in the letters of St. Basil as well as those of Libanius. He could not exercise individual or collective leadership. Christian parents belonging to this class would either have to deny their sons the education traditionally associated with their station and so make them into 'outsiders', or to expose them during some of the most formative years of their life to the influence of a teacher concerned to combat Christianity.[7]

So grave was the situation that Christians sought their own way of insuring that their children would be properly educated. Two men, a father and son, both named Apollinarius, came up with the ingenious idea of rendering the Scriptures in the style and form of Greek literature. They set about the task of writing an epic poem on the antiqui-

7. Robert Browning, *The Emperor Julian* (London, 1975), 172–73.

ties of the Hebrews up to the reign of Saul to take the place of Homer. They wrote comedies in imitation of the playwright Menander,
tragedies modeled on Euripides, and odes in the fashion of Pindar.
Their aim was to take themes from the Scriptures and produce a "set
of works which in manner, expression, character and arrangement are
well approved as similar to the Greek literatures and which were equal
in number and force" (Sozomen *Historia ecclesiastica*, 5.18).

Julian's school law was a well-timed, calculated, and astute attack on
the Christian communities within the Roman Empire. He realized
that Christianity, which had not yet developed its own educational
system, was wholly dependent on the pagan schools and the literary
tradition handed down in these schools. Without the benefit of this
education, Christianity would soon lose one of its most powerful resources, correctly spoken and properly written Greek and Latin. Julian
claimed the Greek intellectual and literary tradition for the exponents
of the traditional religion, thereby hoping to cement the bond between religion and culture which the new Christian movement threatened to dissolve.

AGAINST THE GALILAEANS

The law on schoolteachers was issued in the summer of 362 C.E. Julian spent the following winter in the city of Antioch in northern Syria.
At the end of the fourth century Antioch was one of the most resplen-
dent cities in the empire, a renowned center of Greek culture and
learning. Its educational institutions and mores, its cultural and intellectual life, its festivals and art still breathed the Greek spirit. But
many of the inhabitants of the city were Christians, and Julian was disappointed to discover how influential the Christians there were. It irritated him that they (he calls them "atheists") had no respect for the
"sacred rites which the forefathers observed" (*Misopogon* 357d). The
presence of large numbers of Christians in one of the foremost show-
places of pagan Greek culture only hardened Julian's resolve to rejuve-
nate the ancient rites and strip the upstart religion of its power and influence.

For some months the idea of preparing a literary attack on Christianity, in the style of the works of Porphyry and Celsus, had been brewing in Julian's mind. In a letter written during this period he indicated his intention to write a work in which he would strip "that new-fangled Galilaean god" of the "divinity falsely ascribed to him" (*Ep.* 55). According to Libanius, it was written by the "pious emperor during the long winter nights when other people are usually more interested in matters of sex" (*Or.* 18.179).

Though the work entitled *Against the Galilaeans* included three books, the fragments preserved in Cyril of Alexandria's *Contra Iulianum*, our chief source, contain material only from the first book. Cyril's rebuttal was composed ca. 440 C.E. (i.e., approximately eighty years after *Against the Galilaeans* was written, and long after Julian's death). Furthermore, by the time Cyril wrote, the Roman Empire had become officially Christian (380 C.E.). It would seem that by that time pagan critics would have been silenced. Yet it must be recalled that it was not until 448 C.E. that the works of Porphyry were burned by the Christian emperor Theodosius II.

Julian's work made a deep impression on Christians, and it was still being read in the middle of the fifth century. In the preface to his *Against Julian*, Cyril says that among all the "foes" of Christ Julian was especially to be feared because "before he became emperor he was numbered among the believers; he was worthy of holy Baptism, and he was trained in the Holy Scriptures." In other words, he knew Christianity from the inside and was able to meet Christian apologists on their own terms. He was, says Cyril, also "naturally gifted in rhetoric," not an insignificant gift in an age when rhetorical skill was an indispensable asset in religious controversy. Julian's books had "disturbed many and done much harm," writes Cyril. Simple and impressionable Christians fell sway to his ideas, but what is more, "even those who are strong in faith were troubled because they thought he knew the Holy Scriptures. He heaped up many testimonies from them in the Scripture's own words, although," adds Cyril, "he did not understand what they meant." As a result, many pagans "reproach Christians up and down. They cast his writings against us and assert that they are incomparably skillful and none of our teachers is capable of rebutting or refuting his ideas" (*Patrologia graeca* 76.508c).

It is not possible to say with certainty how Julian's book was constructed. Cyril says that he attacked the Gospels and the Christian religion (*PG* 76.508), but this is too general to be of much help. From the fragments cited by Cyril it appears that a good part of the book was devoted to the Christian interpretation of the Jewish Scriptures (the Christian Old Testament) and ideas about God which Christians, as inheritors of the Jewish tradition, shared with Jews. There were also some passages dealing with the Gospels and the writings of Saint Paul, but in the surviving fragments they do not figure large. A distinctive feature of Julian's book was that he expanded and deepened a line of criticism that went back to Celsus—namely, that Christianity was an apostasy from Judaism.

It is also clear that Julian was familiar with the approach taken by Porphyry in his *Philosophy from Oracles*. The purpose of the work, according to Libanius, was to attack the Christian Scriptures, "in which that fellow from Palestine is claimed to be a god and a son of god" (*Or.* 18.178). Julian wished to strip Jesus of his divinity. This theme appears throughout the work in different forms, including Julian's discussion of the relation of Christianity to Judaism; but the section dealing explicitly with Christ appears to have been lost. Julian does, however, argue, as did Porphyry, that Christians have fallen into the error of worshipping a man (*Gal.* 201e), and he suggests, to the chagrin of Christians, who had been battling over the divinity of Christ in the controversies of the fourth century, that the only writer to call Jesus God was the evangelist John, who did not even do so "clearly and distinctly" (213b). Furthermore, "neither Paul nor Matthew nor Luke nor Mark ventured to call Jesus God" (327a). This statement, though recognized as true by modern scholars, infuriated Cyril (*PG* 76.1004c–d).

Like Porphyry, Julian makes his point against Jesus' divinity by appealing to the Christian Scriptures. His task was made easier by the contemporary dispute within the church on the status of Christ in the years after the Council of Nicaea. During Julian's lifetime the neo-

Arian party, which refused to call Jesus God in the full sense, had articulate leaders and strong support in certain circles. Julian's predecessor Constantius was an Arian sympathizer. Like Porphyry, Julian argued that the notion that Jesus is divine was a fabrication of his followers, not the teaching of Jesus himself; unlike Porphyry, he is surer in his handling of the New Testament text and more discriminating in his use of the biblical data. Only one of the disciples, John, taught the new idea that Jesus was divine. The other Apostles did not. Further, Julian, who realized how important the Christian appeal to the Jewish Scriptures was, makes clear that there is no basis in the writings of Moses for the idea that Jesus is divine. Moses "taught that there was only one God" and the idea that the "Word was first-born son of God or God was one of those ideas falsely constructed by you [Christians] later" (290e).

Julian wished to show that Jesus was a man like other men. He does not even claim that Jesus was a sage, as did Porphyry. After Jesus' death Christians conferred divine status on him. This claim stung Cyril, who had been waging a battle against Nestorius over the question of the nature of Christ's divinity, and in his response to Julian he says: "We have not made a man into God, as you [Julian] think" (*PG* 76.809c), intimating that Julian's argument was precisely that. With these general comments, let us turn first to Julian's criticism of the Christian (and Jewish) idea of God in the Jewish Scriptures and then to his discussion of the apostasy of Christianity from Judaism.

THE TRIBAL GOD OF JEWS AND CHRISTIANS

Julian had an ambivalent attitude toward Judaism and the Jewish Scriptures. He respected Jewish traditions, especially the zeal of Jews to preserve the customs of their ancestors—for example, in observing the ritual requirements of the law—yet he ridiculed the myths and legends of the Jewish Scriptures. In some passages he expresses admiration for the Jewish God and is willing to identify him with the supreme God worshipped by all; yet in others, particularly in the *Contra Galilaeos*, he criticizes the Jews for believing that their God, who is

only a national or tribal deity, should be honored as the one God ruling over all. The point of such comments was, however, not to criticize the Jews but to attack the Christians, who had taken over the
Jewish conception and still used the Jewish Scriptures.

"The god of the Hebrews," writes Julian, "was not the creator of
the whole universe with lordship over all things, but is confined
within limits and since his rule has bounds we must conceive of him as
one among other gods" (100c). Behind this criticism lies the familiar
theological idea which has appeared in a number of the writers discussed in this book. The Greeks conceived of one supreme being who
ruled over all, but they also believed that each nation or people had its
own deities who were to be worshipped along with one God—not,
however, with the same veneration. In Julian's view, the God of the
Hebrews and Christians was a "sectional god," and the proper way to
honor him was to venerate him as a lesser deity subordinate to the one
high God. One should not pretend that he was more than he was.

If the proper object of the highest form of worship is the "God of
all" and not a tribal God, it follows, says Julian, that this high God is
not the property of any particular people, nor can he be known
through a particular revelation. The God of all is known to all humankind.

That the human race possesses its knowledge of God by nature
and not from teaching is proved to us first by all the universal
yearning for the divine that is in all men whether private persons
or communities, whether considered as individuals or as races.
For all of us, without being taught, have attained to a belief in
some sort of divinity, though it is not easy for all men to know
the precise truth about it, nor is it possible for those who do
know it to tell it to all men." [52b]

Julian's view was shared by many philosophers and religious thinkers
in his own day and in the preceding centuries. The reason for intro-
ducing such an argument in the work against the Christians is to expose the foolish idea that this one God revealed himself in a specific
historical revelation. With respect to the Jews, Julian singles out their

concept of election as the most offensive idea. "Moses says that the creator of the universe chose the Hebrew nation, that to that nation alone did he pay heed and cared for it, and he gives him charge of it alone. But how and by what sort of gods the other nations are governed he has not said a word" (100a). This idea of election, Julian observes, was also taken over by the Christians, for "Jesus the Nazarene, yes and Paul also, who surpassed all the magicians and charlatans of every place and every time, assert that he is the God of Israel alone and of Judaea, and that the Jews are his chosen people" (100a).

Julian adds a new twist to Porphyry's arguments against the idea that the God of all would reveal himself to a specific people or through a concrete historical figure. Porphyry asked what was to become of the ancient Romans who knew nothing of Jesus because they had lived long before his lifetime (Frag. 81). Already in the second century Celsus had raised a similar question: "Is it only now after such a long age that God has remembered to judge the life of men? Did he not care before?" (c. Cels. 4.7). Julian, adding his own twist, asks why is Judaea "the only land that he chose to take thought for?" (141c). In another passage, speaking of Jesus, Julian asks why God sent prophets to the Jews, "but to us no prophet, no oil of anointing, no teacher, no herald to announce his love for man which should one day, though late, reach even unto us also? . . . If he is the God of all of us alike, and the creator of all, why did he neglect us?" (106d).

The conflict between Julian and the Christians was not between the polytheism of the Greeks and the monotheism of Christians and Jews. What Julian opposed to Christianity and Judaism was a sophisticated idea of God that he learned from his Platonic teachers. The true God is a spiritual being who is Lord of all and is known by all. "All humankind, without being taught, have come to believe in some sort of divinity" (52b). This God who is far superior to the national or sectional gods of the various nations does not reveal himself at particular times and places. He is known to all men and women of good will who have trained their minds and spirits to contemplate God, and it is insolent for Christians to think that they have received a special revelation unknown to others. Julian, following Celsus and Porphyry, reiter-

ates a fundamental criticism of the Christian theological tradition, and
one that has been expressed over and over again by modern critics of
Christianity, especially since the Enlightenment.

To establish the superiority of the classical conception of God, Julian next offers a comparison between the Greek tradition and the Jewish (and Christian) Scriptures. He devotes considerable space to an
analysis of the creation story in the Book of Genesis and in Plato's
Timaeus. This leads him to discuss the role of myths and legends in
presenting religious truths. Julian readily admits that just as the Jewish
Scriptures present the story of creation in mythical terms, so the
Greeks too have a mythological tradition. What offends him, however,
is that the Jews and Christians do not realize they are dealing with
myths. Instead they insist that the stories be taken literally without
allegorical interpretation. If the myths in the Bible are taken literally
they present an incredible portrait of God and of humankind.

He singles out the story of the serpent in the garden of Eden. What
kind of God is it, he asks, who would create men and women without
the knowledge of good and evil? How can a good God create human
beings without giving them wisdom, the capacity to be able to dis-
criminate between good and evil? If one takes the story at its face
value, it is the serpent who should be praised, for it was the serpent
who taught men and women moral responsibility. The Hebrew myth
teaches the strange doctrine that "the serpent was a benefactor rather
than a destroyer of the human race," for the serpent helped humans to
become responsible agents (93d). But if this is what the myth teaches,
it is clear that the Hebrew Scriptures are "filled with many blasphe-
mous sayings about God. In the first place to be ignorant that she
who was created as a helpmeet would be the cause of the fall; secondly to refuse the knowledge of good and evil, which knowledge
alone seems to give coherence to the mind of man; and lastly to be
jealous lest man should take of the tree of life and from immortal become mortal—this is to be exceedingly grudging and envious" (94a).

This passage hints at another distasteful characteristic of the Jewish
God: the God of the Bible is jealous. The Scriptures explicitly record
God as saying, "I am a jealous God." What kind of God can this be?

"If a man is jealous and envious you think him blameworthy, whereas if God is called jealous do you think it a divine quality?" (155c). In the Greek myths God is never shown to be "angry, or resentful, or wroth, or taking an oath, or inclining first to this side, then suddenly to that, or as turned from his purpose" (160d). But the Jewish Scriptures regularly present God in this way.

If one compares the cosmogony of Plato in the *Timaeus* with the account of creation given by Moses in Genesis, it is clear, says Julian, that Plato had a much clearer grasp of the process by which the world was created. For one thing, Moses is much less thorough in his presentation of creation. He speaks about the heavens and the earth and the creatures who exist on the earth, but he says nothing about the beings intermediary between God and the world, and ignores the nature of angels. He mentions the Spirit but does not say anything about the "generation or the making of the Spirit." He only says that the "Spirit of God moved upon the face of the waters." He also does not say whether the Spirit was "ungenerated" or "generated." Julian is no doubt being sarcastic at this point, for as one who had been raised a Christian he knew that the term ungenerate (*agenetos*) was a point of contention among Christians. For several decades Christian thinkers had been debating whether the son was "ungenerated" or "generated." If the son was generated—that is, came into existence—then he could not be divine. Only God is ungenerated, for he exists eternally without change. At the time Julian was writing his *Contra Galilaeos* the Christians were engaged in a debate as to whether the Holy Spirit was generated or ungenerated—in other words, whether the Spirit was truly divine. Hence he pokes fun at the Christians because Moses did not say anything on the topic, implying that the Spirit must have been generated; if he had been ungenerated (divine) Moses would surely have said so.

It is curious, says Julian, that Christians, who claim to have such a spiritual religion, rely on an account of creation that has nothing to say about spiritual entities. "According to Moses, God is the creator of nothing that is incorporeal, but is only the disposer of matter that already existed. For the words, 'and the earth was invisible and without form' can only mean that he regards the wet and dry substance as the original matter and that he introduces God as the disposer of this matter." Moses is deficient because he only speaks about the creation of the physical world and neglects the angels and other spiritual beings. Plato's account, which includes the noetic (spiritual) and invisible creatures that were begotten of God and proceed from him, is vastly superior, for Moses "has failed to give a complete account of the fashioner of the universe" (99e).

Julian has many more things to say on this topic, and it is likely that Cyril of Alexandria only included a small part of his criticism of the Jewish Scriptures and the legends and myths in the Bible. We know that he also discussed the story of the Tower of Babel, which he calls a "wholly fabulous explanation" (134d) to account for the variety of tongues in the world. He wonders why it is that Christians are so fond of this tale yet refuse to believe the story in Homer's *Odyssey* of the Alodae, who attempted to set three mountains one upon another "so that the heavens might be scaled" (*Odyssey* 11.316). "For my part I say that this tale is almost as fabulous as the other. But if you accept the former [the Tower of Babel] why in the name of the gods do you discredit Homer's fable?" Even though many details of Julian's criticism are missing, his overarching argument is clear. He wishes to show that Jewish and Christian wisdom is no match for the wisdom of ancient Greece. Jews and Christians cannot point to a line of teachers as distinguished as Plato, Socrates, Aristides, Thales, Lycurgus, Archidamus, and so on. *Against the Galilaeans* complements Julian's rescript on the teaching of literature. If Christians are deprived of the Greek intellectual tradition and are forced to rely on their own Scriptures and teachers, they will soon become a laughingstock. They need the wisdom of Greece to enhance their barren and servile tradition.

AN APOSTASY FROM JUDAISM

As important as the above considerations are in assessing Julian's *Contra Galilaeos*, we have still not come to the most compelling arguments set forth there. For the distinctive mark of the *Contra Galilaeos*, in contrast to earlier works on the Christians, is that Julian singles out apostasy from Judaism as the most vulnerable point of Christianity. For Julian this was not simply a philosophical or literary argument; his attack on Christianity was supported by a conspicuous historical gesture, and one that could only have been made by an emperor: the plan to rebuild the Jewish Temple in Jerusalem. More than anything else, this action set Julian apart from other critics and elicited the ire of later Christians. "May his very memory be a curse! Amen!" wrote the medieval chronicler Michael the Syrian.

The Jewish Temple and the city of Jerusalem had been destroyed by the Roman armies under the emperor Titus in 70 c.e. At the time of the Bar Kochba revolt in 132–35 c.e., the Jews briefly recaptured the city of Jerusalem and made efforts to restore the Temple, but when the revolt was finally put down by the emperor Hadrian, plans went ahead to transform the city into a Roman colony called Aelia Capitolina (from Hadrian's family name, Aelius). Jews who remained in the city were driven out, a Roman temple to Jupiter Capitolinus was constructed on the site, and in it was placed a statue of Hadrian. Jerusalem was no longer a Jewish city. It was a city of "Greeks, foreigners, and idolaters," according to Christians (Eusebius, *Comm. in Ps.* 86:2–4; *PG* 23.1044c).

Christians interpreted the fall of the city of Jerusalem and the cessation of sacrificial worship to mean that the Jewish religion had come to an end. From the Jewish Scriptures (Old Testament) Christians knew that the Temple had been destroyed before, the city ravaged, and Jews driven into exile; but each time this had happened, after a reasonable period of time, God had restored the city to his people and allowed the Temple to be reconstructed. This time things were different. Never before, writes Origen, had the Jews been "ejected for so long a time from their ritual and worship" (*c. Cels.* 4.22). God had given the Jewish Law to a people who lived in Jerusalem and the land of Israel, and since the city was now barred to Jews, there was no way that this Law could be observed properly and legitimately. The loss of Jerusalem was thought to invalidate the ancient Jewish Law.

As long as the Temple was in ruins and the city closed to Jews, it appeared to Christians, and to some pagans, that the Christians were correct in claiming that Judaism had lost its legitimacy. Christians appealed to prophecies in the Jewish Scriptures to prove, not only that the destruction of the Temple had been predicted centuries earlier, but that it would never be rebuilt. Its destruction was permanent. The Book of Daniel provided the most important proof-text. In the Greek version used by Christians in the Roman world, Daniel said that "sacrifice and offering will be destroyed" (Daniel 9.27). Jerome, a Christian biblical commentator who was a contemporary (342–420 C.E.) of Julian, interpreted this passage to mean that the Temple would remain in ruins "until the consummation of the world and the end" (*Comm. in Daniel* 9:24).

Not only had the Jewish Scriptures (according to the Christians) prophesied the destruction of the Jewish Temple, but Jesus himself had warned the Jews of their impending doom. Both the Gospels of Matthew and of Luke record Jesus' prophecy: "Jesus left the temple and was going away when his disciples came to point out to him the buildings of the temple. But he answered them, 'You see all these, do you not? Truly, I say to you, there will not be left here one stone upon another, that will not be thrown down" (Matt. 24 : 1–2; cf. Luke 21 : 6). Later in the same chapter Jesus cites a section from the Book of Daniel on the destruction of the Temple (Matt. 24 : 15–16). In Christian circles the prophecy from Daniel together with Jesus' prophecy were interpreted as meaning that the Temple would still be in ruins on the Day of Judgment, as Cyril, bishop of Jerusalem in the mid-fourth century, said in one of his sermons (*Catech.* 15:15).

As if to accentuate the truth of these prophecies and to demonstrate that Jerusalem was no longer a Jewish city and would never again belong to the Jews, Christians, with the spiritual support of Constantine and his mother and the material incentives of the imperial treasury, undertook a massive building program in Jerusalem in the fourth century. Christian pilgrims, for the first time in Christian history, began to travel to Palestine to worship at the holy places in Jerusalem and environs. Eusebius, church historian and bishop of the Palestinian coastal city Caesarea and biographer of Constantine, saw the new buildings, the most splendid of which was the Church of the Resurrection above the tomb of Jesus (*Anastasis*), as visible evidences of the triumph of Christianity over Judaism and the displacement of the Jews by the Christians. According to Eusebius, Constantine had established an "enormous house of prayer and temple in the Palestinian nation, in the heart of the Hebrew kingdom, on the very site of the evidence of salvation" (*Praise of Constantine* 9.16). Constantine's buildings established a "new Jerusalem constructed over against the one so celebrated of old" (*Life of Constantine* 3.33). Significantly, the new city was geographically distinct from the old Jewish city set up against the Temple mount.[8]

From his Christian upbringing Julian was familiar with the Christian interpretation of the city of Jerusalem and its Temple. He knew that the destruction of the Temple was seen as the fulfillment of prophecy, and he realized that Christians looked upon its ruins as evidence of the truth of Christianity. In the Christian view, the Temple had become a symbol of the legitimacy of Judaism and of the observance of the Jewish Law. As long as the Temple was in ruins—and it was presumed that it would always remain so—it seemed that the Christians were correct: the Jewish way of life was invalid and Christianity was the rightful inheritor of the ancient Jewish tradition.

But Julian could see that Judaism was very much alive in his own day. When he visited the great cities of the eastern empire, he saw thriving Jewish communities whose leaders were well-educated and cultured men. He realized that Jews continued to be zealous in the observance of their ancestral traditions, in the teaching of the Law and the study of the Scriptures. And he knew that Jews rejected out of hand the silly idea that the upstart religion had displaced Judaism, or that it could make any rightful claim on the inheritance of their fathers. Only the Christians, and perhaps some uninformed pagans, thought that the Jewish way of life was obsolete or extinct.

In this milieu Julian conceived his strategy against the Christians. He knew that earlier critics of Christianity had attacked the Christians

8. On the Christianizing of Jerusalem, see E. D. Hunt, *Holy Land Pilgrimage in the Later Roman Empire* (Oxford, 1982).

as an apostasy from the Jewish tradition. Celsus had noticed that Christians "despised" the Jewish Law (*c. Cels.* 2.4) yet claimed to be the inheritors of the Jewish tradition. As we have seen, Celsus exposed the contradictions between Jesus and Moses. He asked: Did God give contrary laws, one to Moses, and another to his son, this man from Nazareth? "Who is wrong? Moses or Jesus? When the Father sent Jesus had he forgotten what commands he gave to Moses? Or did he condemn his own laws and change his mind, and send his messenger for quite the opposite purposes?" (*c. Cels.* 7.18).

Celsus's argument presupposed that there were vital Jewish communities that continued to read the Jewish Scriptures and observe the Jewish Law. In Celsus's day, the latter half of the second century, as well as in Julian's time, Jews were a conspicuous feature of life in the cities. They served on the city councils and held posts in the provincial administrations, their sons received a traditional Greek education, their children were given Greek names, and in every other way Jews shared fully in the life of the cities in which they lived. Yet they remained Jews and claimed that they, and they alone, were the descendants of ancient Israel. In the fourth century the Jewish way of life commanded respect. As John Chrysostom, a Christian priest in Antioch, said at the end of the fourth century: "I know that many have high regard for the Jews and think that their present way of life is holy" (*Ad Jud.* 1.3). From the perspective of pagan critics of Christianity, the existence of authentic Jewish communities was a powerful argument against the claims of the Christians. How could Christians claim to be the true successors of the Jews if they did not observe Jewish ways?

Claims about the truth of Christianity and the illegitimacy of Judaism rested heavily on an appeal to palpable events, such as the success of Christianity in winning converts and the presence of ruins at the former site of the Jewish Temple. What would be the impact of Christian appeals on history if the Temple were no longer in ruins and the Jews not only returned to the city but once again offered sacrifices in their Temple? Here lies the germ of Julian's idea to rebuild the Temple. Earlier critics had disputed Christian claims by showing, in such matters as the observance of the Law, that Christianity had apostasized from Judaism. Julian now gave new force to these arguments by announcing that he would rebuild the Temple. What greater proof could there be that Christianity was false and that the Jews, not the Christians, were the rightful inheritors of the ancient tradition of Israel? His predecessors had had only literary or philosophical arguments to cast against the Christians. But why should he rely solely on words? He was the Roman emperor. Why talk about history when he could make history?

Julian's plan to rebuild the Temple also fitted in with his renewal of the traditional religion. He believed, as he had learned from his Neoplatonist teachers, that prayer was not complete without sacrifice. Though Jews no longer offered sacrifices, animal sacrifice had once been a constituent part of Jewish religion. "Abraham used to sacrifice even as we Hellenes do, always and continually" (*Gal.* 356c). Here was a significant difference between Judaism and Christianity. Jews, who in many ways were set apart from other peoples, were in this respect similar to the other nations inhabiting the Mediterranean world. All practiced some form of animal sacrifice. With their ritual of a spiritual or unbloody sacrifice the Christians alone stood apart. Even in our own day, said Julian, the Jews sacrifice in their homes, and "they pray before sacrificing and give the right shoulder to the priests as the first fruits" (*Gal.* 306a). Julian seems to be referring here not to the practice of sacrifice as such but to the ritual butchering (i.e., *kasruth*) that accompanied the preparation of Jewish food.

Why not enlist the Jews as allies in the effort to restore traditional worship to the cities of the Roman Empire? Although the Jews could not embrace the traditional religion of Greece and Rome, they did believe in the efficacy of sacrifices. Let the Jewish Temple be restored to its former glory, and let Jewish leaders reinstitute the ancient tradition of offering animal sacrifices to God. What more effective way to isolate the Christians from all the other citizens of the empire! The Jews, who had shunned the public religion, would now be able to join with other citizens in "offering prayers on behalf of the Imperial office."

Restoration of the Temple in Jerusalem would not only cast doubt on Christian claims to be the true Israel as well as strengthen Julian's program of religious reform; it would also provide additional proof that Jesus was not divine. For if the Temple were rebuilt, Jesus' prophecy that "no stone will be left standing on another" would be proven false.

In the fragments remaining from *Against the Galilaeans* Julian says little about the Temple itself, and it may well be that this section of the work has been lost or that Cyril of Alexandria deliberately suppressed it. Yet the general argument of the book, when complemented by statements in Julian's letters and comments of contemporaries, provides clues to the lines of Julian's thinking. As I have already observed, one of Julian's charges against the Christians was that they had abandoned the teachings of the Greeks and adopted Jewish ways (235d; 207d). But why did Christians, once having adopted the Jewish tradition, not remain faithful to it? "Why is it that you do not abide even by the traditions of the Hebrews or accept the Law which god has given to them? You have forsaken their teaching even more than ours, abandoning the ways of your fathers, and giving yourself over to the predictions of the prophets" (238a).

Julian was well aware that Christians justified their departure from Jewish tradition by appealing to Jewish prophets. So he proceeded to demonstrate that Christians misunderstood the prophets and could not vindicate their new ways by such an appeal. "Since the Galilaeans say that, though they are different from the Jews, they are still, precisely speaking, Israelites in accordance with their prophets, and that they obey Moses above all and the prophets who in Judaea succeeded him, let us see in what respect they chiefly agree with those prophets" (253b). His first example is the birth of Jesus. Moses often said that all humankind should honor the one God, but he nowhere speaks of honoring "another god" (253c). Some might, however, point to the passage in Deuteronomy (18 : 15, 18): "The Lord God will raise up for you a prophet from your brethren as he raised me up. You shall listen to him in whatever he tells you." This text, which is cited in the Book of Acts with respect to Jesus (Acts 7 : 37), was widely quoted by Christians as proof that Moses prophesied the coming of Jesus. Julian was aware of this interpretation from his Christian upbringing. He pointed out, however, that the text nowhere implies that the one who is to be raised up will be divine. Indeed, Moses says explicitly (Deut. 18 : 18) that the "prophet will be like him and not like God, a prophet like himself and born of men, not a god" (253d).

Another well-known prophecy was Genesis 49 : 10: "The scepter shall not depart from Judah, nor a leader from his loins." This text, too, was taken to refer to Jesus. Again Julian is well informed about the Christian exegesis of the passage. The text could be read in two ways: "The scepter shall not depart . . . until *he* comes for whom it is reserved" or "until there comes what is reserved for him." The Christians take the passage in the former sense. But, observes Julian, it is clear that Moses is not thinking of Jesus at all. What the text refers to is the Israelite monarchy, the "royal house of David" which came to an end at the time of Zedekiah. How can the text be speaking of Jesus, who did not come from Judah? Even if Joseph's ancestry can be traced back to Judah, how can this apply when "he was not born of Joseph but of the Holy Spirit?" Moreover, genealogies prove little, because Matthew and Luke disagree concerning the family history (253e; 261e).

Few critics of the Christians could command such inside knowledge of biblical interpretation and theological reasoning. Julian irked the Christians, for he singled out the weak points in the Christian interpretation of the Bible, attacking passages that the most astute Christian exegetes had been wrestling with for generations. In most cases Julian already knew the Christian answers to the questions he raised and thus could anticipate what the replies would be. As Cyril of Alexandria said, his critics were left speechless.

Another example is the famous prophecy in Isaiah 7 : 14: "Behold the virgin [or young woman] shall conceive and bear a son." Christians cited this passage to show that Jesus was divine because he had been born of a virgin. Nothing in the text, however, says anything about a god, nor does Isaiah anywhere state that "a god will be born of the virgin." Why, then, do Christians prattle about Mary being the mother of God if Isaiah nowhere says that the "only begotten Son of

God" or the "firstborn of creation" is born of the virgin? (*Gal.* 262d)

Julian's interpretation of biblical prophecy laid the groundwork for his central argument: Christians, without any warrant from the Scriptures, had instituted a new law and deserted the Law of the Jews. The Jews "have precise laws concerning religious worship" and these are still observed today. Christians do not observe the laws of Moses; indeed, they take pride in having abolished the Law. But where in the Scriptures does Moses teach that a new Law will be established at a later time? Nowhere does God "announce to the Hebrews a second law besides that which was established. Nowhere does it occur, not even a revision of the established law" (320b). Indeed, Moses taught that the Law shall endure forever and that nothing shall be added or taken away from it. "You shall not add to the word which I command you, nor take from it; keep the commandments of the Lord your God which I command you this day" (Deut. 4 : 2; Julian also cites Deut. 27 : 26). The Christians have wantonly disregarded these words of Scripture even though Moses clearly taught (Exodus 12 : 14–15) that "the Law of Moses was to last for all time" (320a).

Another example of Christian transgression of the Law was the neglect of the practice of circumcision. Julian knew very well that Christians had a ready answer to the charge that they did not circumcise. So when he asks the Christians, "Why do you not practice circumcision?" he immediately produces the Christian response: "Paul said that circumcision of the heart but not of the flesh was granted to Abraham because he believed. He was not speaking of the flesh and we ought to believe the pious words that were proclaimed by him and by Peter." But, he continues, it is also clear that the Scriptures teach that "circumcision of the flesh" was given to Abraham as a covenant and a sign, for in Genesis it is written: "This is my covenant which you shall keep, between me and you and your seed after you in their generations. You shall circumcise the flesh of your foreskin, and it shall be in token of a covenant between me and you and between me and your seed" (Gen. 17 : 1–11). Julian not only cited the Jewish Scriptures, he also cited the words of Jesus in Matthew, implying that it was the dis-

ciples, not Jesus, who led Christians to apostasize from Jewish traditions. "I have not come to abolish the Law and the prophets but to
fulfill them" (Matt. 5 : 17) and "Whoever relaxes one of the least of
these commandments and teaches men so, shall be called least in the
kingdom of heaven" (Matt. 5 : 10). Jesus taught men to observe the
Jewish Law.

Finally Julian comes to the matter of sacrifice. "Why do you not
sacrifice" he asks the Christians, when the Scriptures and the Jewish
tradition clearly command sacrifice? "Why is it that after deserting us
[the Greeks] you do not love the Law of the Jews or abide by the sayings of Moses?" (305d). Again, Julian knows what the Christian response will be. "No doubt some sharp-sighted person will answer, 'the
Jews too do not sacrifice.'" To which Julian responds, "Neither do
you observe any of the other customs observed by the Jews," and "the
Jews *do* sacrifice in their own houses, and even to this day everything
that they eat is consecrated; and they pray before sacrificing, and give
the right shoulder to the priests as the first fruits" (305d).

It must be emphasized that Julian's argument, though it is here concerned specifically with sacrifices, deals with the relation of Christianity to the Jewish Law in general. Christians, who claim to be the inheritors of the teaching of Moses, do not observe *any* of the laws of
the Jews. At the same time the Jews continue to keep the laws of Moses. Clearly Christians have no right to claim to be the descendants of
the ancient Israelites.

But Julian's point about sacrifice does not rest on the practice of
eating "clean" meat—namely, on *kasruth*; it is directly tied to the status of the Temple. The reason why the Jews do not offer sacrifices is
that they have no Temple. "Since they have been deprived of their
temple or, as they are accustomed to call it, their holy place, they are
prevented from offering the first fruits of the sacrifice to God." Christians, on the other hand, have "invented a new sacrifice, which does
not need Jerusalem" and for this reason do not sacrifice (306b).
Hence it is clear that Christianity, though it claims Judaism as its origin, has nothing to do with Judaism; it is a new and strange rite

dreamed up recently by Jesus' followers with no claim to antiquity. The Greeks have more in common with the Jews, for they have "temples, sanctuaries, altars, purifications, and precepts" (306b).

In spite of his reservations about Judaism, Julian was able to conscript the Jews on his side against the Christians. The validity of Christianity rested on the credibility of its relation to Judaism. If the Christians were deprived of Jewish Scriptures, or if it were shown that they did not mean what Christians said they meant, and they did not really speak of Jesus of Nazareth as the Christ, Christians lost one of the chief foundation stones of their edifice of belief. Furthermore, if the Jews continued to observe the Law of Moses, and Moses taught that the Law was to be observed for all time and said nothing about a "second law," then the Christians were guilty of repudiating the very teacher they claimed to revere. The Jews, not the Christians, were faithful to the teaching of Moses. Julian's coup de grace was, however, the Temple itself, for in the minds of Christians it had come to be a symbol of the legitimacy of Judaism. The "single excuse" which Christians gave for not observing the Law, said Julian, was that Jews are "not permitted to sacrifice outside of Jerusalem" (351d). If there was no Temple in Jerusalem, Jews had no authority for practicing their religion. If, however, the Temple were restored, then Christians would have to acknowledge that Judaism still had validity, and Christian claims about the truth of their religion would be patently false.

In the winter of 362–63, while staying in Antioch and preparing for his campaign against the Persians, Julian appointed Alypius, a close friend and former provincial governor, to oversee the rebuilding of the Temple. "I will rebuild at my own expense the holy city of Jerusalem" (*Ep.* 51). Amply provided with imperial funds, Alypius set out for Jerusalem to begin the project. The construction, however, was abruptly cut short later in the spring by an earthquake or some other disaster. The pagan historian Ammianus Marcellinus (23.1.2–3) said that balls of fire burst from underneath the foundations, and Christian historians reported that fire came down from heaven to burn the site and the workers (Socrates *Hist. Eccl.* 3.20). The project was abandoned. Possibly Julian's advisors urged him to set it aside because of the impending Persian campaign. In June of the same year, in the midst of a battle with the Persians, Julian was killed, and the project was never resumed.

The failure of Julian's plan did not lessen its significance. In Julian's day and in the generations to follow the idea that the Temple might be rebuilt troubled Christians. In a bitter invective, part of which was cited earlier in this chapter, Gregory Nazianzus said that Julian was planning not only to rebuild the Temple but also to return Jews to the city from which they had been banned for centuries. If the Jews returned to Jerusalem, said Gregory, this would "restore the authority of the ancient tradition" (*Or.* 3.5). A generation after Julian's death the story of the rebuilding of the Temple was still being told in Christian circles, not simply as a past event but as a future possibility. In a sermon preached to Judaizing Christians in Antioch in 386 C.E., John Chrysostom says that Jews in Antioch were still going about the city "boasting that they will get back their city again" (*Jud.* 7.1). This would mean, he said, that Jews would be able to return to their "former way of life" (*Jud.* 5.1).[9]

Julian's dream lived on, and the bitterness of Christian response to him shows that he had touched a sensitive nerve. The Achilles' heel of the Christian tradition was its relation to Judaism. The truth of Christianity seemed to require the demise of Judaism. For if Judaism was still a living religion, an alternative to Christianity, and the ancient Jewish tradition was still observed by Jews, and the Jewish Scriptures were still read and studied in Jewish communities, Christians could not claim to be the rightful inheritor of the patrimony of Israel and Jesus was not the Messiah whom the Jews had awaited. Even though Julian's program to rebuild the Temple was unsuccessful, it was the final, and most brilliant, stroke in the ancient conflict between paganism and Christianity.

9. For the significance of Julian's attempt to rebuild the Temple in later Christian tradition, see David B. Levenson, "A Source and Tradition Critical Study of the Stories of Julian's Attempt to Rebuild the Jerusalem Temple" (Ph.D. diss., Harvard University, 1979; also, Robert L. Wilken, *John Chrysostom and the Jews: Rhetoric and Reality in the Later Fourth Century* (Berkeley, 1983).

In the end, pagan criticism of Christianity based its case not simply on an appeal to the intellectual tradition of classical antiquity but on Judaism. From the beginning pagan critics had sensed that the relation of Christianity to Judaism was an essential aspect of the new religion, but how vulnerable Christianity really was did not become apparent until Christians were faced with a critic who knew the Christian religion from the inside.

EPILOGUE

Adolf von Harnack once wrote that Porphyry's *Against the Christians* was "perhaps the most extensive and thoroughgoing treatise that has ever been written against Christianity. . . . It is not too much to say that the controversy between religious philosophy and Christianity lies in the very position in which Porphyry placed it. Even today Porphyry remains unanswered."[1] Augustine in his time and many scholars in ours would no doubt agree. But it might equally well be argued that the emperor Julian offered as compelling a case against the Christian religion as did Porphyry. "None of our teachers is capable of rebutting or refuting his works," wrote Cyril of Alexandria, his fifth-century opponent.

Julian had been raised a Christian, and though he was a Greek, not a Jew, he charged that Christianity was a false and bastard religion because it had apostasized from its origins in the Jewish tradition. As astute as the analysis of Celsus or Porphyry may have been, and as insightful as Galen's critique of key points of doctrine, none could match the perspicacity of a man who had been baptized a Christian and nurtured in the prayers and liturgy of the church, who had studied its Scriptures and been taught its central tenets since boyhood. Julian saw clearly what others had grasped but dimly—that Christianity had an irrevocable tie to Judaism and that its deviation from the mother religion had left it with a permanently bad conscience.

At the end of a book on pagan attitudes toward Christianity it may appear eccentric to stress the role of Judaism in this ancient dialogue.

1. Adolf von Harnack, *The Mission and Expansion of Christianity in the First Three Centuries* (London, 1908), 1: 505.

197

Yet the tradition of pagan criticism of Christianity, especially as it was formulated by its most articulate thinkers, can be fully appreciated only if the Jews, who lived alongside pagans and Christians in the great cities of the Roman Empire, are included as part of the setting. Julian is the most notable example of a pagan thinker who appealed to Judaism to build a case against Christianity, but the argument developed at length by him had already been adumbrated in the second century by Celsus: if Christianity claims to trace its origin to the Jews and insists that the Jewish Scriptures (Old Testament) really belong to the Christians, why do Christians repudiate the laws that Moses received from God and wrote down in the Scriptures and which the Jewish people revere and observe to this very day? Long after Christianity had severed its ties with the Jews, pagan critics sensed that Christianity's relation to Judaism was one of its most vulnerable points. In this they were surely correct.

But it has not been the purpose of this book to ascertain whether Julian or Porphyry or any other writer advanced the most formidable case against Christianity. My intention has been to understand the attitudes of the ancient Romans toward Christianity in the period when the Christian religion assumed its classical form and to learn from them something about the life and values of the ancient world, as well as about Christianity. In their efforts to understand and evaluate the new religion, pagan critics tell us much about themselves, how they viewed God, the practice of religion, nature, society, history, reason, faith, tradition, and the virtuous life. They also singled out some of the more distinctive characteristics of Christianity: belief in a historical revelation that occurred at a particular place and time; adoration of Jesus, a human being, as divine; belief in a free and transcendent God who created the world by an act of will; a reluctance, at least initially, to relate the new faith to the public life of society and the political realm. One critic has hinted that the reason Christianity succeeded in making its way within the Roman world was due less to what Christians believed than to the way they lived.

I have tried to approach the sources from the perspective of ancient paganism, to present them sympathetically within the framework of the ideas that existed before the emergence of Christianity, not as they might have appeared to later Christian generations. Yet it should be noted that during the almost three hundred years when the critics were most vocal, they did not speak in a vacuum. There was a genuine dialogue, not simply an outpouring of abuse. The credit goes as much to the Christians as to the pagans.

At the outset, of course, no dialogue existed. Pliny and Tacitus did speak in a vacuum. They knew little about Christianity and were preoccupied with other matters when they mentioned the Christians in their writings. By the time Celsus wrote toward the end of the second century, however, Christians had begun to answer back. Celsus seems to have known the writings of the Christian apologist Justin Martyr. Origen studied Celsus's *True Doctrine* and responded to it point by point. Porphyry wrote with full awareness of the intellectual achievement of Origen. Julian knew Christianity intimately. Cyril of Alexandria read Julian's *Against the Galilaeans*, and Augustine answered Porphyry's *Philosophy from Oracles*. Such dialogues were possible because Christians were willing to meet their critics on common ground.

If Christians were susceptible to the charge that they shunned the public responsibility of religion toward society, that was hardly the case in the matter of intellectual debate and argument. Here Christians readily entered the public arena and adopted the accepted standards of truth as the basis for discussion. Celsus poked fun at Christians who boasted that they alone possessed the truth, but other Christians forthrightly took up the challenge laid down by their critics. Although Christianity had initiated a new way of life whose origins were in events that had taken place in Palestine in the first century, Christian apologists believed that the Christian way had significance for all people. If it were to be intelligible it had to be set forth in the universal language of reason. The "teachings of our faith," wrote Origen, are "in complete accord with the universal notions" (*c. Cels.* 3.40). That pagans continued to write books against the Christians for three hundred years is evidence that they took the ideas of Christian thinkers seriously. This made a genuine dialogue possible.

There is, of course, much in the writings of the pagan critics that is off the mark and irrelevant, and some passages are filled with invective, the stuff of ancient polemical literature. But on balance pagan intellectuals knew what they were talking about and understood the new religion remarkably well. That is why the books of these polemicists are worth reading today. They also performed an enormous service to the developing Christian tradition. They helped Christian thinkers to see the difficulties of the positions they adopted, to grasp the implications of Christian belief earlier than would have been possible if they had talked only among themselves—in short, to understand the very tradition they were defending. That Christianity became the object of criticism by the best philosophical minds of the day at the same time when Christians were forging an intellectual tradition of their own was a powerful factor in setting Christian thought on a sound course. Christian theology took shape in dialogue and discussion with alternative points of view.

During the Enlightenment it became fashionable to set Christianity in opposition to classical antiquity. It has always struck me as strange to attack early Christianity because it was supposed to have supplanted reason by faith. From Edward Gibbon in the eighteenth century to Gilbert Murray in the twentieth, this theme has been sounded again and again. To Gibbon the Christians had "debased and vitiated the faculties of the mind" and "extinguished the hostile light of philosophy and science." To Murray they had substituted authority for reason. "Truth was finally made hopeless, when the world, mistrusting Reason, wary of argument and wonder, flung itself passionately under the spell of a system of authoritative Revelation, which acknowledged no truth outside itself, and stamped free inquiry as sin. . . . The intellect of Greece died ultimately of that long discouragement which works upon nations like slow poison."

The very persistence of a dialogue between pagans and Christians over the course of three centuries is, I think, the best refutation of this view. Christians and pagans met each other on the same turf. No one can read Celsus's *True Doctrine* and Origen's *Contra Celsum* and come away with the impression that Celsus, a pagan philosopher, appealed to reason and argument, whereas Origen based his case on faith and authority. One of the things pagans resented most was that Christian thinkers had adopted Greek ideas and methods of thinking to expound Christian teaching. Porphyry said Origen "played the Greek," and Celsus complained that Christians had adopted the technique of allegory, an achievement of Greek reason, to interpret the Hebrew and Christian Scriptures.

Indeed, one might legitimately argue that the debate between paganism and Christianity in antiquity was at bottom a conflict between two *religious* visions. The Romans were not less religious than the Christians. Julian, to be sure, was more zealous in the practice of religion than most men and women of his age. He had known the uplifting power of a transforming religious experience. In the language of a later time, he was a "convert." His paganism was not simply the official religion of the Roman world, but the private and personal faith of a convinced and committed believer. Julian was, however, not only a religious enthusiast; he was also a defender of the traditional religion and, like Porphyry and Celsus and Pliny, he impugned the Christians for deserting the gods. In the Roman world this charge was not simply a matter of "our gods" against "your God." The gods were part of an entire social world into which Christianity could not be fitted. Hence the Christians were called "superstitious," a term they found offensive and would later use derisively of Roman religion, but which struck precisely the right note. It came instinctively to the lips of the earliest observers of the Christian movement. To them, the new way did not foster genuine piety.

In the earliest period these charges were vague and undefined, and the term *superstition* was applied equally to Christians and to other groups foreign to the Romans. As time passed, however, a new generation of critics beginning with Celsus offered a more profound interpretation of this ancient religious vision. Celsus believed that religion was inextricably bound to the unique customs of a people, to the laws of a nation. The ultimate legitimation of religious beliefs and practices did not rest on philosophical arguments about the nature of the gods but on ancient traditions that had been passed on from generation to generation. Age and custom were the final arbiters in religious mat-

ters. As the seer Teiresias says in Euripides' *Bacchae*, "The beliefs we
have inherited, as old as time / cannot be overthrown by any argument." Because Christianity had no homeland and did not belong to
one people or nation, its traditions, such as they were, could make no
claim to antiquity. The one nation to which they could make any
claim, Israel, the Christians themselves had repudiated. Hence there
was no way that Christianity could make a claim on religious truth.
The "old doctrine" was the "true doctrine."

At issue here was not simply the traditional religion as opposed to
the new religion that had arisen in Palestine. Here was also a different
understanding of religion. Pagan critics saw in Christianity a privatizing of religion, a penchant to relegate it to the lives of individuals and
the "voluntary" associations that Christians organized in the cities of
the Roman world. Christianity appeared to be more like a school of
philosophy than a religion. Even after the number of Christians began
to increase, they refused to conform to the expectations people traditionally associated with piety. Critics sensed that Christianity was
loosening the ties that bound religion to the social and political world.
Christians seemed more interested in the moral and spiritual transformation of individuals, in "conversion," to use A. D. Nock's phrase,
and to the gathering of people into a new form of community called
the church, than in fostering public piety. Of course, this situation was
to change profoundly in the fourth century, when Christians eventually assumed the task of giving religious legitimation to the social and
political institutions of the Roman world. The religion that had begun
with the proclamation "Repent, for the kingdom of God is at hand"
became, in the writings of men such as Eusebius of Caesarea, the
Latin poet Prudentius, and in the decrees of Christian emperors, the
public religion of the Roman world and eventually of Western civilization.

I think it significant that the ancient debate between paganism and
Christianity also had as one of its themes the historical character of
Christian revelation. Early on, outsiders began to realize that Christians did not simply look to Jesus as the teacher and founder of their
movement but saw in him the unique revelation of God. What, asks

Celsus, was the purpose of God's descent among humankind? Christians believed that God had intervened in the world, and as a consequence they thought differently about history and the world of nature. This was why pagans charged Christians with ignoring the claims of reason. The new religion seemed to say that reason could no longer be confined to the abstract and logical processes of thinking or appeals to the evidence of nature. It had to embrace the events of history, in particular the history of Jesus.

A corollary to this discussion was a debate over the reliability of the scriptural account of Jesus' life. In the last two centuries the question of "faith and history" has been at the head of the list of theological concerns. This was prompted by the emergence of historical criticism at the end of the eighteenth century and the resultant scrutiny of the gospel tradition. Already in the second century, however, Celsus devoted part of his *True Doctrine* to a critical examination of the accounts of Jesus' life, and Porphyry paid even greater attention to the literary and historical analysis of the Scriptures. His dating of the Book of Daniel is still accepted by critical scholarship. The primary issue in the debate over the Bible was whether the Scriptures could be considered a reliable source for the words and events they record. Did a voice from heaven address Jesus at the time of his baptism and did a bird actually descend on him as he stood in the Jordan River? asks Celsus. "What trustworthy witness saw this apparition?" (*c. Cels.* 1.41).

Pagan critics realized that the claims of the new movement rested upon a credible historical portrait of Jesus. Christian theologians in the early church, in contrast to medieval thinkers who began their investigations on the basis of what they received from authoritative tradition, were forced to defend the historical claims they made about the person of Jesus. What was said about Jesus could not be based solely on the memory of the Christian community or its own self-understanding. As late as the year C. E. 400, Augustine wrote a major work, *On the Harmony of the Gospels*, dealing with the reliability of the Gospels. I do not wish to overstate the importance of this issue in early Christian thought. Many Christian thinkers of that time were

quite oblivious to it. But because it is seldom noticed it is worth
pointing out.

Another dimension of the "historical" argument was the controversy initiated by Porphyry as to whether followers of Jesus, rather
than Jesus himself, were responsible for the distinctive form of the
Christian religion. Porphyry (and Julian) showed, on the basis of the
New Testament, that Jesus did not call himself God and that he
preached, not about himself, but about the one God, the God of all. It
was his followers who abandoned his teaching and introduced a new
way of their own in which Jesus (not the one God) was the object of
worship and adoration. Here, too, the ancient debate anticipated
modern discussion. Porphyry's intention, of course, was to win Jesus
for the pantheon of Greek heroes and to discredit the Apostles and the
Christians who revered him; but he put his finger on a troubling
issue for Christian thinkers: does the Christian faith rest on the preach-
ing of Jesus or on the ideas forged by his disciples in the generations
after his death?

The early Christians considered their critics "enemies of the truth."
Criticism always hurts, and those who took the brunt of it centuries
ago did not find it easy or pleasant. But Christianity needed its critics
and profited from them. They introduced a dialectical element into
Christian thinking. The doctrine of creation out of nothing is a good
instance. Galen was one of the first to sense that the biblical understanding of God implied a different view of the process of creation
than had been worked out in the Greek tradition. Even before Christian thinkers had begun to give the matter careful attention, he realized that a profound, and in his view unfortunate, shift in thinking
was taking place. Christians conceived of God as a free and transcendent being who brought matter into being by an act of his will and
formed it according to his purpose. Through dialogue with the Greek
tradition, first through the work of Gnostic Christian thinkers, Christians began to elaborate the implications of the new revelation and to
formulate a distinctively Christian teaching. Another example was the
presentation of the new movement as a school that led men and
women to a life of piety and virtue. The term *piety*, absent from the

earliest Christian literature, began to be adopted by Christians at the time when pagans charged Christianity with superstition (impiety). By interpreting Christianity as a philosophical school, Christian thinkers were able to speak persuasively to the Roman world and remain faithful to their conviction that Jesus was a moral teacher.[2]

The Christian theological tradition did not develop out of a single original idea like the growth of a plant from a seed. The organic metaphor does not sit easily with historical experience. Ideas and institutions take shape as they interact with forces outside of themselves as well as from internal logic or entelechy. Perhaps this is the one large conclusion to be drawn from the study of pagan criticism of Christianity. Christianity became the kind of religion it did because it had critics like Celsus, Porphyry, and Julian. They helped Christians to find their authentic voice, and without them Christianity would have been the poorer. Christians encountered the traditions of the ancient world not simply as an intellectual legacy from the past, not only in the education they received, but as part of a vital interaction through the vigorous criticism of pagan intellectuals.

When one observes how much Christians shared with their critics, and how much they learned from them, it is tempting to say that Hellenism laid out the path for Christian thinkers. In fact, one might convincingly argue the reverse. Christianity set a new agenda for philosophers.[3] The distinctive traits of the new religion and the tenacity of Christian apologists in defending their faith opened up new horizons for Greco-Roman culture and breathed new life into the spiritual and intellectual traditions of the ancient world.

---

2. Robert L. Wilken, "Toward a Social Interpretation of Early Christian Apologetics," *Church History* 39 (1970): 437–58.
3. See, for example, Stephen Gersh, *From Iamblichus to Eriugena* (Leiden, 1978).

SUGGESTIONS FOR
FURTHER READING

Andresen, Carl. *Logos und Nomos. Die Polemik des Kelsos wider das Christentum.* Berlin, 1955.

Athanassiadi-Fowden, Polymnia. *Julian and Hellenism: An Intellectual Biography.* Oxford, 1981.

Barnes, Timothy D. "Legislation against the Christians." *Journal of Roman Studies* 58 (1968): 32–50.

Bauer, Walter. *Das Leben Jesu im Zeitalter der neutestamentlichen Apokryphen.* Tübingen, 1909. See especially pp. 425–86, on the life of Jesus as seen by Jews and pagans.

Beaujeu, J. *La Religion romain à l'apogée de l'empire romain.* Paris, 1955.

Benko, Stephen. "Pagan Criticism of Christianity during the First Two Centuries A.D." In *Aufstieg und Niedergang der römischen Welt,* edited by H. Temporini and W. Haase. Berlin, 1980. Vol. 23.2, pp. 1054–1118.

————, and John J. O'Rourke. *The Catacombs and the Colosseum: The Roman Empire as the Setting of Primitive Christianity.* Valley Forge, Pa.: Judson Press, 1971.

Betz, Hans Dieter. *Lukian von Samosata und das Christentum.* 1958.

Bowersock, Glenn. *Julian the Apostate.* Cambridge, 1978.

Browning, Robert. *The Emperor Julian.* London, 1975.

Dill, Samuel. *Roman Society in the Last Century of the Western Empire.* London, 1899.

————. *Roman Society from Nero to Marcus Aurelius.* London, 1911.

Dodds, E. R. *Pagan and Christian in an Age of Anxiety.* New York, 1965.

Festugière, A.-J. *Personal Religion among the Greeks and Romans.* Berkeley, 1954.

Friedlander, L. *Roman Life and Manners under the Early Empire.* 1908–13.

Fuchs, H. "Tacitus über die Christen." *Vigiliae Christianae* 4 (1950): 65–93.

Gallagher, Eugene V. *Divine Man or Magician? Celsus and Origen on Jesus* (Society of Biblical Literature Dissertation Series, no. 64. Chico, CA: Scholars Press, 1982.

Geffcken, Johannes. *The Last Days of Greco-Roman Paganism*. Amsterdam, 1978.

Grant, Robert. *The Sword and the Cross*. New York, 1955.

————. *The Earliest Lives of Jesus*. New York, 1961.

————. "The Religion of Emperor Maximin Daia." In Jacob Neusner, ed. *Christianity and Other Greco-Roman Cults*, vol. 4, pp. 143–66. Leiden, 1974.

Hardy, E. G. *Christianity and the Roman Government*. London, 1894.

Harnack, Adolf von. *The Mission and Expansion of Christianity in the First Three Centuries*. London, 1908.

Heinemann, I. "The Attitude of the Ancient World toward Judaism." *Review of Religion* 4 (1940): 385–400.

Janssen, L. F. "'Superstitio' and the Persecution of the Christians." *Vigiliae Christianae* 33 (1979): 131–59.

Kaufmann-Buhler, D. "Eusebeia." In *Reallexikon für Antike und Christentum*, vol. 6, pp. 985–1052. Stuttgart, 1966.

Keresztes, P. "The Imperial Roman Government and the Christian Church. I. From Nero to the Severi. II. From Gallienus to the Great Persecution." *Aufstieg und Niedergang der römischen Welt*, vol. 23.2, pp. 247–315; 375–86. Berlin, 1980.

Labriolle, Pierre de. *Le Réaction païenne. Etude sur la polemique antichrétienne du Ier au VIe siècle*. 2d ed. Paris, 1948.

La Piana, G. "Foreign Groups in Rome during the First Centuries of the Empire." *Harvard Theological Review* 20 (1927): 183 ff.

Liebeschultz, J. H. W. G. *Continuity and Change in Roman Religion*. Oxford, 1979.

MacMullen, Ramsay. *Paganism in the Roman Empire*. New Haven, 1981.

Meeks, Wayne A. *The First Urban Christians: The Social World of the Apostle Paul*. New Haven, 1983.

Meredith, Anthony. "Porphyry and Julian against the Christians." *Aufstieg und Neidergang der römischen Welt*, vol. 23.2, pp. 1119–49. Berlin, 1981.

Momigliano, Arnaldo, ed. *The Conflict between Paganism and Christianity in the Fourth Century*. Oxford, 1963.

Nautin, P. "Trois autre fragments de livre du Porphyre 'Contre les Chrétiens.'" *Revue Biblique* 57 (1950): 409–16.

Nestle, Wilhelm. "Die Haupteinwände des antiken Denkens gegen das Christentum." *Archiv für Religionswissenschaft* (Leipzig) 73 (1941–42): 51–100.

Nock, A. D. *Conversion. The Old and the New in Religion from Alexander the Great to Augustine of Hippo*. Oxford, 1933.

Pannenberg, Wolfhart. "The Appropriation of the Philosophical Concept of God as a Dogmatic Problem of Early Christian Theology." In *Basic Questions in Theology*, 2: 119–83. Philadelphia, 1971.

Pettazzoni, Raffaele. "State Religion and Individual Religion in the History of Italy." In *Essays on the History of Religions*. Leiden, 1954.

Pichler, Karl. *Streit um das Christentum: Der Angriff des Kelsos und die Antwort des Origenes*. Frankfurt-am-Main, 1980.

Rabbow, Paul. *Seelenführung. Methodik der Exerzitien in der Antike*. Munich, 1954.

Radin, M. *The Jews among the Greeks and Romans*. Philadelphia, 1915.

Schoedel, William R. "Christian 'Atheism' and the Peace of the Roman Empire." *Church History* 42 (1973): 309–19.

Smith, Morton. *Jesus the Magician*. New York, 1978.

———. "Pauline Worship as Seen by Pagans." *Harvard Theological Review* 73 (1980): 241–49.

Speyer, W. "Zu den Vorwürfen der Heiden gegen die Christen." *Jahrbuch für Antike und Christentum* (Stuttgart) 6 (1963): 129–35.

Stockmeier, Peter. "Christlicher Glaube und Antike Religiosität," in *Aufstieg und Niedergang der römischen Welt*. Berlin, 1980. Vol. 23.2, 871–909.

Toutain, J. *Les Cultes païens dans l'empire romain*. Paris, 1907–20.

Vogt, Joseph. *Zur Religiosität der Christenverfolger im Römischen Reich* (Sitzungsberichte d. Heidelberger Akademie der Wissenschaft, phil.-hist. Klasse). Heidelberg, 1962.

Waltzing, J. P. *Etude historique sur les corporations professionelles chez les romains*. 4 vols. Brussels, 1895–96.

Walzer, Richard. *Galen on Jews and Christians*. London, 1949.

Wilken, Robert L. "The Christians as the Romans (and Greeks) Saw Them." In *Jewish and Christian Self-Definition*. Vol. 1, *The Shaping of Christianity in the Second and Third Centuries*, edited by E. P. Sanders, pp. 100–25. Philadelphia, 1980.

———. "Toward a Social Interpretation of Early Christian Apologetics." *Church History* 39 (1970): 437–58.

INDEX

Aedesius: as teacher of Julian, 167
Apollinarius: his response to Julian's
school laws, 175–76
Apologists, xv, 66–67, 204–05; argued
the reasonableness of Christianity, 78;
opposed by the average Christian, 78–
79; appeal to miracles, 99–100; on the
nature of God, 151–52; met pagan
critics on common ground, 199
Apuleius: accused of practicing magic, 99
Arians, 178–79
Aristotle: on creation, 90
Aristotle, Ps.: on One God, 106
Arnobius: on Porphyry, 154
Asclepeion: at Pergamum, 69–70
Associations, 12–15; social, recreational,
and religious functions of, 34; members
of drawn from lower classes, 35–36,
40; three main types, 36; bylaws in inscription from Lanuvium, 36–39; provided social cohesion, 40
Augustine: on Roman religion, 53–54;
on trustworthiness of Gospels, 112,
144–46; on pagan discussion of Jonah,
143; on Porphyry and the One God,
151–54

Bacchic rituals, 16–17
Bacchic society: inscription of, 41–44
Basilides: and doctrine of creatio ex
nihilo, 88–89
Bithynia, 1, 7, 8–9; financial troubles of,
10
Burial society: resemblance to Christian-
ity, 44

Callinicus: used by Porphyry, 140
Carpocratians, 19, 20

Cavafy, C. P.: on Julian, 168–69
Celsus: on Gnostic groups, 20; on Christianity as an association, 45; on idea of
God, 90, 102–04; on Christian veneration of cross, 96; on Christian fideism,
97; on Christian proselytizing, 97–98;
on Jesus as a magician, 98, 100; read
Justin Martyr, 101; on resurrection,
103–04, 111–12; on divinity of Jesus,
104–06, 108; his monotheism, 105–
08; on historical Jesus, 108–11; on
Christianity and Judaism, 112–17; on
Christians and civic order, 117–18,
124–25; his devotion to tradition,
121–25; on Logos and Nomos, 121–
25
Christianity: as a privatizing of religion,
124–25
Church: as ecclesia, 32–33
Church history: and Roman history, xiv–
xv
Cicero: on Roman religion, 57, 58–59
Collegia (associations), 34
Conservatism: in Roman religion, 62–
63
Constantius (emperor, cousin of Julian),
170
Contumacia (obstinacy): as a legal charge
against Christians, 23
Conversion: importance to Christian reli-
gion, 202
Coulanges, Fustel de, 64
Creatio ex nihilo, xvi; first developed by
Basilides, 88–89; Galen's critique of
Christian views of, 84–88
Crimes: alleged, of Christians, 17–21
Cyril of Alexandria: on Julian, 177–78

Also Available from Yale University Press

The First Urban Christians
The Social World of the Apostle Paul
WAYNE A. MEEKS

The Origins of Christian Morality
The First Two Centuries
WAYNE A. MEEKS

The Land Called Holy
Palestine in Christian History and Thought
ROBERT L. WILKEN

Christianity and Paganism in the Fourth to Eighth Centuries
RAMSAY MACMULLEN

Christianizing the Roman Empire
A.D. 100–400
RAMSAY MACMULLEN

Books and Readers in the Early Church
A History of Early Christian Texts
HARRY Y. GAMBLE

Paul the Convert
The Apostolate and Apostasy of Saul the Pharisee
ALAN F. SEGAL

From Jesus to Christ
The Origins of the New Testament Images of Jesus
PAULA FREDRIKSEN

Please visit our website at http://www.yale.edu/yup/